HOLLYWOOD'S UNSOLVED MYSTERIES

HOLLYWOOD'S UNSOLVED MYSTERIES

By
John Austin

SHAPOLSKY PUBLISHERS
New York

A Shapolsky Book

For any additional information, contact:
Shapolsky Publishers, Inc.
136 West 22nd Street, NY, NY 10011

1 2 3 4 5 6 7 8 9 10

Library of Congress Cataloging-in-Publication Data

Austin, John, 1922–
  Hollywood's unsolved mysteries.

   1. Homicide–California–Los Angeles–Case studies.
2. Motion picture actors and actresses–California–
Los Angeles–Death. 3. Motion picture producers and
directors–California–Los Angeles–Death. 4. Hollywood
(Los Angeles, Calif.)   I. Title.
HV6534.L7A98   1989   364.1'52'0979494   89-24327
ISBN 0-944007 49-X

Book Design and Typography by: Woodmill Press, NJ

ALSO BY

JOHN AUSTIN

The World I Lived In (The George Jessel Story)

Sex Is Big Business

Surrogate

How To Syndicate To Newspapers

Dedication

For LISA...

On April 24, 1984
That one great love entered my life.
Her patience with me and
Everything in life has
No boundaries...

Acknowledgements

The author wishes to acknowledge Ian Shapolsky for his careful guidance and enthusiasm in bringing this project to publication.

And thank you to the diligent Julian de Rothschild-Blau, a New York editor with a Hollywood soul.

In addition, many thanks go to Marvin Paige's Motion Picture and Television Research Service for his help and close friendship over the years; also to Sue Gianforte for deciphering and typing the manuscript.

"Because it is so unbelievable,
the truth often escapes being known."

—Heraclitus
540-470 BC

"There is not a reporter in Hollywood
who could not rock the country
by sitting down at his typewriter
and recording merely a portion of the things he knows ."

— Douglas Churchill
Editor & Publisher
August 10, 1935

Hol-ly-wood (hol-e-wood), n. the NW part of Los Angeles, California; *center of the American motion picture industry.*

Hol-ly-wood-i-an (hol-e-wood-e-an, hol-e-wood) n.
1. a person who works for the motion picture industry located in Hollywood, California. 2. a person born or living in Hollywood, California. —. 3. of, suitable to, or characteristic of the motion picture industry or of the people who work in it, esp. in Hollywood, California; *tawdry, emphasizing effect rather than content.* 4. *of or pertaining to Hollywood or Hollywoodians.*

Hol-ly-wood-ish (hol-e-wood-ish), adj. of, pertaining to, *or resembling Hollywood, Hollywoodians, or the highly romanticized and unrealistic.*

— Random House Dictionary

Oligarchy: n. pl. *-chies: -ical*: a form of government in which the power is vested in a few persons, *or in a dominant class or clique.* Government by the few. *A state or organization so ruled. The person or persons so ruling.*

— **Random House Dictionary**

Contents

3 MARILYN MONROE: THE CONSPIRACY UNCOVERED ... *67*

4 THE STRANGE AND LONELY DEATH OF WILLIAM HOLDEN ... *105*

5 ROY RADIN: "THE DAY OF THE LOCUST" REVISITED ... *129*

Was the Swedish Beauty, With Her Career in High Gear, Depressed and Commit Suicide; Was It An Accident, or ...? • *Why Could No Trace of Her Supposed Marriage to Isaac Jones, a Black Musician, Be Found By Los Angeles County Authorities?* • *Why Did Jones Present Witnesses At the Second Hearing To Obtain Control of Inger's Estate, and Not the First?* • *And Why Did He Not Use the Money For What He Told the Court He Would?* • *Was There a Conflict Between Inger Stevens, Burt Reynolds and Ike Jones?* • *And Why Did Inger's Marriage Plans With Bing Crosby Go Awry?*

Did the Husband of Toni Mannix Plan the Death of TV's First "Superman", George Reeves? • *Reeves and Mannix Had Been Having An Affair For Years Behind the Back of MGM and Theatre Executive Eddie "The Ape" Mannix* • *Reeves Underwent Three Strange "Accidents" in the Months Prior to His Death* • *Studio Stunt Men Could Have Had The Expertise to "Arrange" Them* • *Was a Real Bullet Slipped Into Reeves' Pistol, the Weapon He Used To Stage "Mock Suicides" When He Was Upset?* • *Why Did the Beverly Hills Police Department, "The Friend of the Stars," Call the Death a "Probable Suicide" When All Indications Pointed To Murder?*

Other Unsolved Mysteries of Earlier Decades Are Yet To Come in Another Volume • *Who Shot Thomas Ince, the Movie Pioneer, to Death? Charles Chaplin or Wm. Randolph Hearst?* • *Why Did the Los Angeles Times "Kill" the Story After It's First Edition and Go Along With the Oligarchy?* • *The Unexplained and Mysterious Death of Steve Cochran Aboard His Yacht Off Guatemala With An All Girl Crew* • *Why Did Cynthia Bouron, Later Murdered in a Market Parking Lot, Claim Cary Grant Was the Father of Her Unborn Child? It Turned Out to be the Child of a Black Father* • *Why We Quit "The*

Business" as a Successful Second Generation Entertainment Journal-ist For Life in California's Countryside and in Ireland For Several Months Each Year.

Prologue . . .

"There are many unsolved mysteries . . .

Nearly two decades ago, the author wrote a series of articles for magazines and newspapers in Germany, Canada, Australia, and some other countries. The series was titled **Hollywood's Unsolved Mysteries!**, and proved so popular that what started out to be a series of three articles mushroomed into eight.

None of *those* eight unsolved mysteries, except an update on Marilyn Monroe, appear in this book. Many of those I wrote about then will be incorporated into another volume for a new generation of readers.

Strangely enough, we received a tremendous amount of fan mail from that series of articles; more fan mail, in fact, than we had ever received before for anything we had written until that time. Because the volume was so heavy, most of the letters (and postcards) could not be acknowledged individually. But, if you who are reading this book were among those letter writers — we thank you now!

So many deaths of Hollywood notables of yore: William Desmond Taylor; and Paul Bern, the ill-fated husband of Jean Harlow with a penis so small it made Harlow laugh on their wedding night, are just two. Then there was the case of Thomas H. Ince, the movie pioneer who "died" aboard the W.R. Hearst yacht. All of these unsolved deaths remain open on the blotters of several police departments.

To answer some of those questions and the anxieties registered in those letters, this book has been written. The contents have also been chronicled for those tens of thousands of film fans around the world, those who have asked us in writing and personally, "What ever happened to...?", "Is so and so still alive?", or, "How did so and so actually commit suicide?"

There have been many, many deaths of Hollywood figures, some famous, some infamous, some not so well known. At least thirty of them to our knowledge were of the "unsolved" variety. We have selected for this book some of the most notorious of those unsolved mysteries which occurred within the last 25 years or so; most of them will be well remembered.

Others will be held over for a soon-to-be-released additional volume.

Only a few of these "Hollywood-connected" deaths, supposed suicides, or even murders, have ever been solved to the complete and total satisfaction of relatives, the film-going public, or the police departments in and around Los Angeles as well as those in other states.

In some cases — especially in the twenties through the forties, these police departments "covered up" the crimes, suicides or whatever at the behest of well-heeled Hollywood figures, or at the urging of their political sycophants. This also includes the Los Angeles Police Department — for at least four decades the finest in the country, but prior to then, very corrupt.

Even Los Angeles County District Attorneys were reportedly not above accepting bribes and/or Hollywood-promoted lifetime judgeships through the industry's campaign contributions to the right Governor or President.

William Holden, Natalie Wood, Bob Crane, Inger Stevens, Freddie Prinze, Vicki Morgan — all died under more-than-mysterious circumstances. Most of these deaths, if not all of them to some degree, have never been closed with definitive *reasons* or *motives* to satisfy everyone.

☆ ☆ ☆

Hollywood — used throughout as a generic term — is an oligarchical society which relies on the whims and favors and tastes of the general public to swell the box office coffers and increase ratings on television series. These, in turn, finance its opulent lifestyle of two-Mercedes-in-every-garage-tennis-court-in-the-back-of-every-house-with-a-swimming-pool-alongside syndrome.

Because of the huge amounts of money involved in success, it is in Hollywood's own best interests to keep as much dirty laundry, scandals and behind-the-scenes machinations from the public as possible. Anyone within the industry who tells what he knows is considered a pariah, an outcast, who will find it hard to obtain any work within the industry, or connected with it.(*)

The Washington *Post's* Bob Woodward found out how Hollywood works. In the matter of his book, **Wired**, about the life and drug-induced death of John Belushi, Woodward had to defend himself against the attacks of Hollywood about his "insensitivity" Said Woodward, in rebuttal:

> "What I did in that book was hold a mirror up to those people and drew attention to their responsibility for Belushi's death. *They didn't like it.* [Author's italics]
> "Film people are used to getting a free ride in the press, particularly out there in Hollywood. If we covered Washington like the Los Angeles *Times* covers Hollywood, we would be out of business.
> "There is no curiosity at all about the abuses, the stuff in **Indecent Exposure**, or any of the drug stuff in **Wired**.
> "They just don't touch it (out there).
> "They just don't ask the hard questions about these people!"

Indecent Exposure is the story of David Begelman's forgery of actor Cliff Robertson's signature to a $10,000 check Begelman ordered drawn and given to him, personally, while he was president of Columbia Pictures. The fraud was discovered when Robertson received a "routine" income tax form from Columbia stating that his "earnings" were in that amount from the studio in 1976. Robertson had done no work for Columbia during that year.

There were also other embezzlements by Begelman to cover his gambling losses, which were hardly mentioned in the Los Angeles newspapers or the toadying trade papers — *The Hollywood Reporter* and *Daily Variety*. At his trial, Begelman pleaded *nolo contendere* on a plea bargain and was placed on *unsupervised probation*. He was also ordered to perform community service in the form of an anti-drug film.

After a few months, Begelman went on to bigger and better things. He

---

(*) An example: Those witnesses who testified for the prosecution, either under subpoena or voluntarily, in The **Twilight Zone** manslaughter case which killed actor Vic Morrow and two Vietnamese children, found that out the hard way. Few, if any, of those prosecution witnesses have ever again worked in the industry to which they had devoted their lives. One, a top cameraman, who just told what he saw, and who had worked steadily for 26 years, has not received a work call in over two years as of this writing. Thanks to an inept prosecution by Lea Purwin D'Agostino, The Dragon Lady, the defendants were acquitted of all charges.

has continually been hired by members of the oligarchy, including MGM, and placed in more powerful and higher paying positions.

The victim — Cliff Robertson ... ?

He was more or less "banished" from the industry and did not work in feature films for over five years.

We talked to Robertson in Cannes in 1980 about the situation. "Just what the hell was I supposed to do? Pay income tax on money I hadn't earned?" he asked.

"I had no choice but to call Columbia and find out what was going on! That was the worst thing I ever did for my career. It came to a screeching halt sometime in 1977."

This aspect of the Begelman affair — the "indecent exposure" of the oligarchy to outsiders — was hardly mentioned in the Los Angeles media. It is just one more example of how the industry protects its own and rids itself of those who "go against the grain."

☆   ☆   ☆

The earnings of a great many members of this oligarchical society of Hollywood have been called, and are, obscene, compared to all other industries. This has helped to create an "us against them" mentality in order to protect those earnings. This attitude creates an atmosphere which breeds mystery and isolates its subjects in the upper echelons from the *real* world. In a broader sense it also breeds utter contempt for the laws of human behavior which govern every person outside the oligarchical society, the "civillians," as they are referred to.

To those people who *want* to tell the truth, such as in **The Twilight Zone** trial, it is an economic fact of life that they will lose their livelihood if they do, and many have, in this and other cases.

Dr. Thomas Noguchi, the Los Angeles County Coroner for many years, and recognized around the world as a brilliant medical examiner, tried to explain the possible and/or probable reasons for many Hollywood-connected deaths, suicides and over-doses, accidental or otherwise. Because of language and cultural differences, Noguchi lacked the tact and diplomacy required to deal with such a high-profile industry and its deaths. Noguchi was dismissed from his job upon the urging of the L.A. County Board of Supervisors, three of which — a majority — are pawns of the Hollywood establishment.

Noguchi challenged his firing in a Civil Service hearing and civil law suit which he lost. The cards were stacked against him. (*)

(*) In 1969, a previous attempt to oust Noguchi failed. He managed to overturn that decision and retain his job, much to the chagrin of the Board. The Supervisors have been greatly influenced by "campaign contributions" from within the industry, as an inspection of their campaign documents will attest.

Many observers say that the "evidence" against Dr. Noguchi was obviously "tainted," probably a lot of it perjured, and a great deal of behind-the-scenes maneuvering occurred to see that he *was* removed from office — this time permanently. Noguchi was demoted to Pathologist within the Los Angeles County Coroner system. Once again, Hollywood had survived the dictum of PYOA — Protect Your Own Ass.

Because of this and many other factors which will be brought out in various mysteries herein, the truth will probably never be known in many of those recounted. A case in point is the murder of Bob (Col. Hogan of **"Hogan's Heroes"**) Crane in a Scottsdale, Arizona, apartment. When found, Crane's apartment was full of videotapes of the actor performing acrobatic sex with various females — many of them. His suite also contained enough video camera equipment, VCR, dubbing paraphernalia, and even a photo darkroom in the bathroom to have made a professional lab envious.

Crane used to cart all this stuff around the country while playing dinner theatres between film and TV roles. Our beliefs as to why Crane was killed, and who killed him, will be gone into in depth.

Before our semi-retirement, we were a second generation entertainment journalist, broadcaster and the International Editor of two famous "trade papers" catering to the egos of the industry. Because of this we were able to "stay on top" of these mysteries and unsolved deaths and what have you, on a daily basis in preparation for their recounting in this work.

The unsolved mysteries on the following pages will, we hope, elicit as much interest and fan mail, as that original series of articles.

Enjoy!

—John Austin
Killarney, Ireland
1989

William Desmond Taylor. It took over 60 years to find a solution to his murder. It had been hushed up by the oligarchy and by crooked District Attorneys. (John Austin Collection).

Fade In . . .

Director King Vidor who believes he solved the Unsolved Murder of
William Desmond Taylor before he died.   (AP/Photo)

"Many people in Hollywood have, since its inception, believed the motion picture industry to be an oligarchical society, an island, which does not have to live by the rules of an organized and lawful community."

—*Editorial Page*
Hollywood Citizen-News
September, 1935

1 ... Background To Mystery

HOLLYWOOD is envisioned the world over as the epitome of glamour, money, sex, beautiful women, handsome men and affluent gays, but not necessarily in that order. It has also provided the cyclorama for some of the most mysterious deaths, suicides and murders in the annals of Los Angeles crime.

Some of these "mysteries" are still considered "open" in police files, although the chance of clearing up any of them is, at the very least, remote at this stage.

The closest anyone has come to solving a previously "unsolved mystery" of a noted Hollywood figure was King Vidor. The famed director, who spanned several decades from silent to sound films as both actor *and* director, undertook two years of research into the February, 1922, slaying of British-born director William Desmond Taylor. Vidor intended to use the material as his "comeback" film after several inactive years.

Vidor had to abandon the project eventually because he realized that no studio in Hollywood would touch the material. He had, in effect, been hoisted by his own petard by discovering that Taylor was not only gay, but that Charlotte Selby, the overly protective and avaricious mother of silent star Mary Miles Minter had shot Taylor in the back in the presence of her daughter.

Vidor also discovered that the sitting District Attorney of the day, Thomas Woolwine, had been paid many thousands of dollars by Selby to quash any possible indictment of her or her daughter for the murder. His successor as District Attorney, Asa Keyes, (who later went to jail for corruption in another case) also jumped on the bandwagon of greed and lined his pockets at the expense of Selby and Minter.

A Deputy District Attorney, Buron Fitts, succeeded Keyes in this very powerful post and he, too, proceeded to shake down Selby. Fitts guaranteed that he would destroy whatever evidence remained to link her or her daughter to the murder. This included the Smith and Wesson pistol Selby used in the shooting. Fitts also kept quiet about the fact that Paramount Pictures, in concert with Woolwine, had been allowed to "sanitize" the crime scene so that Taylor's death would appear to have been the work of a burglar. (*)

In many of the cases recounted herein, we may never know who or why; we can only conjecture, guess, explain, explore, discuss and outline what we *feel* really happened. An educated guess after many years of covering the Hollywood scene and discussing the cases with those who survived and investigated them, such as police officers and sheriff's deputies who "worked" the cases.

In a lot of deaths recounted herein, Hollywood's societal structure was responsible for "keeping the lid on" the real cause of death to "protect the industry" no matter what the cost in truth, money, ruined reputations, or careers down the tubes, in the same fashion as the Taylor murder was hushed up and the crime scene sanitized.

Again, in many of the cases there is a common thread overlooked by many people - scholars of film, writers of Hollywood lore and others - or else purposely ignored: in the deaths of Bob Crane; William Holden; Lana Turner's late lover, gangster John Stomponato; and several others, either press agents, managers, sycophants, or household help were the first ones to find the body or bodies.

Whenever anything went wrong, and under the emotional circumstances of the moment, studio heads, studio security chiefs, agents or lawyers, were usually the *first* to be notified. Rarely the police. In several cases, this allowed enough time for "the scene of the crime", so to speak, to become totally sanitized and vital evidence *planted* or *destroyed*.

In the case of gangster Stomponato's killing in Lana Turner's Beverly Hills home, famed filmland damage-control specialist, lawyer Jerry Giesler was called first. Several hours elapsed before the Beverly Hills Police Chief, Clinton H. Anderson, was notified by Giesler. Anderson personally "took care" of the crime scene before calling in his detectives for the "official" investigation. This resulted in Lana's daughter, Cheryl, being held in protective custody after admitting killing Stomponato. Following a Juvenile Court hearing, Cheryl was placed in a foster home

---

(*) Fitts, who was later appointed a Superior Court Judge (!!) in Los Angeles, committed suicide in 1973 with an antiquated Smith and Wesson revolver similar to that used in the Taylor slaying.

Thelma Todd and her first husband, agent-cum-bootlegger-cum-pimp for Louis B. Mayer, Pat De Cicco. (Marvin Paige's Motion Picture and Television Research)

after pleading self defense, and later released to the custody of her maternal grandmother.

If there had been any inkling that Turner had been in the room when the hoodlum was stabbed, there was a strong possibility that Turner *could* have been charged as an accessory in the killing of the two-bit hood. He was constantly beating Turner when she would not do his bidding such as "loaning" him thousands of dollars at a time. It was so bad while Turner was on location for a film in England that she had to call in Scotland Yard. It was "suggested" that Stomponato leave the country by the first available aircraft. He did.

As a result of delays such as that which occurred in this killing, the *gendarmes*, like the cuckolded husband, were the last to find out or be told that a crime was suspected or a suicide had taken place in or at one of the "deodorized" crime scenes. Nevertheless, Cheryl Crane did Hollywood, and civilization in general, a favor by ridding the town of one of mobster Mickey Cohen's nastier, blackmailing, extortionate, woman-beating goons.

In the earlier decades of Hollywood, and even into the wartime forties, and even really, since the fifties, such cover-ups were and are particularly important. At the time, for instance, of the murder of the Ice Cream Blonde, Thelma Todd, famed choreographer Busby Berkeley was on trial for the drunk-driving murder of three people. The accident occurred, ironically, on Pacific Coast Highway, just a few hundred feet north of Thelma's cafe.

At about the same time, there was Mary Astor's explosive and dynamite-laden diary of her Hollywood and New York extramarital affairs — and all rated on a scale of one to ten. This was divulged during her divorce trial from Dr. Franklyn Thorpe. One passage read, "I don't know where George gets his staying power! (*) he must have cum three times in an hour!"

The diary was about to be incinerated on the orders of Superior Court Judge Goodwin J. Knight, but not before the foregoing and several other "purple passages," as they were dubbed because of the color of the diary, had been "leaked" to the sob sisters of the Hearst press. Knight, who presided over the case, did eventually order the destruction of the diary. This helped to keep the lid on the scandal in those days of semi-Victorian and Bible Belt morals. Knight also heard some of the more sordid evidence behind closed doors.

*Playwright George S. Kaufman, the partner of Moss Hart.

Thelma Todd's Cafe as it looked in 1957. It has changed very little since her death and is now the headquarters for a religious film producing company. (John Austin Collection)

(It should be pointed out that divorce in California in the thirties and into the forties was extremely hard to come by. Proven adultery was generally the only acceptable reason, except mental illness or imprisonment of one of the spouses. In fact, in keeping with the Wild West nature of California of that era, a cottage industry grew up around paid "professional adulterers" — those who would allow their pictures to be taken in bed with the divorcing spouse.)

Knight was later known as *Governor* Goodwin J. Knight for his handling of the Astor-Thorpe divorce and other little favors to the oligarchical society.

Another scandal at the time might, the moguls felt, cut into their industry's bloated profits which, even during the depths of the depression, were obscene as compared to others and the general economy of the 1930's.

This would also have been a catastrophe for the then well-oiled police departments of Los Angeles, and the outlying communities of Santa

Monica, Beverly Hills, Culver City, etc. It would also have shut off the Golden Faucet for city and state political leaders. Most of them, during those years, had a long history of "accommodating" the film industry in most, if not all of its requests. These included the appointment of District Attorneys under its contol such as Thomas Woolwine, Asa Keyes and Buron Fitts, and the appointment of judges including Knight. These appointees generally rendered verdicts and decisions in favor of the industry when called upon to do so.

Hollywood money, influence and high-powered publicity campaigns orchestrated by the experts of the film industry, assured the election of Knight as Governor of California — as it did many years later for another Favorite Son, Ronald Wilson Reagan, eventually propelling him into the White House.

One of the "fixers," whose job it was to notify judges of the "preferred outcome" of a case, divorce, or what have you, was the late William "Doc" Bishop of 20th Century-Fox. He was known as "Doc" by everyone because of this sideline to his regular job as director of Foreign Publicity and liaison with Hollywood's Foreign Press Corps. Bishop's boss, the director of publicity for Fox, was Harry Brand, whose brother was the late Edward J. Brand, the all powerful judge in West Los Angeles.

Pre-World War II Los Angeles had only one real industry apart from the fledgling aircraft factories just gaining a toehold — in Burbank, Lockheed Aircraft; and in Santa Monica, the Douglas Aircraft Company, which was then busily turning out the workhorse DC-3 transports for the world's airlines.

That one other real industry associated with Los Angeles was film-making. Apart from a City Hall bloated with fat cat civil servants, most of them political appointees and relatives of other corrupt elected officials of that era, the Make Believe Factories were the area's largest employer. In order to keep that industry on an even keel, a "neat and tidy" solution, *regardless of the truth*, was desperately needed in the Thelma Todd case and, later, the Mary Astor-Dr. Franklyn Thorpe divorce.

In both cases, that "neat and tidy" solution *was* found, thanks to the deep pockets and influence of the industry. It was also applied to several other cases over the years, including the murder of Marilyn Monroe.

Hedda Hopper, one of the "piranhas" of Hollywood of the thirties and forties, Gossip columnists rode high, wide and handsome in the Golden Era of Hollywood and could make or break an aspiring or established actor. (Marvin Paige Mot. Picture and TV Research Svc.)

Some background...

The motion picture industry is a business which sees the emotions and feelings of its stars, executives, and even lower echelon employees stripped bare by the largest concentration of reporters, radio and television commentators and gossip columnists in the world outside of Washington, D.C.

Many observers have surmised that the Hollywood press corps *is* the largest in the world concentrating on just one industry. This is so when you include the *maitre d's*, head waiters, car-wash jockeys, waiters, valet parking attendants, accountants, and Consuls for obscure, autonomous islands in the Caribbean, and the banana republics of Central America.

Some members of these categories of employment make up the bulk of the Hollywood Foreign Press Association — about 60% of the (non-voting) membership. Many of them arrived in Hollywood with dubious credentials from foreign publications in order to secure their "accreditation" to the Motion Picture Association of America, Inc. Without such "accreditation", no one is allowed inside a studio or on a movie set.

This is just one more method of Hollywood's *manipulating* people who work in, with, or for the industry. One bad word about the business, or revealing a hushed-up scandal, and the journalist finds himself/herself discredited or at the very bottom of a list. The only exception(s) to this rule are the three television networks and a few major metropolitan newspapers such as the Los Angeles *Times*, The New York *Times* and a few others of their ilk. They just have too much power. But even those have one eye cocked on the extensive advertising outlays of the studios in their publications and on their networks. Because of derogatory reports on the industry in some of them, advertising in those papers has been cancelled anywhere from three months to three years.

That is just the way the oligarchy works.

Some journalists, and especially the two major columnists of the thirties, forties and fifties, the vain and ignorant piranhas Louella Parsons and Hedda Hopper, had no regard for emotions — generally doing the bidding of the moguls — *regardless* of the damage to careers or the accuracy of their stories. It was — and still is — one of Hollywood's ways of ridding itself of people who betrayed or who betray its trust.

Parsons and Hopper terrorized Hollywood for decades. Hedda eventually died at her typewriter with a fruit bowl of a hat on her head. Eventually, "Lolly" Parsons could no longer control her bladder and was forced to retire. She had a very disconcerting habit in her last years of urinating while sitting on bar stools, and on chairs at cocktail and dinner parties. Many Hollywood hostesses, obliged to entertain her, heaved a sigh of relief at no longer having to call in the carpet and upholstery cleaners after every Parsons visit.

Louella (Lolly) Parsons, shown here with Claudette Colbert during a radio broadcast, was the other "piranha" of gossip columnists of the thirties, forties and fifties. It has always been said that Parsons secured her "lifetime" tenure with The Hearst Press by witnessing the shooting death of Thomas H. Ince by either Charlie Chaplin or by Hearst himself. Parsons retired only when she could no longer control her bladder and started "peeing in place," as her detractors remarked. (Marvin Paige's Mot. Picture & TV Research Svc.)

Franchot Tone (L) and Robert Taylor on the set at MGM during an interview with Hedda Hopper for her nationally syndicated "gossip" column. (Marvin Paige's Mot. Picture & TV Research Svc.)

Regardless, it was their business, as it was mine for thirty-odd years, to get news of the greats and near-greats of Hollywood. The appetites, insatiable as they are, of movie-goers and fans, and television addicts around the world, have to be sated on a regular basis. Most of the Hollywood Press Corps are well paid and well entertained by the studios and press agents. This manages to keep the names of their pictures and their clients and TV series fresh in the minds of movie and TV fans around the world.

We agree that it is hard for people engaged in an industry that so taxes their mental, moral and physical fibre with twelve- to fourteen-hour days not to become embroiled in scandal now and again. At least those at the very top. It is almost impossible for them to have a well-ordered home-life. This is one of the major reasons for so many divorces in Never-Never Land, Tinseltown, Baghdad-on-the-Pacific, or whatever you want to call Hollywood. Perhaps "Babes in Toyland" would be a good nomenclature for its denizens.

But those who have reached the pinnacle as stars, top executives and the like, earn — if that is the correct word — obscene amounts of money. One studio head in 1988 received over $30 million in salary, bonuses and stock options. Others regularly receive anywhere from $5 to $7 million. Is it any wonder that those salaries and perks have to be protected by fair means or foul?

But because of these vast sums and the power that goes with them, is it also any wonder that "insecurity" is the operative word in Hollywood? One breath of scandal can blow them out of the catbird seat and those multi-million-dollar paychecks. It can cost them careers, estates in Beverly Hills, Bel-Air, and Pacific Palisades, and million dollar homes in Malibu, not to mention a garage full of exotic automobiles.

That is why in so many instances within the pages of this book, murders and suicides have, as you will see, been covered up or disguised, as was that of Marilyn Monroe, resulting in **Hollywood's Unsolved Mysteries.**

And let the chips fall where they may!

Undone By Ambition

Victoria Lynn Morgan, the girl from Montclair, California who parlayed a .25 cent cup of coffee into becoming the mistress of Alfred Bloomingdale, one of the most powerful members of former President Ronald Reagan's "Kitchen Cabinet." He had sado-masochistic tendencies which, after a while, bored Morgan in spite of the $10,000 to $18,000 per month "allowance" she received from Bloomingdale until his death. (Wide World).

"The audio tapes began to tell deep dark secrets of members of the Reagan administration as well as Reagan himself. Vicki had no chance to survive after she put on (audio) tape what she knew."

— *Anonymous*

"It really is an ugly mess, more than anyone will ever really know..."

— *Victoria Lynn Morgan*
August 13, 1982

2 ... Who *Really* Killed Vicki Morgan...?

The bottom line on Victoria Lynn Morgan can be summed up as:

The Girl Who Knew Too Much!

Those six words provide the most powerful of all motives for her murder on July 7, 1983, in a rented condominium at 4171-D Colfax Avenue, Studio City, California, from which she was about to be evicted for non-payment of rent. The condo was located just 12 miles from a luxurious home at 1611 Tower Grove Road, Beverly Hills. Morgan had paid the rent for the house in an exclusive area of Beverly Hills out of the generous allowance provided her by department store heir and Diner's Club founder Alfred Bloomingdale. It is a murder San Fernando Valley residents still talk about several years after a self-admitted homosexual, Marvin Pancoast, walked into the North Hollywood Division of the Los Angeles Police Department and said that he had "...just killed someone."

But had he?

Pancoast was, after all, "mentally disturbed" and had spent some time in a mental hospital. It was there that he first met Vicki Morgan. She had checked herself into the facility "for therapy and observation for depression." According to friends and relatives, including his long-suffering mother, Pancoast was very easily brainwashed.

The "someone" Pancoast confessed to killing turned out to be Vicki Morgan, the 30-year-old daughter of a U.S. Air Force recruiter, Delbert Morgan, and a British mother, Constance. While Vicki was still an infant,

Vicki Morgan's condo in Studio City where she was murdered.   (John Austin Collection.)

Morgan deserted the family, leaving Constance, Vicki and two other children virtually penniless.

After living off welfare checks and odd jobs for four years, Constance married Ralph Laney, a tool and die maker from Montclair, California. The bedroom community of lower middle-class families in the foothills of the San Gabriel Mountains lies 50 miles due east from Baghdad-on-the-Pacific.

Several years later, Laney keeled over and died of a heart attack just one month after his life insurance policy had lapsed! Vicki, by then, was a blossoming 13-year-old who was left with little supervision while her mother went to work to support her brood. At 16, Vicki became pregnant and bore a son, Todd, around her 17th birthday. The child was fathered by Vicki's high school sweetheart, now a doctor in Santa Barbara. She later married him in order to give the child a name.

When Todd was about a year old, Vicki decided her life was going nowhere and decided to try her luck in Hollywood. She left Todd to be raised by her long-suffering mother, his father contributing to the child's support.

Entrance to condo units where Vicki Morgan met her death. (John Austin Collection.)

So started the trail of the destruction and early death of Victoria Lynn Morgan.

Vicki first met Alfred Bloomingdale in a Sunset Strip coffee shop, The Old World, a hangout at that time for Hollywood *roués* looking for some action with nubile aspiring actresses who used to hang out at the outdoor tables because of their proximity to many agents and casting offices.

Vicki was killing time over a cup of coffee between appointments for potential modeling assignments when Bloomingdale struck up a conversation. Following the usual small talk, he convinced the still naive child-woman from Montclair that he could, with his connections, land her some modeling and acting assignments. This was the sort of conversation heard many times a day at The Old World. Nevertheless, Vicki, who had been making the rounds for several months, gave Bloomingdale her telephone number, believing she would never hear from him again.

But hear she did and, as he promised, Bloomingdale had made an appointment for her with famed producer Mervyn LeRoy. Over a breakfast meeting, LeRoy had agreed to see Vicki to see if he could further her career. After the meeting, LeRoy realized that she was too inexperienced for him to do anything for her. All that came out of the meeting was that Vicki met Cary Grant, a business associate of the producer. That introduction resulted in a short-lived affair with Grant at his Beverly Hills home and in Malibu, and a few hundred dollars in Vicki's pocket.

A few weeks after she stopped seeing Grant, Vicki agreed to become Bloomingdale's mistress. It was then she began receiving checks of $10,000 to $18,000 per month. These came from several different companies controlled by Bloomingdale. He made it quite clear to Vicki that the money was in return for her full-time companionship and for "therapy" for what Vicki later learned to call his "Marquis de Sade" complex. The Morgan-Bloomingdale relationship reached a point where Vicki even accompanied Bloomingdale on extensive overseas business trips. She often followed him in secret when his socialite wife, Betsy, a close friend of Nancy and Ronald Reagan, was along. While Betsy was, as usual, shopping, Bloomingdale and Morgan found plenty of time for their trysts in London, Paris, and in a hotel near the Vatican in Rome.

Bloomingdale's initial sexual attraction grew into genuine affection for Vicki and her willingness to accommodate his sado-masochistic desires. One might say that $10,000 to $18,000 per month will finance an awful lot of desire.

Vicki's first sexual encounter with Bloomingdale involved two prostitutes who were called in by Alfred. Once there, they proceeded to beat the hell out of each other and Bloomingdale. All this was in Vicki's presence so that the aging Lothario could get a hard on and mount his new and voluptuous toy.

☆   ☆   ☆

Bloomingdale had been a very early supporter of Ronald Reagan, even before Reagan became Governor of California. He was also a member of Reagan's "Kitchen Cabinet," a club made up of wealthy and influential Southern California businessmen and political leaders.

During the 1980 Presidential campaign, Bloomingdale installed his mistress as a Republican campaign assistant. He saw to it that she acted as driver and guide for the then Vice Presidential candidate, George Bush, during his three campaign swings into California. She once told her "palimony" lawyer, Marvin Mitchelson, that she overheard and was told secrets which would make Watergate look like pre-school.

With the help of Vicki and her friends, Bloomingdale was able to service the often bizarre sexual appetites of the rich and famous throughout the world, especially when they came to the City of the Angels.

One player in the high stakes fun and games in the house Bloomingdale owned in the Hollywood Hills was Marvin Pancoast. Unbeknownst to Vicki or Pancoast at the time, Bloomingdale had the house equipped with state-of-the-art video cameras in every room and hidden behind false walls. Even the three johns were "wired" behind two way mirrors. Pancoast was becoming known in the theatrical agency where he worked in the mail room and around Hollywood as quite a character. Vicki and Pancoast, at the request of Bloomingdale, would often "share" a high ranking member of the late Administration. Pancoast would then, shall we say, give a "blow by blow" account to his friends or anyone else willing to listen.

Anyone who was important in the pre-Administration and the administration of Ronald Reagan and who wanted *divertissement* called on Alfred, regardless of what his particular fetish might be. At the start, it appeared that Bloomingdale just wanted to indulge his fantasies while maintaining some control over the political climate in America, using Vicki's and Marvin's genitalia for the purpose. Everything that took place in the Hollywood Hills house was recorded on video tape. It was these tapes which eventually figured in the destruction of Vicki Morgan.

As Confucius is said to have written centuries ago, *The penis is the axis upon which the world revolves*. It is obvious that Alfred Bloomingdale believed in that adage wholeheartedly. He was, at the time, becoming very concerned about the life insurance policy that these tapes would represent for Vicki if anything happened to him. But Vicki's sophistication in survival tactics was non-existent and she never prepared for such an eventuality by stashing the tapes where they would serve as her life insurance policy. But, by this time, the relationship between Victoria Lynn Morgan and Alfred Bloomingdale had developed into a love story of epic proportions.

Once she became Alfred Bloomingdale's mistress of record, Vicki's life changed radically; she lived in the fast lane which only those with inborn sophistication and street smarts could survive. Vicki had neither, merely an educated sexual appetite in order to pay the bills. She had come a long way, nevertheless, from the working class neighborhood of Montclair. She had learned early in life how to use her voluptuous body and bedroom charms to get what she wanted.

ALFRED BLOOMINGDALE
1888 CENTURY PARK EAST, SUITE 1018
LOS ANGELES, CALIFORNIA 90067

February 12, 1982

Mr. William McComas
Marina Bay Hotel
2175 State Road 84
Ft. Lauderdale, Florida 33312

Dear Bill:

As per our conversation, if we finalize Showbiz
Pizza, then Vicki Morgan, now residing at 1611
Tower Grove, Beverly Hills, California, is entitled
to ½ (one-half) of my interest in the above. Her
name should be included in all contracts so that
this cannot be taken away from her, in the event
of my incapacitation or absence.

Regards,

Alfred Bloomingdale
cc: Vicki Morgan
    David Rousso
    Barry Rubin

WITNESS   WITNESS

Alice Valenzuela   Charles F. Charles

1918 PLANT AVE   2615 Hampton Ave

Redondo Beach, CA   L.A. CA 00016
        90278

Letters from Alfred Bloomingdale authorizing payments to Vicki Morgan after his death.

ALFRED BLOOMINGDALE

1888 CENTURY PARK EAST, SUITE 1018
LOS ANGELES, CALIFORNIA 90067

February 12, 1982

Miss Vicki Morgan
1611 Tower Grove
Beverly Hills, Ca. 90210
Dear Vicki:
I agree to pay you $10,000 a month for two years
beginning March 1, 1982. This money will be paid
to you by the 28th of each month from the proceeds
of my profit from Marina Bay, etc.
Bill McComas has been authorized to do this.

Regards,

Alfred Bloomingdale
cc: William McComas
    David Rousso
    Barry Rubin

WITNESS   WITNESS
Alice Valenzuela   Charles F Chandler
1918 PLANT Ave   7615 Arlington Ave
Redondo Beach, CA   Lt. Co. 90774
91278

43

Over the long haul, Vicki was being turned off by Bloomingdale's ever-increasing appetite for Sado-Masochism. She was also tired of, and bored with beating him with thongs, straps, whips and anything else that came to hand.

Sometime around 1974, Vicki was in one of her "I hate Al" moods and moved into the Beverly Hills harem of financier Bernie Kornfeld, whom she had met while with Alfred. The diminutive Kornfeld installed Vicki in a bedroom connected to his via a secret passageway. She soon became tired of being just another of Kornfeld's toys, as well. She escaped from his clutches and drove to New York in one of the financier's cars and with one of his credit cards, and several of Alfred's which he had given to her.

In New York, Morgan took on modeling assignments from the top-drawer Ford agency, where she had been introduced by Kornfeld several years before. She stayed away from Alfred.

Vicki worked with another beautiful model who is now Mrs. Cristina Ferrare Thomopolous, formerly Cristina De Lorean (and, before that, as Cristina Ferrare while under contract to 20th Century-Fox). Both were flown to far-flung modeling assignments — of a sort — in a Kornfeld jet piloted by William Hetrick. It was on one of these assignments that Morgan met and had an affair with the King of Morocco, and became one of his palace favorites because of her ability to please him sexually. He "rewarded" Vicki with many thousands of dollars in jewelry.

(Hetrick, the pilot, is the same William Hetrick who, in 1982, was charged along with auto manufacturer John Z. De Lorean (then Cristina's husband) in a bungled FBI "sting" operation for dealing in cocaine. De Lorean plead "Not Guilty" and was acquitted.

(De Lorean's acquittal came after the Federal Court Jury had viewed video tapes of De Lorean receiving a suitcase full of the nose candy in a hotel room near the Los Angeles International Airport. Hetrick, charged in the same case, plead "Guilty," cooperated in the prosecution, so called, of De Lorean, and went to jail for several years!)

A Federal Agent provided another glimpse of Vicki Morgan during another of her many separations from Bloomingdale. The agent asserted he met her at the now defunct Rotunda Restaurant on Washington's Capitol Hill. This was an elegant spa with a clientele of Congressmen and Senators where many of them could be observed by a practiced eye walking out with briefcases with which they had not arrived. It also served as the hangout for government officials of all ranks, call girls, and many mobsters of note.

Vicki Morgan with defrocked financier Bernie Kornfeld at his Beverly Hills estate. Vicki once "escaped" from Bloomingdale and went to Kornfeld's estate before leaving in one of his cars and becoming a model in New York. (Wide World).

It was the agent's job to hang around the watering hole because it was considered at the time as a Big Bird intelligence nest. Vicki, our agent friend recalled, seemed to be a warm and friendly person, and she was part of a "sexpionage" ring operating out of the restaurant. It was never definitely established whether or not Bloomingdale put Vicki up to this to further several of his Machiavellian schemes. It is firmly believed that he did. The agent noted that one day while browsing in the Woodward and Lathrop department store, he bumped into Vicki just as she was planting a kiss on the cheek of one Alexei Goodarzi who presided over the Rotunda as *maitre d'*. Vicki then introduced a second, distinguished looking man as "my father". The agent subsequently learned that he was Alfred Bloomingdale and that he often introduced Vicki as "my daughter".

It was alleged in many circles that Goodarzi was a high ranking Washington pimp, a procurer and a dual agent of the Shah of Iran's secret police, the dreaded SAVAK, as well as the CIA. You could say it was sort of a fox-guarding-the-chicken-coop situation.

Three years after he first met Vicki Morgan and Alfred Bloomingdale, Goodarzi's body was found behind the wheel of his new Porsche, his brains decorating the dashboard because of three well-placed bullet holes in the back of his head. The Iranian's "trick book" and other potential blackmail material were later found in his apartment, but his killer, or killers, were never found; perhaps, as some have said, on purpose.

"The Goodarzi Connection," as it came to be known, demonstrates that Vicki Morgan was getting in knee-deep with high stakes players whose death might only be a telephone call away. Many have said her position at the time was not unlike that of Judith Campbell Exner, a one-time Hollywood and New York party girl. Exner carried on a clandestine affair with the late John F. Kennedy in and out of the White House bedrooms, at the same time that she was the mistress of Mafia mobster Sam Giancana. During the same period she was also servicing Giancana's lieutenant, Johnny Roselli, a long-standing friend of Alfred Bloomingdale dating from the 1940's.

(Campbell had been introduced to JFK in 1960 by Frank Sinatra. Bloomingdale had once been an agent for Sinatra during the singer's salad days as a big band crooner. Because of Bloomingdale's association with Roselli, the FBI had opened a file on the department store scion in the early 1960's.)

Vicki should have been able to foretell her future at the time of Goodarzi's death because three of that circle's principals died violent and non-accidental deaths.

- John F. Kennedy was assassinated in Dallas on November 22, 1963;

- Sam Giancana was shot point blank in the head in the kitchen of his Chicago mansion. (This was just a few days prior to his testifying before a U.S. Senate Committee probing the joint CIA-Mafia adventure in Cuba in which it was planned to put out the lights of Fidel Castro once and for all);

- Johnny Roselli's body was found stuffed into a fifty-gallon oil drum floating in Biscayne Bay near Miami in 1976. (This was shortly after Roselli had testified, briefly, before a House panel investigation which had re-opened the JFK assassination).

- Only Exner and Sinatra are alive today.

Following Ronald Reagan's ascendancy to the White House, Bloomingdale was looking forward to his long-hoped-for Ambassadorship to France. Unfortunately, it was discovered that his wife, Betsy, had been caught red-handed in 1975 attempting to smuggle tens of thousands of dollars worth of Dior gowns into the United States by the "Doctored Invoice Ploy" to cut down on customs duty.

Betsy, who had always been considered a paragon of virtue and a pillar of the Washington, D.C.-Beverly Hills-Palm Springs society axis, was, in spite of Alfred's power and connections, sentenced to one year's probation and a stiff $5,000 fine. The Judge in the case excoriated Betsy Bloomingdale, telling her, "...you deserve the contempt of this court and of the society which has served you so well!"

This conviction of Betsy made the Bloomingdales ineligible for such a sensitive position as an Ambassadorship, even though his affair with Vicki Morgan *could* have been overlooked. Nevertheless, Ronald Reagan named his old California backer to a far more important post: The Foreign Intelligence Advisory Board, an organization that still oversees covert actions, dirty tricks, and CIA undercover operations of every kind. It is, perhaps, the single most sensitive intelligence apparatus in the U.S. Government. (This Commission was hurriedly called into play during

Alfred Bloomingdale, one of the original members of Ronald Reagan's "Kitchen Cabinet." On his marriage to Betsy Bloomingdale in September, 1946, he remarked to friends: "One morning I was a Democrat and a Jew. The next morning, a Catholic and a Republican!"

the Iranscam scandal in 1986-1987 to help alleviate some of the damage to the Administration, and to Ronald Reagan.)

The life of Alfred Bloomingdale, when it is broken down, dissected and analyzed (and one conjectures about the information and state secrets he *must* have shared with Vicki Morgan), reads like an intelligence or crime *dossier* you might find in a John Le Carre or Ian Fleming novel. There is one more very strange connection which came to light for the first time following Bloomingdale's death, and the revelation is believed to have originated with Vicki - something she should not have known for her own protection.

When Bloomingdale married the former Betsy Newling in 1946, he changed his religion from the Jewish faith to Catholicism. He was, it turned out, a member of the world-wide Knights of Malta. Major figures in both the Reagan Administration and the Bloomingdale-Morgan affair, in short, in the murder of Vicki Morgan and the resultant cover-up, are all associated with the Knights of Malta. Johnny Roselli and Sam Giancana, Neil Reagan, the President's brother, and William Clark, the President's former Secretary of the Interior, are or were members. Membership was also enjoyed by the late William Casey, the CIA chief until his death in 1987.

Bloomingdale was also much more than a prominent Catholic layman; he was nothing less than a Papal Knight. According to Sheldon Davis, his biographer, "Alfred was a frequent visitor to the Vatican with tremendous influence." It was not very well known until the Banco Ambrosiano-Vatican Bank-Richard Calvi-Bishop Marcinkus conspiracy that the Vatican is — or was — the center of a world-wide intelligence and diplomatic network, and Bloomingdale was at the very center of that network.

Bloomy, as he was known, was an enigma wrapped inside a riddle.

When Alfred Bloomingdale, who had been ill for years, finally realized that he did not have long to live, he took steps to provide Vicki with both financial and — he believed — physical security. They had been together for about twelve years. He knew that the assets of his estate, including the Bloomingdales Department Store stock, would be tied up in the family trust. Therefore, he wrote a letter to Vicki and advised her that she would be paid $10,000 per month from several companies he controlled outside the Trust. This included the Marina Bay Hotel in Fort Lauderdale, Florida.

Bloomingdale then wrote a letter to William McComas, the general partner of the hotel property instructing him that Vicki was to receive one half of his interest in another business, Show Biz Pizza Parlors. "Her name," wrote Bloomingdale, "should be included in all contracts so that this cannot be taken away from her in the event of my incapacitation or absence." He was obviously referring to his impending death from cancer.

Following his death, Vicki prevailed upon palimony attorney Marvin Mitchelson to file a $5 million suit against the estate of Alfred Bloomingdale which served to publicize the lurid details of the sado-masochistic tendencies of her benefactor. Betsy Bloomingdale, upon learning of the secret letters to pay Vicki a monthly allowance, vigorously opposed the payments and cut them off.

For physical insurance, Bloomingdale is said to have supplied Vicki with the video tapes from the Hollywood Hills home, several of which revealed major figures in politics and the Reagan Administration in action with Vicki, Marvin Pancoast, and other males and females.

Bloomingdale never realized that the possession of the tapes could cut both ways. In the end, Victoria Lynn Morgan, the 17-year-old from Montclair, California, who made the big time through a 25c cup of coffee at The Old World Coffee Shop, became a two-time loser within a very short period.

Several weeks after Bloomingdale's death, Judge Christian E. Markey, sympathetic to the Reagan Administration and its sycophants, tossed out the bulk of Vicki's palimony suit, including the letter to McComas. Markey ruled that Vicki's relationship with Alfred Bloomingdale was "no more than that of a wealthy, older man, married paramour and young, well-paid mistress." With this pompous pronouncement from the bench, Markey reduced Vicki Morgan to no more than a hooker who had been paid by the trick.

And in the early morning hours of July 7, 1983, someone cashed in Morgan's life insurance policy with a baseball bat. The Louisville Slugger later turned up with *no blood stains* and having *never been dusted for fingerprints*. (When noise is a factor in detection, a baseball bat is a favorite method of hired killers.)

In the pursuit of the killer or killers of Vicki Morgan — **and nobody for**

one minute believes that Marvin Pancoast killed Vicki Morgan, in spite of his (later recanted) confession — the trail winds circuitously. It runs through the garbage dump of America's organized crime and into the back alleys of sinister covert actions, and even Washington politicos.

☆   ☆   ☆

The Morgan-Bloomingdale liaison was an *affaire d'amour* of power and its absolute corruption. Vicki Morgan was caught in the middle and was too naive to realize what was happening to her. The girl was taken out of the country, but the country was never taken out of her, to paraphrase an old cliche.

Following Pancoast's strange and rambling admissions to the desk sergeant at the North Hollywood Division, LAPD radio car officer Kenneth Henckle was dispatched to the condo on Colfax Avenue. Henckle found the front door unlocked, and the living room littered with packing boxes preparatory to Vicki's move.

Henckle made his way cautiously upstairs to the master bedroom on the second floor of the three-story structure. On entering the bedroom through the partially opened door, he discovered a body wrapped in a bloodstained yellow shirt and bikini panties, its right arm entangled in the bed sheets, lying on one side of a king-sized bed.

It was the body of Victoria Lynn Morgan, thirteen years removed from Montclair, California, now brutally undone by ambition for a life in the fast lane!

Blood, according to Henckle, was everywhere. On the walls, the ceiling, the floor. The baseball bat of light-colored wood was resting across the body. Without concerning himself with fingerprints, which might have been on the bat, Henckle placed it against the wall so he could check the pulse for any sign of life. There was none, and Henckle advised his Desk Sergeant by walkie-talkie of the situation as it appeared to him.

The Watch Commander of the Homicide Division, Detective William Welch, left the questioning of a distraught, confused and rambling Marvin Pancoast to Detective Jay Rush, and headed for the Colfax condo. It was noted at the time that Pancoast did not have a spot of blood on him anywhere. This fact was never brought out during his trial. But, if he had killed Vicki, he could not have helped but be covered in the substance. No bloody clothes from which he might have changed *were ever found in the condo, either*.

When Welch entered the bedroom he, too, noticed the blood everywhere and had to push aside boxes and cartons to inspect the homicide scene. Welch also found zipper clothes bags emblazoned with the distinctive logos of world famous hotels and airlines, as well as *couturiers*, belongings strewn everywhere, dresser drawers on the floor, their contents scattered as though the apartment had been ransacked in a frenetic search for something. If he had planned to confess, Pancoast would never have gone to the trouble of creating such chaos over and above the moving arrangements already made.

On a night stand, Welch recounted in his report, there were a quantity of drugs and pill cases but, as he would testify later on, he left them there. The so-called experienced homicide investigator did nothing to secure the probable cause of Morgan's death, *twenty or more video cassettes*, VCR and video camera in a cabinet against the wall. As far as Welch was concerned, they were tapes of movies and labeled as such. (What better place or method to "hide" anything. In plain sight and, in this case, cassettes marked with movie titles?) Welch admitted at Pancoast's trial that he did not list, catalog or scan any of those tapes. When asked what he did with them, Welch replied, "They were left in the residence!"

Welch did admit that he did take the baseball bat after initialing it with a marker pen he found on the night table and placed it in a plastic bag he had also found in the apartment. As many members of the press, and others pointed out later, it was indeed a strange and unorthodox way to conduct a serious murder investigation, a "confession" notwithstanding. It appeared to many people that Welch, in the true tradition of supporting the oligarchical society and the tenets of the Hollywood community, was trying to sanitize the scene and wrap up the investigation with the least amount of speculation.

But, in even more remarkable revelations, Welch was asked, "Did you either personally, or did you request anyone, to check the deceased's residence for fingerprints? Or the baseball bat? Or have the pills found beside the bed analyzed for their drug content?" Welch replied, to the astonishment of everyone, "No. I did not!"

☆   ☆   ☆

During the time Vicki lived at the Colfax Avenue address, she was considering the possibility of writing a book with a writer she knew, a Gordon Basichis. She had met the writer several years earlier and contacted him following a turn-down by a major talent agency to represent her on a major publishing contract.

Before contacting Basichis, Vicki seriously considered writing *Alfred's Mistress* herself following his death in August, 1982. She felt that with her bankroll dead and buried, she could not afford to pay a writer up to 50% of any proceeds the book would fetch. She needed the money because Vicki Morgan, who never realized there would be a tomorrow, did not invest or save one dime of the monthly allowances she received from Bloomingdale over many years. (She had asked Alfred to advise her on this many times, but he always put it off. He obviously wanted to keep Vicki under his thumb and could not if she developed an outside income.)

Pancoast arranged a meeting for Vicki with a lower echelon agent at the William Morris Agency, his employer for several years. The agent began negotiations to represent Morgan in the sale of the book rights, along with the movie and/or TV sales which might result. Vicki visited the agency three times, so far along were the negotiations.

But then in September or October of 1982, we learned that a senior executive of the agency, which already represented General Alexander Haig and ex-President Gerald R. Ford, along with many important people of their ilk, received a call from a highly placed client. The executive was told that if the William Morris Agency represented Vicki Morgan, dire results from Government agencies, including the Internal Revenue Service, could ensue.

☆　　☆　　☆

Pancoast, a homosexual with a long history of psychological problems, first met Vicki Morgan in 1979 when both were patients at a private Southern California mental hospital. He worked and helped Vicki gather information and material for her palimony suit because she couldn't afford to hire private investigators.

Following Judge Markey's dismissal of her suit, Vicki, whom many friends described as "Gucci'd and Giorgio'd to death," was forced to sell most of her jewelry and her Mercedes convertible. Pancoast agreed to move in with her in the condo as a sort of bodyguard, and to split the $1,000 per month rent.

Basichis testified at the trial that Pancoast came in late the night before Morgan's death and paced back and forth in the third floor bedroom. "This was not like him," the author testified, "and then at 2 a.m., he was on the telephone talking to someone. I stayed, made love to Vicki and then we talked until 7:30 a.m. and recorded some more of her memoirs."

"Before I left," he continued, "Vicki confided in me that she was afraid of being murdered. I have a feeling," he told the court, "that someone with knowledge of the Bloomingdale 'tapes' had approached her, possibly through Pancoast, with a proposal for blackmail." He did not elaborate any further.

Vicki Morgan was murdered the following night about 2 a.m., according to the Los Angeles County Coroner. She was, his report said, beaten to death with a blunt instrument. "I read the confession of Marvin," Basichis continued. "He (Pancoast) walks into a police station and voluntarily confesses. (It) covered eight or ten loose-leaf pages. Nobody ever asked him, 'Was anyone with you in the apartment?' Nobody said, 'Should we go over this again?' It seems strange. A poor approach to a murder investigation," Basichis told the court. "Why, he never even had any blood on his clothes and blood was all over the bedroom according to the police report. He couldn't have helped but get splattered with Vicki's blood!"

On the surface, it would appear that the LAPD detectives wanted to sweep the Morgan investigation under the rug, get it into court and disposed of as quickly as possible. Perhaps they were being pressured by early morning telephone calls when the news got out of Vicki's death, or someone was contacted by someone involved in Morgan's death, or by someone who had wanted her dead. That contact could possibly have been Jay Paul, a suspended LAPD officer who had been playing footsie with U.S. Intelligence Agents while he was a member of the LAPD Intelligence Unit. No one ever expected Marvin Pancoast to recant his confession.

The co-author of yet another book on Victoria Lynn Morgan, **Vicki**, Anne Louise Bardach, commented, "This is really a story of police negligence. The scene of the crime was NOT sealed by the LAPD until 24 hours following the murder. What kind of police work is that? It's unheard of," she said. "People could just walk in and walk out. And they did. If there were any 'sex tapes' in the condo, then they could easily have disappeared during those 24 hours."

What Bardach, Basichis or anyone else failed to point out is the fact that when Pancoast went to the North Hollywood Police Station, "to confess," he had left the door to the condo unlocked or ajar. This explained the easy access to the condo by Officer Henckle. However, what has also never been explained, nor has anyone ever questioned it: *how did Pancoast get to the police station, four miles away, without a car?* His old blue Oldsmobile was found where he parked it when he arrived home earlier in the evening. Did he walk? No, the time element rules that out. Did he take a taxi? This was never checked *by the media or the police*. Did someone in the apartment at the time drive him there and then take off, perhaps convincing the mentally disturbed Pancoast that he either killed or contributed to Vicki's death? *In other words, brainwash a disturbed mind under drug induced hypnosis?*

We learned from friends of Vicki's and neighbors following her death that Pancoast went out around midnight on the murder night. When he returned a short time later, they said, he was accompanied by Basichis and four other men, the group arriving in two cars. Since the Coroner placed the time of Vicki's death as early as 2 a.m., *possibly* before, this development is intriguing in the extreme. There was at least an hour and a half from the supposed 2 a.m. death of Vicki until Officer Henckle arrived at 3:30 a.m. (There was no one in the condo when Henckle arrived).

Who were those other people who arrived with Pancoast, and where were they while Vicki was having her skull crushed with a Louisville Slugger in the master bedroom? Did "they" aid and abet Vicki's death for an ulterior motive such as obtaining possession of the so-called "sex tapes?" Could Pancoast, in his confused mental state have mentioned the tapes and their value to those in power?

It would have been a relatively simple matter in that hour and a half for anyone to have walked upstairs, searched (and ransacked?) the bedroom and gone through the twenty or so cassettes in Vicki's bedroom, even viewing two or three or more minutes of each tape to find the incriminating one, and then leave with one or more cassettes under their arm. It will be recalled that Detective Welch never mentioned how many tapes there were in his investigation.

There is precious little physical evidence, if any, to link Marvin Pancoast to the death of Vicki Morgan — even though he was found guilty by a jury. His "confession" was recanted within hours after it was dictated to detectives at North Hollywood. Further, Pancoast *had no motive*. In homicide cases all over the world, police look for a suspect with a motive, then means and the opportunity. With Pancoast having no motive, the chain was broken at its most important link.

But it is those tapes of alleged orgies which still have many people in high places very concerned over their eventual fate and who might have them.

Writing in the *Rebel*, a defunct magazine of the early 1980's, investigative reporters William Turner (a former FBI agent) and Donald Freed wrote:

> "The Police disinterest in the video tapes lasted precisely four days following Vicki's death. On the night of July 11, a wake was held for Vicki at the home of Sally Talbert, one of her oldest friends. Michael Dave, Vicki's personal

attorney who had drawn up the **Alfred's Mistress** contract with Gordon Basichis for Vicki, was there.

"Around 10 p.m. Dave received a call from LAPD homicide detective Bill Welch, who was in charge of the murder investigation, so called, of Vicki Morgan. He and Dave had attended school together.

"Welch wanted to know where the video tapes were that had been in Vicki's condo. Dave verified with Vicki's mother, Constance Laney, that they were among Vicki's possessions at her Montclair home. Welch told the attorney to have Mrs. Laney get them at once and bring them to him.

"Dave argued that it was late and a two-hour round trip to Montclair would be made in the morning. Listen, Mike, I want you to know that I'm prepared to get a search warrant tonight and get those tapes,' Welch warned the attorney.

"After much *hondling* back and forth, it was agreed that Dave would call a Stanley Weisberg, the Deputy District Attorney in charge of the Pancoast prosecution, who had been putting the heat on Welch. Weisberg, who had gone to law school with Dave, allowed him to promise to bring in the tapes first thing in the morning. The attorney complied without viewing them."

What undoubtedly triggered the frantic interest in Vicki's video tape collection was another attorney, Robert K. Steinberg, and his startling disclosure that someone had delivered to him two of the tapes two days previously which showed some of the then Reagan administration at play. But, later, at Pancoast's preliminary hearing, Welch and Weisberg did a tap dance around the court room that made it seem as if the tapes were still out at Montclair where Victoria Lynn Morgan, as a young teenager, first learned the joy of sex in the back seat of a hot rod.

"When you last saw them (the tapes) they were still in the condo on Colfax Avenue. Is that correct?" Weisberg asked Welch.

"Yes, sir," was the answer from the witness stand.

And was that apartment and its contents released to some person?" the Deputy D.A. inquired, rather gingerly.

"Yes, it was," replied Welch, brushing an imaginary speck from his polyester suit. "To Mrs. Laney as the deceased's executor."

"Have you, at any time since, seen any of those video tapes again?" Weisberg wanted to know.

"No! I have not!" Welch answered quietly.

Weisberg's intent to keep the tapes from being entered into evidence is understandable. It was a wise career move. He could have found himself prosecuting claim jumpers and dog-nappers in the Mojave Desert.

Prior to Pancoast's preliminary hearing, Steinberg, a showboat of the legal profession of Beverly Hills, held a press conference to announce the existence of the two tapes in his possession. He said that he and two others, one a lawyer, the other a Federal employee, had viewed them over the weekend. They appeared to be a year or two old and showed Bloomingdale and five other men, one a former U.S. Congressman, and two others holding high posts in the Reagan Administration. The sex tapes, Steinberg asserted at the press conference, "...could bring down the present administration!"

A few days later, Steinberg's bombshell was reduced to shrapnel when, faced with a court order to turn the tapes over to the police and/or the Federal Bureau of Investigation, Steinberg alibied that they had been, "stolen from a gym bag in my office during a press conference."

A mocking Los Angeles press corps turned the tapes into the **Maltese Falcon** of the Vicki Morgan case.

Again, in the *Rebel*, Turner wrote:

> "The *Rebel* has interviewed a person close to the situation (not Steinberg) who contends that the tapes DO exist and show three separate sessions: (1) Vicki Morgan, Alfred Bloomingdale, and an unidentified female; (2) Barry Goldwater, Jr. (the former Congressman) and Edwin Meese III, one of Bloomingdale's old time playmates; and (3) unnamed Reagan associates with various females and Vicki Morgan engaging in oral sex."

Because of the explosive nature of this statement, the tale of the tapes went largely unreported in the Los Angeles media, print or electronic. Only the left wing throwaway with a huge circulation, the *LA Weekly*, ran an article by Anne Louise Bardach, (the co-author, with Joyce Milton, of **Vicki**) which named names. In a sidebar to the Bardach article, the editors of *LA Weekly*, further buttressing the fact that the tapes did (or do) exist, stated:

> "Sources the *Weekly* would tend to believe are reliable say that Meese almost certainly appears to be one of the men on

such tapes, even given the difficulty of making a positive identification of someone on a video tape.

"According to a second extremely reliable source, Vicki knew Meese and met with him both before and after the 1980 Presidential election. Meese, it might be noted, was a friend of Bloomingdale's who met Vicki through him and, according to the *Weekly's* source, saw her several more times after that."

What the fate of those tapes is, or has been, in the intervening years since Vicki's death, is anyone's guess. However, from the author's informants, they still do exist. They could be, we are told, being held back by some powerful individual with megabucks to play with, who purchased the tapes and is protecting the Administration. They could be being held also, to use as a pawn in legislation of some benefit to the owner. This is what we have been told by people privy to the situation.

So, the question still remains, and probably always will, *who killed Victoria Lynn Morgan*, the voluptuous young courtesan who emerged from a small, working-class bedroom community of Southern California and into the bedrooms of some of the wealthiest and most powerful men in the U.S. and Europe?

It is very doubtful that Marvin Pancoast, now allegedly dying of AIDS in a California prison, committed the murder; he had no motive and had always been very protective of Vicki. When he walked into the North Hollywood police station, there was not a trace of blood on him, even though the murder scene was a bloody mess. There were no fingerprint checks made of the baseball bat or the murder scene itself. When one was made *several days after the murder*, none were found.

It has also never been learned, even from Pancoast, how he reached the police station, over four miles from the condo, when his car was later found parked on Colfax Avenue.

It has never been discovered (except for Basicihis, who said he only returned to the apartment courtyard to pick up his car and never went into the condo) who the other people were who arrived at the unit with Pancoast two or more hours before Vicki Morgan had her lights put out. Pancoast's attorney, Arthur Barens, was to learn who they *might* have been in mysterious telephone calls following Pancoast's arrest and "confession!"

58

After he had been jailed and settled into a steady routine, and treated by a psychiatrist employed by Los Angeles County, Marvin Pancoast appeared to be a different person.

The psychiatrist studied Pancoast's medical history and then restored him to a regime of major tranquilizers — a favorite tool of this branch of the medical profession. These tranquilizers had a calming effect, according to those at the L.A. County Jail and the few visitors Pancoast had while in the Hall of Justice.

While in the lock-up, Pancoast told Arthur Barens that he had no memory at all of beating Vicki Morgan to death. Vicki was dead when he came out of his (drug induced?) stupor at the condo *and he had assumed he must be responsible! Hypnotized*?

He said that the last time he saw Vicki Morgan alive was shortly before midnight. She was sitting up in bed dressed in a yellow shirt and bikini panties and watching the **Tonight Show**. In the middle of the monologue — with apologies to Johnny Carson — Marvin says he dropped off.

Sometime later, he said, he awoke feeling dizzy and nauseated. He was aware, he claims, of a sweet, sickish odor in the room, a smell that reminded him of medicine (chloroform?) or, possibly, very strong nail polish remover.

Still only "half conscious," he told Barens, he saw Vicki's body on the far side of the huge bed, her head a bloody mess. The hall light was on and there was, he remembered, water running in the bathroom. (Could this have been the murderer or murderers washing off tell-tale bloodstains who didn't realize Pancoast had awakened? **Had** he been hypnotized while under?)

Disoriented, Pancoast said he quietly staggered down the stairs and out the front door. It was closed but not locked and he left it that way.

The next thing he remembers is being at the North Hollywood Police station and cannot explain how he got there.

☆ ☆ ☆

As with all sensational murder cases, the Vicki Morgan homicide generated a swirl of rumors which continue on and off even today. An attorney, Robert Steinberg, is believed to have seen one (or more) of the "Bloomingdale Tapes" but never had total and complete control over their destiny for more than 24 hours.

A powerful cabal, we have been told by sources who must remain anonymous, selected Steinberg to "broker" the tapes to the highest bidder. But when he went "public" with the press in a fit of show-boating, the cabal which, some say is, or was, headquartered in Pennsylvania, decided Steinberg "had blown it!"

A "deep cover" Federal Agent, according to William Turner in *The Rebel*, using the *nom de plume* "David Phillip Habersheim," is believed to have pilfered the tape (s) from Steinberg buttressed by the fact that later on he boasted to cronies that Steinberg "was an easy victim!"

On the fringes of the conspiracy was a source who originally contacted William Turner. This "someone" claimed to be an ex-spook from the CIA and talked to the ex-FBI Special Agent about Morgan's connecton with the renegade CIA agent Frank Terpil.

The same source also constantly called Arthur Barens and at all hours of the day and night. The caller poured out, supposedly, an incredibly complex tale of intrigue, like something out of an early Graham Greene novel. The gist of the calls was that Vicki Morgan had participated in a sex and espionage ring with CIA connections while in Washington, D.C. This was operated by Alexei Goodarzi, the slain *maitre 'd* of The Rotunda, according to the caller.

On the night of her death, the spook said another ex-spook, who had been working undercover on the De Lorean drug case (which he called entrapment by the Government) had received a call ordering him to Vicki's condo to retrieve some "compromising tapes."

"David Phillip Habersheim?"

Barens said later that he did not know what to do or to make of these clandestine telephone calls. But the man, to confirm his "*bona fides*," had sent Barens a photocopy of a memorandum which he said dated back to the days of Watergate. The memo, apparently written by John Dean to John Ehrlichman, which discussed Barens source by name, read, in part, "This guy is trouble!"

It was this which started the attorney believing there was some foundation to it all, a conspiracy in the Morgan death. But without corroboration none of it could be used in Pancoast's defense or to allow him to "cop a plea" for his client. Charles "Ted" Mathews was brought into the case by Barens as co-counsel about a week following Pancoast's arrest, and also agreed.

Barens said later on that "My client is an innocent man," and then went on to contend that Vicki Morgan was killed by a "person or persons unknown" who then ransacked the apartment and left it in the disarray found by Officer Henckle at 3:30 a.m. All this went on while Pancoast slept, or was drugged into a deep sleep by chloroform or some other drug available to spooks all over the world.

"David Phillip Habersheim?"

☆ ☆ ☆

But, did those tapes really exist?

Yes, according to Marvin Pancoast. He said he first heard of the tapes from Vicki while watching TV one evening in her bedroom. Pancoast said he started talking about renting some porno tapes. He claims Vicki said that wasn't necessary. "I've got some stuff here!"

It was then that she went to the black laquer cabinet against the wall, the same cabinet Detective Welch said contained tapes of "old movies." Pancoast said Vicki than removed three Betamax cassettes from the twenty or more tapes on the shelves. According to Pancoast, one of the "porn" tapes featured Vicki performing with Bloomingdale; another had Bloomingdale with two other women; and a third, Pancoast claimed, featured Vicki with a prominent, grey haired member of the (former) Reagan administration.

Barens also received feedback from Marvin Mitchelson with whom Barens had worked closely for three years. Mitchelson by now had come around to thinking that the tapes actually existed. He came to his conclusions with some other oligarchy gossip and from an ex-CIA acquaintance, and also was told that the White House knew about them.

☆ ☆ ☆

Vicki Morgan had been travelling recklessly for many years in a very fast lane for which she was not equipped mentally; neither was her friend, Pancoast. In her Montclair naiveté she did not realize the ramifications to herself and to those around her. If Vicki Morgan had had any sophistication or street smarts at all, those Betamax cassettes would have been in a bank vault or some safe place as a life insurance policy. She should never have had then in her immediate possession.

It is almost certain that "David Phillip Habersheim" was at Vicki's condo as one of the four arrivals the night the beautiful, voluptuous courtesan received six or seven healthy whacks to the cranium with an ash blonde Louisville Slugger baseball bat.

And so might have been Jay Paul, the LAPD detective suspended two years previously for copying police intelligence files in his garage. He had been turning over the copies to a private spy organization, Western Goals, headed by a former member of the John Birch Society, and former

Congressman, Larry McDonald. The latter was one of the unfortunate victims of the shooting down of Korean Air Flight 007!

Those intelligence files had been ordered destroyed by the (civilian) Los Angeles Police Commission, made up mostly of ultra-liberal political cronies of the entrenched Mayor of The City of the "Angels," Thomas Bradley, an ex-cop. (Bradley was badly beaten in two attempts at the Governorship of California even though he had been backed politically and financially by most influential members of the oligarchy).

Those "intelligence" files had been "stored" in Paul's garage for some unknown reason, ever since the unit had been ordered disbanded, because of the "invasion of privacy" of the individuals who were the subjects of those files.

Undoubtedly, there were *dossiers* on Alfred Bloomingdale, Vicki Morgan, Johnny Roselli and probably even "Phillip Habersheim David" but under his real name *and* his *nom de plume*, and many others in Paul's possession.

However, the slaying of Vicki Morgan will forever remain one of the most complex and politically charged of all of Hollywood's Unsolved Mysteries.

Defense Counsel's Hands Tied...

IS IT THE END OF THE BIZARRE VICKI MORGAN SAGA?

Prosecutors at Marvin Pancoast's trial succeeded in what they intended to do from the outset: they prevented the defense, through an obliging Judge of the Superior Court, from turning Pancoast's trial for murder into an expose of the relationship between Vicki Morgan, Alfred Bloomingdale and other prominent men.

The prosecution claimed there was no conspiracy behind Morgan's sad and shabby death contrary to the beliefs of many people. The prosecution wanted the trial of Pancoast to be quick, not to be sensational and, therefore, attempted to and succeeded in tying the hands of his defense counsel in many facets of the trial.

Beyond Pancoast's repudiated confession, there was no hard evidence presented against him at his trial. A strong motive was never established if any, a cornerstone and important link in any murder trial.

Court observers said that the investigation of Vicki Morgan's murder was "strikingly inept!" The police neglected to seal off the "scene of the crime." No fingerprints were recovered, even Marvin Pancoast's from the Morgan condo. Strange, when Pancoast had been living in the condo as long as Vicki.

Deputy District Attorney Stanley Weisberg never interviewed a number of material witnesses at the time. Weisberg explained, very lamely for a Deputy D.A., "We had other cases at the time more important than this one!"

Pressure from above ... ? From Washington ... ?

The Jury never bought the defense argument nor Pancoast's claim that someone else had murdered Morgan and framed him by using hypnosis to convince him that he had committed the crime!

There is more, much more, to Vicki Morgan's murder than meets the eye — or was allowed to be brought out at Marvin Pancoast's trial.

WAS MARVIN PANCOAST MERELY A PAWN ... ?

Pancoast's defense counsel, Arthur Barens, really felt his client to be innocent of Vicki Morgan's brutal slaying. Barens had known Pancoast from the age of fourteen and recalled in an interview that Pancoast had once tried to confess to the murders committed by the Manson clan.

A lot of people "in the know", and that includes Barens, believe that Marvin Pancoast was nothing more than a pawn in the entire Bloomingdale-Morgan affair — a patsy who took the fall.

This time Pancoast's "confession" was believed — even though he repudiated it later — and prior to his trial.

A Conspiracy Unmasked

Marilyn Monroe in a scene from her final film, **Something's Got To Give** — the film was never completed. Monroe was fired from the film and then murdered after being reinstated. (John Austin Collection)

> "Conspiracies no sooner should be formed than executed ..."
> — *Joseph Addison*
> *1672-1719*
> *English Essaayist*

> "It makes me wonder how much more scandal has been swept under the rug. The industry is very closely knit and it's hard to get people to talk because of retaliation by the industry."
> — *John Van de Kamp*
> **(Former) District Attorney**
> *Los Angeles County*

3 ... Marilyn Monroe:
The Conspiracy Uncovered

Since the cover-up to suppress the truth of Marilyn Monroe's murder on the night of August 4-5, 1962, many facts have emerged. The conspiracy was to cover up Marilyn's secret, long-time affair with then Senator, and later President, John F. Kennedy, and later his brother, the Attorney General of the United States, Robert F. Kennedy.

What was whispered about for so many years has, in the last decade, exploded and come out into the open. The whispers from Marilyn's grave became shouts to bare the truth to the world about power and its absolute corruption. This was practiced by the Kennedy family at the time, as well as their friends in the oligarchy — and that other oligarchy in Washington, D.C.

The power of the Kennedy family, at the time of the death of the sex goddess has emerged from the investigation of many people. These have included world renowned investigators such as Fred Otash, investigative reporters from Britain's BBC-TV and U.S. tabloids such as the *National Enquirer, Star* and *Globe,* and ABC-TV's *20/20.* The segment scheduled for airing on the popular events program was "spiked" and forbidden to be aired by Roone Arledge, a close and dear friend of Bobby Kennedy's widow, Ethel.

The investigations have finally allowed the massive conspiracy and cover-up of 1962 to be overridden. This includes the suppression by the Los Angeles Police Department of certain evidence — at least certain high ranking officials of the LAPD — and including its then Chief, William H.

Parker. Until the Monroe fiasco, Parker was supposed to have been "lily white." He reorganized the Department into the efficient machine it is today, as compared to the ragtag, corrupt police force of the 1940's, and as far back as the 1920's.

The suppression of evidence also included the Los Angeles County Coroner, Theodore J. Curphey, who *forced* a Deputy Coroner to sign a false "cause of death." It also included a former Kennedy in-law, the tosspot and drug addict, Peter Lawford, and many others, as we shall see.

The conspiracy over the years, which started immediately following Marilyn's murder — and up to ten hours before the police were notified of her death — can be compared to a Big Lie. It can be likened to an attempt to keep a Big Lie alive and then compounding that one by telling dozens and dozens of other lies to make the first Big Lie believable. It never has worked; it never will work. It has definitely not been accomplished in the suppression of the real method or cause of Monroe's death.

The conclusions, in summary, reached by the investigators and their probing for the facts, and ours, over the years, include:

- Marilyn, furious at being discarded by both Kennedy brothers, and "being passed around like a piece of meat," had threatened to hold a press conference on Monday, August 6, to tell the world about her involvement with both. Also the fact that she had recently (July 20) had a pregnancy termination at Cedars-Sinai Medical Center in Los Angeles.

- Marilyn's incriminating "Little Red Diary" which mysteriously disappeared following her death, contained important government information as well as a running account of her love life.

- With world peace and stability at stake, a plot to "eliminate" or "silence" Marilyn Monroe was allegedly devised in the highest cabals of the country.

- The Kennedys were at the peak of their power at the time of her death. If Marilyn held such a press conference, and told what she knew and about her affairs with the married brothers, Bobby and John F. Kennedy, it is probable that they could have been derailed. It would have made Watergate, a decade later, look like a kindergarten exercise.

Robert F. Kennedy studying at home in 1959. (Wide World)

- The Kennedy family was not about to give up the power Kennedy, Sr. developed and trained them for for decades.

- Mafia leaders, led by Chicago mob boss Sam Giancana, were deeply involved with the government figures to silence Monroe.

- In fact, so involved was Giancana with John F. Kennedy that they shared the favors of the same mistress, Judith Campbell Exner — this by her own admission on talk shows and in a book over a decade ago which was suppressed and recalled from sale because of "outside pressures" on the publishers.

- During the Campbell-Exner affair, while Bobby Kennedy was supposed to be on a campaign to "rid the country" of mob infiltration, she was carrying messages back and forth between Giancana and John Kennedy. At the same time, Campbell-Exner was also servicing another mob figure, Johnny Roselli.

☆ ☆ ☆

Neither the President nor Bobby, nor the country for that matter, could afford to be "smeared" or involved in a sizzling, sex-oriented Hollywood scandal. With Marilyn Monroe involved, perhaps the most famous of all of Hollywood's legendary "Sex Goddesses" throughout the world, that is exactly what it would have been — sizzling.

This was just at the time the country was very, very close to a nuclear conflict over the Cuban missile crisis. Bobby discussed this with Marilyn, or so it is said, or at least told her about it; probably JFK as well.

To illustrate how serious was the crisis, it was revealed at a Nuclear Conference in Moscow in January, 1989, that the missiles in Cuba had warheads available. Fidel Castro was begging Nikita Khrushchev to fire them at U.S. cities such as New York, Washington and other major centers. Because of the seriousness of the situation, neither Kennedy, the country, nor anyone else could survive a sex scandal involving two top officials of the United States Government.

On the home front, the missiles of John and Robert Kennedy had been a little too active with Marilyn Monroe and she was about to turn the key to disarm them.

Marilyn's "Little Red Diary," it has been said over the past decade or so, and by Robert F. Slatzer, (*) to whom Marilyn once showed it, contained such explosive secrets of State such as the plot to kill Castro. (This was the plot being hatched by Sam Giancana and the mob in order to regain the gambling concessions in Havana).

Slatzer had said many times, as have others, that Marilyn said she kept the diary—more of a daily journal—in order to recall conversations with her lovers such as Bobby or JFK. This enabled her to carry on a "sensible discussion" with them. After he had read it, Slatzer told her to destroy it. She never did.

It was discovered, following her death, that the diary had disappeared from Marilyn's effects at the Coroner's office after her corpse and a sackful of possessions which were in her bedroom at the time of her death were delivered for the autopsy. A coroner's assistant, who inventoried the contents, swore it was on the inventory that he recorded. Sometime on Sunday it disappeared and the inventory altered.

It is fairly well accepted that Chief Parker ordered it delivered to him by one of the Coroner's flunkies who was in on the impending cover-up. The Chief had been "courting" the Kennedys ever since their advent to power and had hoped to be named Chief of the Federal Bureau of Investigation. Bobby, according to those in the inner circle, had told many people, including Parker, that he intended to get rid of his arch enemy, J. Edgar Hoover. Therefore, Parker was trying to score brownie points in order to secure the position. But Kennedy, like others before him, found out Hoover could not be fired.

When Travellin' Sam Yorty was first elected Mayor of Los Angeles, he told the Los Angeles *Times* that Parker had conveyed to him the news that Bobby Kennedy was in Los Angeles the night of Monroe's murder. He was supposed to have been in Northern California for a Bar Association meeting.

Yorty also recalled for the *Times* in a 1985 interview, "I just remember at this late date that we talked about the case. I don't think there *is* any file on that. I believe the Chief kept it separately. While I was still Mayor, and when the Chief died, I sent for it, and they didn't have it."

(*) Robert Slatzer was a close friend of Marilyn's for many years and, at one time, they were married for a short period. Slatzer remained Marilyn's confidante and close friend until her death.

Marilyn with her closest friend and husband of a few weeks Robert F. Slatzer. Slatzer also claims that Marilyn was murdered and that her death was "covered up" by the oligarchy and the Kennedy family, and Los Angeles Chief of Police at the time, William H. Parker. (John Austin Collection)

An early publicity shot of Marilyn. (John Austin Collection)

☆   ☆   ☆

A now retired Los Angeles police officer, a sergeant, who was the first on the scene when the police were finally notified of her death, is Jack Clemmons. He was the Watch Commander at the West Los Angeles station when the call came in. As it was "a high profile case," Clemmons answered the call himself.

When he arrived, Clemmons said Mrs. Murray, the housekeeper, looked "very scared." He has also pointed out several times over the years that Marilyn's doctor, Hyman Engelberg, (*) looked very subdued.

Clemmons has never had "any doubt" that Marilyn Monroe was murdered. He has said so several times over the years on talk shows, and in various interviews.

When he arrived at Marilyn's home on 5th Helena in Brentwood, he said he found her, "stretched out, face down, catty-corner to the bed, and the house full of people. Obviously, she was placed in that position. I was shown the night stand by her doctor with eight or ten empty pill bottles that had contained barbiturates. Her doctor said she must have swallowed them all!

"I looked around the room instinctively, and in the bathroom, for a glass used for the ingestion of so many pills. There was none in either room. And there was no suicide note.

"In my opinion, Marilyn Monroe was murdered that night. In fact, it was the most obvious case of murder I ever saw. Everything was staged. The body was rigid and artificially placed. It was not the sort of position in which you die."

Clemmons also recalls that when he arrived Mrs. Murray was using the washing machine. It was a strange time of night (or early morning) and under even stranger circumstances to be doing the family wash — unless she was ordered to wash away some evidence by someone connected with Marilyn's demise.

"I asked Dr. Greenson," said Clemmons, "who appeared to be pale and shaken, why it had taken three hours to call the police. Greenson said that they *had to get permission from the studio publicity department before they could tell anybody!"*

Even in death, the Oligarchy must prevail!

It was also during those early morning hours that Bobby Kennedy

---

(*) Engelberg was another of the left wing liberal clique Marilyn was introduced into by Paula and Lee Strasberg, her drama coaches. Dr. Ralph Greenson, her psychiatrist, his wife, who studied socialism in Switzerland, and Marilyn's ex-husband, Arthur Miller, all expounded the liberal philosophy to a mind which perhaps could not absorb the innuendoes of such obtuse thinking.'

escaped from the area by helicopter to the Bates ranch in Gilroy, California, about 30 miles south east of San Jose. On the Sunday morning at 9:30 a.m., Bobby attended Mass at the local Catholic church.

The former sergeant of the LAPD believes Marilyn was murdered by someone *she knew and trusted who administered Nembutal by suppository or injection directly into her bloodstream, or by enema.*

Clemmons was shocked to high heaven, he says, when the verdict of suicide came down from the Coroner. Clemmons also says the original homicide reports were changed, evidence disappeared and the Police chief (Parker) rushed to Washington to see Bobby Kennedy — probably with the complete Monroe *dossier*, including the Red Diary from Marilyn's effects. It is probable that everything was destroyed while Parker was in the nation's capitol.

☆ ☆ ☆

Dr. Thomas Noguchi, then a Deputy Medical Examiner and pathologist, arranged for a toxicological study to be made of Marilyn's liver, kidney, stomach and its contents, urine, intestine, and a sample of unembalmed blood.

The tests were to be made for alcohol and barbiturates. The Los Angeles *Herald-Examiner* of August 18, 1962 quotes Coroner Theodore Curphey, as stating:

"Toxicologist Raymond Abernathy found a lethal dose of Nembutal and an equally fatal dose of Chloral Hydrate."

The report of chemical analysis, Los Angeles County Toxicology Laboratory, Hall of Justice, Los Angeles, is dated August 6, 1962, and is signed by Abernathy, Chief Toxicologist. The document shows material submitted for tests: (1) quantity of blood; (2) kidneys; (3) liver; (4) stomach; (5) urine; (6) intestines; and (7) drugs — prescriptions found in containers on deceased's night table.

In the report we find this important information:

Blood - Ethanol absent. Blood — barbiturates 4.5 mg percent. Phenobarbitol is absent.

The findings, therefore, show no traces of barbiturates in kidney, liver, stomach, urine or intestines; only in the blood sample. No alcohol was found anywhere nor was any phenobarbitol.

76A890— Cdb 2-62

"ORIGINAL COPY"

81128

File # _____

OFFICE OF COUNTY CORONER

Date Aug. 5, 1962   Time 10:30 a.m.

I performed an autopsy on the body of   MARILYN MONROE

at the Los Angeles County Coroner's Mortuary, Hall of Justice, Los Angeles,

and from the anatomic findings and pertinent history I ascribe the death to:

ACUTE BARBITURATE POISONING

DUE TO: INGESTION OF OVERDOSE

EXTERNAL EXAMINATION:

The unembalmed body is that of a 36-year-old
well-developed, well-nourished Caucasian
female weighing 117 pounds and measuring
65½ inches in length. The scalp is covered
with bleached blond hair. The eyes are
blue. The fixed lividity is noted in the
face, neck, chest, upper portions of arms
and the right side of the abdomen. The
faint lividity which disappears upon pressure
is noted in the back and posterior aspect
of the arms and legs. A slight ecchymotic
area is noted in the left hip and left side
of lower back. The breast shows no significant lesion. There is a horizontal 3-inch
long surgical scar in the right upper
quadrant of the abdomen. A suprapubic
surgical scar measuring 5 inches in length
is noted.

DIGESTIVE SYSTEM:

The esophagus has a longitudinal folding
mucosa. The stomach is almost completely
empty. The contents is brownish mucoid
fluid. The volume is estimated to be no
more than 20 cc. No residue of the pills
is noted. A smear made from the gastric
contents and examined under the polarized
microscope shows no refractile crystals.
The mucosa shows marked congestion and
submucosal petechial hemorrhage diffusely.
The duodenum shows no ulcer. The contents
of the duodenum is also examined under
polarized microscope and shows no refractile
crystals. The remainder of the small
intestine shows no gross abnormality. The
appendix is absent. The colon shows
marked congestion and purplish discoloration.
The fecal contents is light brown and formed.
The mucosa shows no discoloration.

Portions of Marilyn Monroe's autopsy report.

SPECIMEN:

Unembalmed blood is taken for alcohol and
barbiturate examination. Liver, kidney,
stomach and contents, urine and intestine
are saved for further toxicological study.
A vaginal smear is made.

T. Noguchi, M.D.

T. NOGUCHI, M. D.
DEPUTY MEDICAL EXAMINER

TN:ag:G
8-13-62

THE FOREGOING INSTRUMENT IS A CORRECT

COPY OF THE ORIGINAL ON FILE AND/OR

OF RECORD IN THIS OFFICE.

ATTEST ....MAY 1 4 1964..............

THEODORE J. CURPHEY, M.D.
CHIEF MEDICAL EXAMINER-CORONER
COUNTY OF LOS ANGELES

BY........R. H. Rathbun.........,DEPUTY

STATE OF CALIFORNIA, }
  County of Los Angeles } ss.   N° 28182

    On this....14th....day of........May................in the year nineteen hundred and...sixty-four........,
before me, HAROLD J. OSTLY, County Clerk and Clerk of the Superior Court of the State of California, in
and for the County of Los Angeles, residing therein, duly commissioned and sworn, personally appeared

      R. H. Rathbun................, DEPUTY CORONER,
known to me to be the person whose name is subscribed to
the within instrument, and acknowledged to me that he
executed the same.

      IN WITNESS WHEREOF, I have hereunto set my hand
and affixed the official seal of said Superior Court the day
and year in this certificate first above written.

      HAROLD J. OSTLY, County Clerk,

      By.........................Deputy.

76C821—2/57

> **The report of the toxicologist does not support the statement attributed to the Coroner in the Los Angeles Herald-Examiner report on August 18 that "... a lethal dose of Chloral Hydrate was also found."**

The toxicologists report also does not indicate that **any** tests were made to detect Chloral Hydrate. This drug, also known as "knockout drops" is a powerful one which causes unconsciousness in a very short time and causes death if given in quantity.

Among the containers of drugs found in Marilyn's bedroom was one containing ten green capsules with the prescription Number 20570, which had been filled by the same pharmacist on July 25, 1962, and called for fifty caps of 0.5 gram doses of Chloral Hydrate. On the same day **another** prescription was filled for her - Number 20569 — which was for 36 tablets of Sulfathallidine, an antibiotic. The Chloral Hydrate prescription was **renewed** for an additional **fifty capsules** on July 31, *six days after the first prescription.*

Knock out drops???

Why would have been a good question to have asked at the time, *if anyone had been at all interested in getting at the truth.*

At the time of her death, ten caps of Chloral Hydrate remained in their containers on her night stand. This would mean a total of ninety caps had been used in ten days.

What happened to them?

That was enough Chloral Hydrate to put a herd of African elephants to sleep, if not kill them.

Why did Curphey say she had taken a "lethal dose" of the drug, when the toxicologists did not find **any** evidence of it or even make such tests when the drug was found beside her bed?

The findings of the toxicologist do not agree with the "official statement" of Curphey. The report of his pathologist, who performed the toxicology test, *clearly show no signs of drugs in Marilyn's body organs and this alone indicated the need for a full investigation at the time.*

That answer came seventeen years later in the Los Angeles *Sunday Mirror* of April 22, 1979: A Deputy Coroner at the time, Lionel Grandison, was quoted as saying that: "in spite of his reluctance, his superiors had **forced** him to sign the death certificate on the 36-year-old movie star which said that on 5 August, 1962, she had taken a fatal dose of Nembutals."

He now admits the investigation of Marilyn Monroe's death was a farce ...

STATE FILE NUMBER	CERTIFICATE OF DEATH STATE OF CALIFORNIA—DEPARTMENT OF PUBLIC HEALTH	LOCAL REGISTRATION DISTRICT AND CERTIFICATE NUMBER 7053 17716

1a NAME OF DECEASED—FIRST NAME Marilyn **1b** MIDDLE NAME **1c** LAST NAME Monroe **2a** DATE OF DEATH—MONTH DAY YEAR August 5, 1962 **2b** HOUR 3 40 a.

3 SEX Female **4** COLOR OR RACE Cauc. **5** BIRTHPLACE—STATE OR FOREIGN COUNTRY Los Angeles, Calif. **6** DATE OF BIRTH June 1, 1926 **7** AGE 36

8 NAME AND BIRTHPLACE OF FATHER unk unk. **9** MAIDEN NAME AND BIRTHPLACE OF MOTHER Gladys Pearl Baker —Mexico **10** CITIZEN OF WHAT COUNTRY United States **11** SOCIAL SECURITY NUMBER 563-32-0764

12 LAST OCCUPATION Actress **13** NUMBER OF YEARS IN THIS OCCUPATION 20 **14** NAME OF LAST EMPLOYING COMPANY OR FIRM 20th Century-Fox **15** KIND OF INDUSTRY OR BUSINESS Motion Pictures

16 ARMED FORCES GIVE WAR OR DATES OF SERVICE none **17** WIDOWED DIVORCED Divorced **18a** NAME OF PRESENT SPOUSE **18b** PRESENT OR LAST OCCUPATION OF SPOUSE

19a PLACE OF DEATH—NAME OF HOSPITAL **19b** STREET ADDRESS 12305 -5th Helena Drive

19c CITY OR TOWN Los Angeles **19d** COUNTY Los Angeles **19e** LENGTH OF STAY IN COUNTY OF DEATH 3* **19f** LENGTH OF STAY IN CALIFORNIA 3*

20a LAST USUAL RESIDENCE—STREET ADDRESS 12305 -5th Helena Drive **20b** INSIDE CITY CORPORATE LIMITS **21a** NAME OF INFORMANT Mrs. Inez C. Melson

20c CITY OR TOWN Los Angeles **20d** COUNTY Los Angeles **20e** STATE Calif. **21b** ADDRESS OF INFORMANT 9110 Sunset Blvd.

22a PHYSICIAN I HEREBY CERTIFY THAT DEATH OCCURRED AT THE HOUR DATE AND PLACE STATED ... Theo. J. Curphey M.D. Coroner **22b** PHYSICIAN OR CORONER SIGNATURE By *Lionel Grandison* Deputy **22c** DEGREE OR TITLE

22 CORONER ... autopsy ... ON THE REMAINS OF DECEASED AS REQUIRED BY LAW **22b** ADDRESS HALL OF JUSTICE LOS ANGELES **22c** DATE SIGNED 8-28-62

23 BURIAL ENTOMBMENT Entombment **24** DATE Aug. 8, 1962 **25** NAME OF CEMETERY OR CREMATORY Westwood Memorial Park **26** EMBALMER—SIGNATURE Edward... L.B

27 NAME OF FUNERAL DIRECTOR Westwood Village Mortuary **28** DATE ACCEPTED BY LOCAL REGISTRAR SEP 12 1962 **29** LOCAL REGISTRAR—SIGNATURE

30 CAUSE OF DEATH PART I DEATH WAS CAUSED BY IMMEDIATE CAUSE (A) ACUTE BARBITURATE POISONING DUE TO (B) INGESTION OF OVERDOSE DUE TO (C) | APPROXIMATE INTERVAL BETWEEN ONSET AND DEATH

PART II OTHER SIGNIFICANT CONDITIONS CONTRIBUTING TO DEATH BUT NOT RELATED TO THE TERMINAL DISEASE CONDITION GIVEN IN PART I (A)

31 OPERATION—CHECK ONE **32** DATE OF OPERATION **33** AUTOPSY—CHECK ONE X

34a SPECIFY ACCIDENT, SUICIDE OR HOMICIDE Probable Suicide **34b** DESCRIBE HOW INJURY OCCURRED As Above

35a TIME OF INJURY HOUR 3 40 a 8-5-62 **35b** INJURY OCCURRED ☒ NOT WHILE AT WORK **35c** PLACE OF INJURY Home **35d** CITY TOWN OR LOCATION Los Angeles COUNTY L.A. STATE Calif.

This is a true certified copy of the record if it bears the seal of the County Recorder imprinted in purple ink.

FEE $2.00   SEP 24 1964

Ray E. Lee COUNTY RECORDER
AND DEPUTY COUNTY HEALTH OFFICER
LOS ANGELES COUNTY, CALIFORNIA

"False" Certificate of Death of Marilyn Monroe showing Dr. Lionel Grandison signature and cause of death as acute barbiturate poisoning when none was found in her organs. Dr. Grandison's signature appears on line 22c.

A then member of the Los Angeles County District Attorney's Office, on duty that weekend, John Miner, confirmed that because of the importance of the case and the rumors of a crime a thorough autopsy was performed but no barbiturates were found in Marilyn's stomach. What's more, Miner added, the tissue samples sent out by Dr. Noguchi, *"mysteriously disappeared."* Miner's report questioning the suicide verdict of Curphey also "vanished in a day or two."

"From the information I had available to me as a Deputy District Attorney, it was only logical to draw the conclusion that she did *not* commit suicide."

It was also known that Marilyn, in order to help her keep her weight at a certain level, was fond of taking enemas; a great many of them during her career.

Nembutal, blamed by Curphey for Marilyn's death, over which he should have been prosecuted for issuing a false report and for perjury, can be dispensed in different ways. According to **The Complete Guide to Prescription and Non-Prescription Drugs**, Nembutal can be dispensed by suppository or by enema, and it takes effect within 60 minutes.

Two different theories have emerged over the years, which have been advanced by various people. One is that, because of a bruise on Marilyn's right hip noted during the autopsy, but brushed off as a "transportation bruise," it *might* have been administered by an injection into the bloodstream.

But the more likely theory advanced was that as the autopsy showed, "some discoloration of the colon," it must indicate that it was administered in the area by *suppository or by enema*, possibly by "someone she trusted." In this case, it was probably Dr. Greenson. (It will be remembered that Jack Clemmons advanced the theory that someone she trusted administered the drug).

One of Peter Lawford's ex-wives, Deborah Gould, was quoted as saying in an interview that Lawford told her: "Marilyn took one last, good enema!" In his more lucid moments toward the end of his life, Lawford denied making any such statement. But then he later denied a good many things he had said "under the influence!"

Sergeant Clemmons added to his theories in another statement, "Greenson never admitted what we (the LAPD) know to be true, on account of Bobby Kennedy's deposition (*) to having injected Monroe in any form — even *accidentally*."

(*) Bobby Kennedy gave the LAPD a cursory and private deposition about his "friendship" with Marilyn and events leading up to her death.

Marilyn's bedroom after the body had been removed.
(John Austin Collection)

**Broken window which was broken by
Dr. Greenson to gain entrance to
Marilyn's bedroom.**
(John Austin Collection)

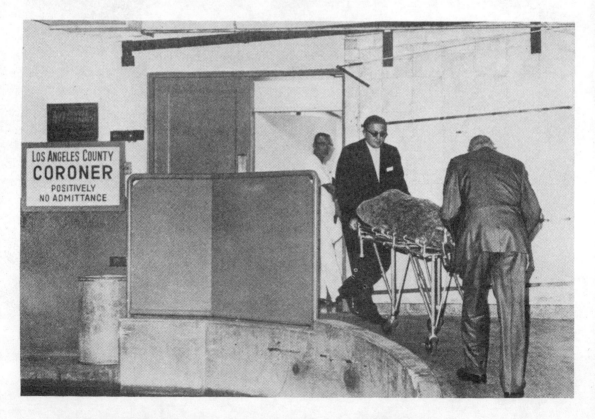

Body of Marilyn Monroe at the L.A. County Coroner's Office.

(John Austin Collection)

Patricia Newcomb, Marilyn's press secretary, at Monroe house following Monroe's death after being denied entrance. (John Austin Collection)

Picture of Dr. Ralph Greenson and socialist wife. Greenson claimed he saw Marilyn on 28 days from July 1 to August 4. At least that is the billing he submitted to the Probate Court. (John Austin Collection)

Joe DiMaggio, Marilyn's divorced husband, and Joe, Jr. at Marilyn's funeral. DiMaggio banned Peter Lawford and others close to Marilyn from attending the funeral.
(John Austin Collection)

Marilyn's casket leaving Westwood Memorial Park chapel for tomb.
(John Austin Collection)

Don Murray and Marilyn Monroe on location during the shooting of **Bus Stop**. (John Austin Collection)

Peter Lawford, the former brother-in-law of John and Robert Kennedy. It was Lawford who was always "scrounging" for girls to satisfy JFK and RFK's insatiable appetites for female companionship. It was Lawford who also helped to engineer the cover-up and was the last person known to have spoken with Marilyn Monroe on the night of her death. He is seen here with his last wife, Patricia Seaton Lawford. (People In Pictures, Ltd.)

"Why didn't Greenson admit it? That is, if it was an accident?
"Why the lies?"

☆   ☆   ☆

The oligarchy — as well as the other one in Washington, D.C. —
managed to sweep Marilyn Monroe's murder under the rug for at least
twenty years. It also managed to keep quiet the fact that the star was
having affairs with both John and Bobby Kennedy. Many people have
denied orally and in writing that she was having an affair with Bobby —
as well as with John. This is because of the "Kennedy mystique" which
decrees that their names must not be tarnished. Why not?

Most of us in the Hollywood community knew about it at the time, but
kept it quiet — but for a different reason. There was just no sense in being
imprudent enough to not do so if we wished to maintain a steady cash
flow into our bank accounts. Therefore, being the hypocrites we were
forced to be by the structure of the oligarchical society in order to survive
financially, we kept our typewriters silent and our mouths shut for many
years.

The two people closest to Marilyn during her final days were her
obsequious publicist, Patricia Newcomb, who worked for the respected
Public Relations firm Arthur P. Jacobs and Co., and Eunice Murray, (*) "a
professional housekeeper." Patricia Newcomb was invited by Marilyn to
spend the weekend with her at the house.

Newcomb said, in a statement later, that she arrived at the house at
6:30 p.m. Friday and left at the same time on Saturday, August 4th. Both
Murray and Newcomb left town following Marilyn's funeral.

The case of Newcomb, however, is the most interesting:

She left for Hyannis Port, Mass., on August 12 or 13, 1962 at the
"urging" of Kennedy in-law Peter Lawford. Following a few days at the
Kennedy compound, she left for Europe and between the last week of
August, 1962, and February, 1963, she visited Germany, France, Italy,
Holland, Denmark and Switzerland.

On her return to the United States, she was placed on the Government
payroll as an "Information Specialist" at the United States Information
Agency with a GS-13 rating and a salary of $12,245.00 per year. On her
employment application, Newcomb gave as references Mr. and Mrs.

(*) Mrs. Murray was a long-time friend of Dr. Greenson and had the same left wing leanings as Greenson,
her mentor. She was hired by Greenson for Marilyn, probably to keep an eye on her.

David O. Selznick, and Mr. and Mrs. Peter Lawford, 625 Ocean Way, Santa Monica, California.

But the interesting part about Newcomb's employment with the Government was exposed in a Walter Winchell column of late 1963:

> **"A certain Hollywood female was given employment with the United States Information Agency on May 6, 1963. She did not get around to filling out her application until October 10, 1963.**
>
> **"This is supposed to be a sensitive agency requiring security clearances. Can the Secret Service or the CIA explain that?"**

When Pierre Salinger, President Kennedy's former Press Secretary, decided to run for Senator from California — he was defeated by S.I. Hayakawa — Newcomb left her employment on a leave of absence from the USIA. She came to California to act as "Information Specialist" for Salinger's campaign. Patricia Kennedy Lawford and her husband, Peter also worked on the campaign, and it was allegedly financed, in part, by Robert Kennedy.

Following Salinger's defeat, Newcomb again left for Washington and re-employment in a "Special Unit" of the U.S. Justice Department, a unit presided over by Bobby Kennedy personally. Her office was five doors away from her mentor.

☆   ☆   ☆

One of the reasons for Newcomb's sudden departure from the oligarchy was that immediately after the removal of Marilyn's corpse, she had a run-in with the reporters and photographers who were covering the story of the decade.

Pat Newcomb committed the cardinal sin of PR people — or "Information Specialist" as she preferred to call it — she became hysterical. Her efforts to prevent photographers from taking pictures and reporters from getting stories caused considerable difficulty for her employer with members of the media. This feud became so rancorous that Arthur P. Jacobs fired her.

PR firms hired by members and firms of the oligarchy are expected — *at all costs and at all times* — to maintain friendly and cordial relations with the media.

John F. Kennedy, with Jackie, John and Caroline Kennedy, at Hyannisport. Jackie was well aware of his assignations with many females around the country. Months before JFK's assassination she also became aware of his affair with Marilyn Monroe by Monroe's several telephone calls to the White House. (John F. Kennedy Library.)

Jacobs, one of the most powerful and respected public relations figures of the era, was attending a Hollywood Bowl concert on the night of August 4. It was his wife, Natalie's, birthday.

Natalie Jacobs, in an interview with ABC's **20/20**, said that somewhere around 10:30 p.m. — *at least six hours before the police were notified* of Marilyn's death, someone approached her late husband in their box at the Bowl and said he had an urgent telephone call.

In the interview, Jacobs told **20/20** "Arthur came back to the box and told me that something was going down at Marilyn's house and that he had to go."

The segment of **20/20** during which this interview with Natalie Jacobs was to appear, was spiked — cancelled — by Roone Arledge of ABC-TV. Arledge was a close friend of Ethel Kennedy, Bobby's widow. One of the on-air personalities who worked exhaustively on the Marilyn Monroe cover-up segment resigned, and several other employees quit the network because of what they considered "censorship" by Arledge.

Natalie Jacobs said she stayed until the end of the concert and then went home. A little before one in the morning, she recalled, Artie — as he was known to the industry — telephoned and said he wouldn't be home that night because he had a lot of work to do.

When he called Natalie at one a.m. or thereabouts, it was still three and a half hours or so before Jack Clemmons took the telephone call about Marilyn's death. If Marilyn *was* dead when Jacobs received the call at the Bowl, which is probably closer to the time she died — it would make it at *least* six and a half hours before the police were finally called at 4:25 a.m.

It is not surprising, in view of this, that in the parlance of the Coroner, Marilyn's body had to be "bent" in order to get it on the gurney. *Rigor mortis* had set in.

Natalie Jacobs said that her husband did not come home for two days. And when he did, he said he helped "to fudge the Press" and the whole scene to cover everything up on behalf of the Kennedys.

The Big Lie was starting, and being compounded on an hourly basis.

☆   ☆   ☆

Fred Otash, in his prime, was one of the most famous of Hollywood's private eyes and investigators during the "swinging era" when the studios really made Hollywood a "company town."

In September, 1985, Otash, from his retirement villa in Cannes, France, consented to a telephone interview with the Los Angeles *Times*.

He said that shortly after midnight on August 5, 1962, still several hours before the police were notified of Marilyn's death, Lawford telephoned him to say that a very traumatic situation had arisen.

Otash said he agreed to meet Lawford at his Laurel Canyon office. He said the actor arrived at about 2 a.m. looking half-crocked and nervous.

"He said he had just left Monroe's house and that she was dead, and that Bobby (Kennedy) had been there earlier. Lawford said they had gotten Bobby out of the city via helicopter, and back to Northern California."

"He asked me," said Otash, in his first known public statements about *l'affaire* Monroe, "if I would go on out there and arrange to do what was necessary to remove anything that might be incriminating from the house.

"He said, `I took what I could find and destroyed it'," Otash related, "But then Lawford added, `I'm so out of it, I would feel better if you went there'."

Otash said he told Lawford that he would not go to the house, "because I'm too well known."

But he telephoned an operative skilled in installing listening devices with whom he (Otash) had worked over the years and sent him to the house along with a moonlighting LAPD officer to assist him.

"When they got out there," said Otash, "the place was swarming with people — and the police had not yet been called. It was impossible to sweep the place or anything else."

Otash said in the same interview that Lawford told him that Monroe and Robert Kennedy had had a fight earlier in the evening over their relationship — whether he was going to marry her — and he then left Monroe's house.

"He (Kennedy) went over to Lawford's place and told them, `She's ranting and raving. I'm concerned about her *and what may come out of this*'," Otash said, quoting Lawford.

"According to Lawford, he had called her and she had said to him that she was passed around like a piece of meat. She had had it. She didn't want Bobby to use her anymore. She called the White House and there was no response from the President. She was told he (John Kennedy) was in Hyannis Port and she didn't connect with him. She kept trying to get him. (*)

(*) The FBI, on the orders of Bobby Kennedy, seized all of Marilyn's telephone records of her long distance calls that she made on August 4. Several records were later released showing calls to the Justice Department on an earlier date, some to Kennedy's private line.

A scene from a documentary on Monroe's career, **Marilyn.** (John Austin Collection.)

Marilyn modelling a swimsuit before she achieved fame. (John Austin Collection.)

Marilyn modelling another swimsuit in her early days before stardom.
(John Austin Collection.)

An early publicity shot of Marilyn believed to have been taken at the time of her first "walk-on" in John Huston's **The Asphalt Jungle** at MGM. (John Austin Collection.)

Continued Otash, "He (Lawford) had tried to reason with her to quiet down and come to the (Lawford's) beach house and relax. She said, `No, I'm tired. There is nothing more for me to respond to. Do me a favor. Tell the President I tried to get him'."

Otash said Lawford tried to call Monroe back but the phone was off the hook. (It has to be presumed that Lawford did not have the number for the second line into the house, the number used by the housekeeper).

"He said Bobby got panicky," Otash recalled. "Bobby asked, `What's going on?' He (Lawford) said, `Nothing. That's the way she is'."

Otash, to everyone in Tinseltown, is, or was, the quintessential private eye of the 1950's — he was known to be tough, hard-drinking, and very street smart — hence his decision not to go to the Monroe house that night. He admitted to having had run-ins with the Kennedys over the years. He told the *Times* he had investigated them from time to time while doing some work for the Teamsters.

Otash also said he had remained silent over the years about the Monroe case because "I didn't see any purpose of getting involved."

Lawford didn't live long enough to reply to Otash's recall of the events of that evening.

Lawford's widow, however, confirmed that her husband told her that he had gone to Otash for assistance *sometime after Monroe's body was discovered*. This is another confirmation of the fact that Marilyn Monroe died *many hours* before the police were notified.

☆   ☆   ☆

A few days before Pat Newcomb left for Hyannnis Port, Mrs. Murray checked out of the Santa Monica apartment which she shared with her daughter. She had been telling friends for several days that she "had come into some money" and wanted to go to Europe for a long holiday. Before she left, she continued to deny that Bobby Kennedy had visited Marilyn on that fateful Saturday of August 4, 1962. She also insisted that Marilyn's body was not discovered until 3 or 3:30 a.m. Sunday morning," obviously a blatant lie. The police report about Mrs. Murray stated, "...she was nervous and appeared to be evasive." That was the under-statement of the year.

It was not until several years later that Murray, in an interview, finally admitted that Kennedy had been at Monroe's the afternoon of her death; but that is all she would say.

From another of Walter Winchell's columns from sometime in 1963:

"Puzzlement Dept.: Sgt. Jack Clemmons (of the Los Angeles Police Department) was the first officer on the scene when Marilyn Monroe died. He can verify that the psychiatrist and the housekeeper first stated that the time was 10 p.m. when the housekeeper awakened — and midnight when she summoned the doc ... Later detectives were told that the woman woke up at midnight and called medics at 3:30 a.m. ...Mighty strange, indeed, if true."

Many more rumors — or lies — have surfaced over the years about the enigma of Marilyn Monroe's death. It is obvious that it was a murder, or at the *very least* an accidental death.

Some of the rumors have been checked out and led into a *cul-de-sac*. Others were so far-fetched they weren't even worth bothering with.

But what is patently obvious is, there was a massive cover-up about Marilyn Monroe's death. Whether it was murder, the most likely theory, or accidental, will never be known.

Dr. Greenson appeared to be a very sad man from the day of Marilyn's demise, a very troubled man, until he finally passed away. Whenever he was asked to discuss the case of Marilyn Monroe, he told everyone, "Discuss that with Bobby Kennedy. Not me!"

In the same article in the Los Angeles *Times* of September 29, 1985, Deputy District Attorney Ronald H. Carroll, who headed a 1982 reinvestigation of the Monroe case for the District Attorney's office, said had he known of Fred Otash's statements at that time, Peter Lawford's actions would have been scrutinized more closely.

(Because Otash, being the street smart investigator that he was, refused to go to Monroe's house that night, it was not known to anyone that Otash was involved in the case, albeit from a distance.)

Carroll said Lawford's actions would have been pursued if he had known about them. "However, whether it would have been included in our report would have depended upon whether it had relationship to circumstances of her death."

(Typical lawyer legalese to skirt the issue at hand.)

STANDARD FORM 57
REVISED MARCH 1961
U. S. CIVIL SERVICE COMMISSION

APPLICATION FOR FEDERAL EMPLOYMENT

57-10:

1. Kind of position applied for, or name of examination	Announcement No.
Federal Administrative and Management Examination	167

2. Options for which you wish to be considered (if listed in examination announcement)
Information Specialist (Motion Pictures)

3. Primary place(s) of employment applied for (City and State)
Washington, D.C.

4. Name (First, middle, maiden, if any, last)
Margot Patricia Newcomb

5. Address (Number, Street, City, Zone, State)
2920 P Street, N.W.
Washington, D.C.

6. Home phone	7. Office phone
452-8901	DU 3-4160

8. Legal or voting residence (State)
California

9. Height without shoes	10. Weight
5 feet 6 inches	114

11. Sex	12. Marital status
☐ Male ☒ Female	☐ Married ☒ Single (Incl. widowed, divorced)

13. Birthplace (City and State, or foreign country)
Washington, D.C.

14. Birth date (Month, day, year)	15. Social Security Number
July 9, 1930	559 45 8494

16. If you have ever been employed by the Federal Government, indicate last grade and job title:
GS-13 Information Specialist
(Motion Pictures)

Dates of service in that grade
From May 6, 1963   To Present

DO NOT WRITE IN THIS BLOCK
For Use of Examining Office Only

☐ Appor.	Material	Entered Register:
☐ Nonappor.	☐ Submitted	
	☐ Returned	

Notations:

App. Reviewed:

App. Approved:

Option	Grade	Earned Rating	Preference	Augm. Rating
			☐ 5 points (Tent.)	
			☐ 10 points Comp. Dis.	
			☐ Other 10 Point	
			☐ Disab.	
			☐ Being Investigated	

Initials and date

17. AVAILABILITY INFORMATION

A. Lowest grade or pay you will accept GS-13
$ ____ Per ____ or grade

B. Will you accept temporary appointment? (Acceptance or refusal of temporary employment will not affect your consideration for other appointments.) ☒ Yes ☐ No If "Yes," indicate by "X" in appropriate box or boxes.
☐ 1 mo. or less ☒ 1 to 4 months ☐ 4 to 12 months

C. Will you accept less than full-time employment (less than 40 hours per week)? ☐ Yes ☒ No

D. Are you willing to travel? ☐ Not at all ☐ Occasionally ☒ Frequently

E. Will you accept employment: In Washington, D.C.? ☒ Yes ☐ No   Outside U.S.? ☐ Yes ☒ No

F. Will you accept appointment only in certain locations? ☒ Yes ☐ No If "Yes," list locations: Washington, D.C., ___ City

18. ACTIVE MILITARY SERVICE AND VETERAN PREFERENCE

A. List Dates, Branch, and Serial or Service Number of All Active Service
From ____ To ____ Branch of Service ____
NONE

B. Have you ever been discharged from the armed forces under other than honorable conditions? ☐ Yes (Give details in Item 39) ☐ No

C. Do you claim 5-point preference based on wartime military service? ☐ Yes ☐ No

D. Do you claim 5-point preference based on service during peacetime campaign? ☐ Yes (Complete and attach Standard Form 15) ☐ No

E. Do you claim 10-point preference? ☐ Yes ☐ No If "Yes," check type of preference claimed and complete and attach Standard Form 15, "Veteran Preference Claim" TYPE: ☐ Compensable disability ☐ Disability ☐ Wife ☐ Widow ☐ Mother

[stamp: OCT 10 1963 U.S. CIVIL SERVICE COMMISSION]

THIS SPACE FOR USE OF APPOINTING OFFICER ONLY

The information given in answer to Question 18 has been verified with the discharge certificate and/or other proof which shows that the separation was under honorable conditions.
VETERAN PREFERENCE ALLOWED: ☐ 5-point ☐ 10-point Comp. Disab. ☐ Other 10-point ☐ None

Signature and title	Agency	Date

16-76819-1

Federal Employment Application of Patricia Newcomb.

ATTACH SUPPLEMENTAL SHEETS OR FORMS HERE

● ANSWER ALL QUESTIONS CORRECTLY AND FULLY

20. SPECIAL QUALIFICATIONS AND SKILLS

A. Kind of License or Certificate (For example, pilot, teacher, registered nurse, lawyer, radio operator, C.P.A., etc.)	B. State or other licensing authority	C. Year of first license or certificate	D. Year of latest license or certificate

E. Special skills you possess and machines and equipment you can use. (For example, short wave radio, multilith, comptometer, key punch, turret lathe, transcribing machine, scientific or professional devices)	F. Approximate number of words per minute:
	Typing Shorthand

G. Special qualifications not covered in application. (For example, your most important publications (do not submit copies unless requested); your patents or inventions; public speaking and publications experience; membership in professional or scientific societies, etc.; and honors and fellowships received.)

21. EDUCATION

A. Place "X" in column indicating highest grade completed												B. If you graduated from high school, give date	C. Name and location of last high school attended
1	2	3	4	5	6	7	8	9	10	11	12	---	---
											X	June, 1948	Immaculate Heart Hollywood, California

D. Name and location of college or university	Dates attended		Years completed		Credit hours		Degree received	Year received
	From	To	Day	Night	Semester	Quarter		
Mills College	1948	1952	4				BA	1952

E. Chief undergraduate college subjects	Semester Hours Credit	Quarter Hours Credit	F. Chief graduate college subjects	Semester Hours Credit	Quarter Hours Credit
Psychology major					
History &					
Government					
Liberal Arts Course					

G. State major field of study at highest level of college work

Psychology

H. Other schools or training (for example, trade, vocational, Armed Forces, or business). Give for each the name and location of school, dates attended, subjects studied, certificates, and any other pertinent data.

22. FOREIGN TRAVEL

Have you lived or traveled in any foreign countries?

☒ Yes   ☐ No

If "Yes," give in Item 39 names of countries, dates and length of time spent there and reason or purpose (military service, business, education, or vacation).

23. FOREIGN LANGUAGES

Enter foreign language and indicate your knowledge of each by placing "X" in proper column	Reading			Speaking			Understanding			Writing		
	Exc.	Good	Fair	Exc.	Good	Fair	Exc.	Good	Fair	Exc.	Good	Fair
French			X			X			X			X

24. REFERENCES

List three persons living in the United States or territories of the United States who are NOT RELATED TO YOU AND WHO HAVE DEFINITE KNOWLEDGE of your qualifications and fitness for the position for which you are applying. Do not repeat names of supervisors listed under Item 19.

FULL NAME	PRESENT BUSINESS OR HOME ADDRESS (Number, Street, City, Zone, and State)	BUSINESS OR OCCUPATION
David O. Selznick	1400 Tower Grove Rd. Beverly Hill, California	Producer
Lois Weber	Allan-Weber Co. NYC	Public Relations Exec.
Mr. & Mrs. Peter Lawford	625 Ocean Front Santa Monica California	Actor
George Stevens, Jr.	1330 New Hampshire Ave. N.W.	Director, IMS

Education and references of Patricia Newcomb on Federal Employment application.

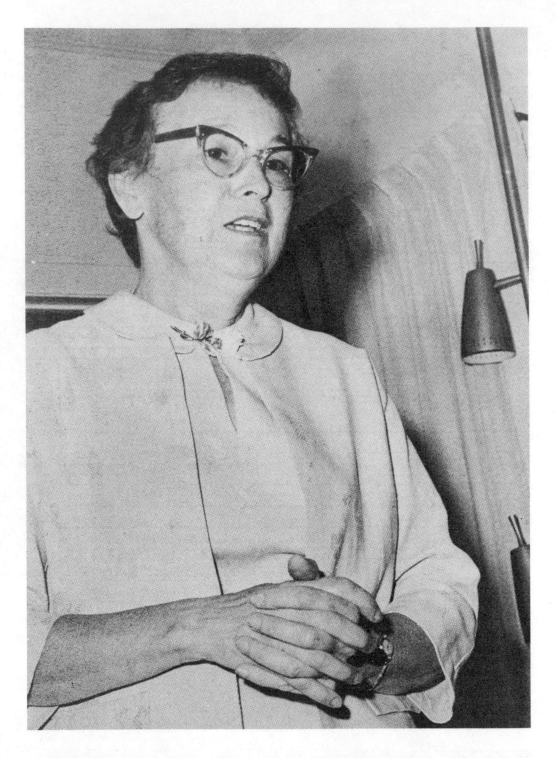

Eunice Murray, Marilyn's housekeeper hired by Dr. Ralph Greenson, one of his very left-wing, liberal cronies. She was hired by Greenson to keep an eye on Marilyn and aided in the "cover-up." (John Austin Collection.)

"If it had to do with conduct after her death that was not criminal, such as a delay in calling police, it would not have had an impact on our report. If there had been a crime to begin with, and there was a cover-up, clearly that would have been criminal!" said the Deputy District Attorney.

Just what the hell did he think had been going on for over 23 years; an exercise in semantics?

Carroll, whose investigation took three and a half months, concluded that there were insufficient facts to warrant the opening of a criminal investigation into Monroe's death.

The power of the Kennedys had reached out again, this time from the grave(s).

There it stands today.

It appears that no one will ever come forward to lay the entire Monroe affair to rest. Even though those whispers from her grave, her fans, her friends, all want the truth to be known once and for all, it never will be.

It is the American way — or is it — that money + power = "I can do whatever I want and you can't stop me?"

Based on that question, which it has to be, the death of Marilyn Monroe will forever be just another of Hollywood's Unsolved Mysteries.

Marilyn with her husband of the time Arthur Miller in 1958 at a London night club following a film premiere. During the marriage, Marilyn was still carrying on a clandestine affair with John F. Kennedy, which led to the breakup of the marriage with Miller. (John Austin Collection.)

THE DECISION TO 'SPIKE' THE SEGMENT DREW CRITICISM FROM THE CO-ANCHORS, HUGH DOWNS AND BARBARA WALTERS, AND THE EXECUTIVE PRODUCER

When a decision came down from the office of Roone Arledge to kill a 13-minute report on the Marilyn Monroe story in 1986, it left a lot of unhappy staff members of the ABC-TV show.

The report was the result of a two month investigation by correspondent Sylvia Chase — who resigned from the network following the decision by Arledge. The producers of the original 26-minute segment — which was cut to 13 for airing — were Stanhope Gould and Ene Riisna. It was largely based on the book, **Goddess: The Secret Lives of Marilyn Monroe** by Anthony Summers.

The book contained information — not drawn upon herein — on the romantic links between Monroe and both Bobby Kennedy and Jack Kennedy. Her affair with the latter started long before he became president and was largely responsible for Marilyn's divorce from Arthur Miller. The affair continued between Marilyn and Jack Kennedy during her short marriage to the playwright.

Arledge, president of ABC News & Sports at the time, said that he had "killed" the piece because it was "gossip column stuff" and "it does not live up to its billing.

"It set out to be a piece which would demonstrate that because of alleged relations between Bobby Kennedy and John Kennedy and Marilyn Monroe, the presidency was compromised because organized crime was involved." said Arledge, and then added, "based on what has been uncovered so far, there was no evidence."

(Arledge never mentioned the connection between Chicago mob boss Sam Giancana and Judith Campbell Exner, the mistress who, by her own admission, was servicing both President Kennedy and Giancana).

Hugh Downs, the anchor of the popular series, took issue with Arledge's judgement: "I am upset about the way it was handled," he said in an interview with Sally Bedell Smith of the New York Times News Service.

"I honestly believe that this is more carefully documented than anything the network did during Watergate.

"I lament the fact that the decision reflects badly on people I respect and it reflects badly on me and the broadcast."

Arledge made his decision after executive producer Av Westin had given his approval following the addition of several clarifications in the script.

This came from an ABC staff member familiar with the review of the segment.

Anthony Summers accused ABC of "pulling" the piece because Arledge is a close personal friend of Ethel Kennedy, the widow of Bobby, and because David Burke, an ABC-TV vice president, at one time worked for Senator Ted Kennedy.

About the same time, another strange coincidence was occurring 2,700 miles away in Los Angeles. Police Chief Darryl Gates decided to release "The Marilyn Monroe File" to the press and general public. It was considered a joke by those "in the know!" More than half the file (which was sold by the LAPD for $12.60) was devoted to documents from 1975 (including several chapters from a book by Robert F. Slatzer; and Internal Investigative Report, and an interview with Peter Lawford.

The only documents contained in that file that reflect any police work in 1962 are the routine Death Report (one page), summaries of interviews with five people regarding the "times of various phone calls received by Miss Monroe on the evening of her death" (five pages), "reinterviews" of Monroe's doctors concerning the "time sequence of their actions" one page; (Where, one should wonder, are the original interviews?), a sketchy chronology of the night's events (one and a quarter pages), and a list of Marilyn's phone calls from June, 1962 to August, 1962.

That list does not contain most of the calls Monroe made on her last day on earth. However, we saw a list of some of the calls and they were to the east coast. The records were removed by the FBI — (some were later released) — the following morning, obviously on the orders of their chief, the Attorney General of the United States.

We have confirmed that the file released by Chief Gates represents only a tiny part of the original file. According to those who worked on it, there "...was a blizzard of paper work."

Just what DID happen to that original file? It was probably destroyed on Chief Parker's visit to the Justice Department in Washington, D.C. with just a few innocuous documents — such as those released — retained by the L.A.P.D.

This was confirmed by Anthony Summers, who interviewed Lt. Marion Phillips, the former senior desk man in Police Intelligence — which handled the case. He said he was told in 1962 that Chief Parker — the supposed lily white Chief for whom Los Angeles Police Headquarters are named "had taken the file to show someone in Washington. That was the last we heard of it."

When Gates released "the file," he remarked, "I don't think it's going to change anything. The legend of Marilyn Monroe will continue!" We assume he made those remarks with his tongue in his cheek.

Summers also claims — as do several other investigative reports — that Marilyn was taken by an ambulance of the Schaeffer Ambulance Service to the Santa Monica Hospital and that she died en route.

Then the body was brought back to her house, at which point Peter Lawford, aided by a detective, mounted a cover-up operation to hide the (Kennedy) connection.

Summers, who was interviewed on camera for the ABC piece, suggested upon its cancellation that Arledge's friendship with Ethel and the rest of the Kennedy clan, led to the "axing" of the **20/20** story. Arledge later denied both this and Summers' asertion that the story's cancellation "was the result of biased news management and political pressure."

The Mystery of Marilyn's "Little Red Diary"

Lionel Grandison, the Deputy Coroner who said he was "forced" to sign a false death certificate and cause of death, spoke out several years after Marilyn's death.

"The diary came into my office with the rest of Miss Monroe's personal effects," he told a Los Angeles newspaper, now defunct.

"The next day," said Grandison, "the diary not only had disappeared, but its very existence had been struck from the inventory."

Grandison is one of the only people who have ever admitted that Marilyn Monroe's diary survived her and disappeared a few hours after her body and personal effects had arrived at the Los Angeles County Forensic facility.

A Lonely And Ugly Death

A partially bare-chested William Holden and Kim Novak in a scene from **Picnic**, one of the star's most notable films. (Marvin Paige's Mot. Picture & TV Research Svc.)

"Man's unhappiness comes of his greatness; it is because there is an infinite in him; which, with all his cunning, he cannot quite bury under the finite."

— *Thomas Carlyle*
1795-1881

4 ... The Strange And Lonely Death of William Holden

William Holden, the Oscar-winning actor, was a giant among super-stars and within the industry. But he died at the age of 63, alone in his Santa Monica *pied-a-tierre*. When found by the building manager and a Santa Monica police officer, Holden had been dead "for four or five days!"

When he was "in town", either from his Palm Springs home or from a world jaunt, he resided on the fourth floor of the twelve-story Shorecliff Towers on Ocean Avenue in Santa Monica. Holden had purchased a forty-percent interest in the building eighteen years previously. His fourth-floor apartment and balcony overlooked the tall, swaying palm trees lining Santa Monica's Palisades Park and looked across the beach to the shimmering Pacific dotted with sail boats from Marina Del Rey, just a few nautical miles downwind from the beach city. The Pacific was an ocean Holden had crossed and criss-crossed so many times during his lifetime he had lost count.

One friend of Holden's said no one had heard from him in almost two weeks. But they all knew he was preparing to star as the coach in the filmization of Jason Miller's hit Broadway play **That Championship Season**. Further, Holden often took off for somewhere in the world without telling anyone and they chalked up this "disappearance" to one of those unannounced jaunts and paid little attention to his silence. They were also well aware that the actor made many "mysterious" trips to faraway lands on very short notice — sometimes less than a day — and for no apparent business or personal reasons. At least not on the surface, to his friends and associates.

Nevertheless, Brian Keating, Holden's butler at his Palm Springs

Front entrance of Holden's Shorecliff Towers apartment building in which he owned a 40% interest. It is on Ocean Avenue in Santa Monica. (John Austin Collection.)

house, worried more than usual. At the request of his employer's very close friend, Patricia Stauffer, Keating drove from the desert to the Shorecliff. But the manager would not admit Keating. The Santa Monica Police Department was then called and Sergeant Dick Tapia "requested" the building manager to let him into Holden's apartment to ascertain whether the Oscar winner was there or not. The manager said Holden was "in residence" but as Holden did not answer the telephone, he might have gone away for a few days unknown to the building manager.

On entering the luxury apartment, Tapia found Holden's lifeless body in the bedroom lying supine on the floor at the right side of the bed with the arms at the sides. Underneath the body there was a huge pool of blood. If nothing else, Tapia was sure, Holden probably died from a loss of blood.

The Coroner's initial reaction was that the actor had been drinking and had tripped on a throw rug in the bedroom. On falling, he had hit his head on the corner of a nightstand. Thomas Noguchi, who personally conducted the Coroner's investigation because of the high profile of the case, said the impact was so great that the nightstand was jammed into the wall and made an indentation of two or three inches into the plaster.

Holden, Noguchi told the media, suffered a deep and jagged gash on the right side of the forehead. The nightstand had cut right through to his skull. *"A very strange wound,"* said the Coroner, *"for someone who tripped over a small throw rug."*

Noguchi then added, "Mr. Holden bled profusely and had tried to staunch the flow of blood with Kleenex in a period of, perhaps, five or ten minutes." Then, according to the Medical Examiner's calculation, Holden passed out from the loss of blood spurting from the wound. Twenty minutes later, the examiner said, and based on estimates from Holden's size and weight, he was dead.

According to the Coroner's final report, the alcohol content of Holden's blood was .22. A person is considered intoxicated under the law when the alcohol content reaches .10.

"It seems that Mr. Holden was not aware of the severity of his injury. By the time he realized it, it was probably too late. It seems strange, but the telephone, less than an arm's length away on the nightstand, was never touched." the report concluded.

Why?

The question was asked of Noguchi how someone of Holden's status and bank account did not have a maid to come in every day to at least make the bed and tidy up. A minimum of five days had elapsed since Holden's "accident." According to the building manager, the maid chose

Holden's apartment was on the fourth floor facing the Pacific Ocean.   (John Austin Collection.)

that week, with, apparently, Holden's concurrence, to take a vacation.

If that had not been the case, Holden might still be alive.

Again, the question was asked and never answered: Why did his maid choose to take off the week Holden would be in the apartment? Why not any one of the other thirty-five or forty weeks of the year when he was not?

☆   ☆   ☆

William Holden's life was a whirlwind of romances and adventures with such glamorous film queens as Grace Kelly and Audrey Hepburn. Towards the end of his life, there was television personality Stefanie Powers. Then there was Acapulco socialite Pat Morgan Stauffer, the former wife of an Acapulco businessman, Teddy Stauffer.

It was Pat Stauffer who urged Holden's butler, Brian Keating, to drive to Santa Monica to check on his employer when he had not been heard from for several days. Stauffer then admitted that she and Holden were planning to marry on New Year's Eve, six weeks hence; on the seventeenth anniversary of their first meeting. From her home in Newport Beach, Stauffer confirmed this for the Los Angeles *Herald-Examiner* a few days following the discovery of Holden's body.

"Bill was planning to go on safari in the Sudan in January because **That Championship Season** had been postponed until sometime in May. I was supposed to go with him. He told me on the telephone the week before he died that we would pick up my daughter in Rome, and be married at the Mount Kenya Safari Club on New Year's Eve, the seventeenth anniversary," explained Stauffer.

"Bill and I were very close and it had been all over between him and Stefanie (Powers) for over a year when we reached this decision. The last time we were together, about two weeks before he died, he talked about how lucky we were to have had a love so few people ever experience, and that it was now time for 'Ma and Pa Kettle' to settle down."

She went on, "Bill was a very private person and we kept our relationship very, very private from the world. I was in the center of a very guarded world of Bill's that consisted of just a few close people. He kept in touch with Glenn Ford, his old friend from their days at Columbia together, Brian Keating, his butler, with whom he always kept in contact, Stefanie Powers, and myself!"

☆   ☆   ☆

A still partially shirtless Holden and Rosalind Russel in another scene from **Picnic**. (Marvin Paige's Mot. Picture & TV Research Svc.)

Holden's lifestyle also included hair-raising adventures in Africa, and a manslaughter conviction in Italy following an automobile accident in which the driver of a small car was killed.

Then there was international intrigue in his life as well. He was a contact and a runner for the CIA. This had long been rumored, but never made public until after his death.

The Oscar winner's last years were a sickening downward spiral of drugs, booze and violence. These bouts were interlaced with futile attempts to save his romance with Powers. These ended about a year and a half before his death and proposal to Pat Stauffer.

Immediately following his death, there was a flurry of "William Holden anecdotes" and many facts revealed from behind the veil of secrecy which had surrounded the star's decline.

Holden in a scene with Ernest Borgnine from **The Wild Bunch**, one of his best Westerns. (Marvin Paige's Mot. Picture & TV Research Svc.)

- He had twice attempted suicide and once held a loaded gun to his head for 90 minutes because Stefanie Powers had refused to marry him;

- He brutally slapped Powers around on numerous occasions in drunken rages. Then got on his knees begging for her forgiveness;

- When Grace Kelly's father broke up his romance with Grace because he didn't think he was good enough for her, and that everyone in Hollywood was "rotten," he was a totally shattered person, which may have started his downward decline, many people believe;

- Audrey Hepburn dumped him after learning he had a vasectomy because she was always talking about marrying him and bearing "his child";

- He wrecked several of Stefanie Powers' parties by arriving roaring drunk and making an ass of himself;

- He had become impotent sexually because of his constant boozing, and tried to make up for it with macho exploits such as attempting to lasso a rhino in Africa from a jeep while drunk;

- He allegedly shot over the head of a man because he had asked for Holden's autograph;

- He nearly pushed actress Jacqueline Bisset off a 200-foot cliff in Hawaii during a binge;

- He had a terrifying premonition that he would die an ugly death.

According to a psychotherapist with whom Holden had become friendly and whom he consulted professionally, much of Holden's problems could also be traced back to the pain and hurt he felt as a young boy, being ignored by his father, a prosperous manufacturing chemist. He was also painfully shy and took up acting to help overcome this at the urging of a friend while he was in Pasadena Junior College.

The psychotherapist, Michael Klassman, in a magazine interview two and half years following Holden's death, said that, "in my sixteen years of dealing with chronic drug and alcohol abusers, Bill was the sickest person I ever treated. He was the sweetest, classiest guy you could ever want to meet, but when he was strung out on drugs and alcohol, he could be a monster."

Said Klassman, "Stefanie Powers tried for years to straighten him out. In the end, she had to break off the long-standing romance and love affair because she just couldn't take it anymore.

During the stormy years together of Holden and Stefanie Powers all over the world, he slapped Stefanie around while he was drunk. Remorse overtook him when he was sober and he begged the **Hart to Hart** star to forgive him. She usually did.

One Christmas time, however, he sorely tried her patience. Holden was not invited to Stefanie's Christmas party and was deeply hurt. He decided to go anyway and turned up at her house roaring drunk. She was shocked. There were all kinds of people there, people important to Stefanie's career. Holden staggered around the house, cussing the people out and insulting them. Stefanie freaked out when he threw up all over the place. After cleaning him up, she sat him in a corner and he kept quiet. Soon after that, according to those who were there, the party broke up.

The quart of vodka plus per day, along with pills, such as Percodan and Demerol, and some marijuana, also took their toll on Holden's relationship with the actress. She refused to marry him unless he stayed off the pills and the vodka for a solid year.

Holden knew he could not do this. By this time in his life, he was in a state of chemical dependency and shock. Powers was sick of it; his love affair with vodka and pills had started to interfere with her career; during a lot of their time together, Powers was involved in a very demanding role with Robert Wagner in **Hart to Hart**. At times, she would say following his death, Holden would lie in a corner and wet his pants. He'd cry like a baby and howl like a dog.

Holden's problems were rooted deep in his past life. The actor said many times that he came from a family that didn't put much emphasis on touching and loving. "Dad never showed me any love or caring," he explained to interviewers.

In addition to this psychological problem, Holden was haunted by the failure of those two romances with Audrey Hepburn and Grace Kelly. As far as Audrey was concerned, he felt it was her fault, not his. He once said, "One of Audrey's greatest desires was to have my child. She was always talking about it. In our intimate moments, at dinner, while we were driving around. I told her I did not feel at this stage in my life, I would be successful as a father."

To spite Hepburn's desire to become pregnant with Holden's child, he underwent a vasectomy. She broke off the relationship. Why Holden felt he would not be a good father is conjectural. He had two fine children with Brenda Marshall, the Paramount contract actress he had married in Arizona in 1941; Peter, now aged 46, and Scott, now 42.

If William Holden had married Audrey Hepburn, Grace Kelly, or Stefanie Powers, or later in his life, Patricia Stauffer, maybe he would have straightened out his life. Instead, it kept on going downhill.

☆　　☆　　☆

It is not surprising that wanderlust was in Holden's blood. He was born in O'Fallon, Illinois. While still a child, the family moved several times to various parts of the country, finally settling in Pasadena, California, the home of the famed Tournament of Roses.

With nothing in his family background to suggest a career in acting, Holden, at the suggestion of a friend who knew how shy he was, tried out for some of the plays staged weekly by the drama department of Pasadena Junior College. He was seen by a talent scout from Paramount Pictures and persuaded to take a screen test which resulted in a contract for $50 per week.

At that time, 1938, producer-director Rouben Mamoulian was actively searching for an actor to play the young boxer-violinist in Columbia Pictures' **Golden Boy**. Holden won the lead in the filmization of the Clifford Odets play following a test for Mamoulian.

This was Holden's first major film assignment and he never did return to college to prepare for a career in the family chemistry business.

It was before the release of **Golden Boy** that Holden acquired that name. Born William Beedle, his film studio bosses wanted him to change his last name. While standing in the studio publicity department one day, the publicist assigned to his career at the time received a call from a man named "William Holden," the night managing editor of the Los Angeles *Times*. William Beedle liked the sound of the name, and adopted it as his *nom de theatre*.

Paramount and Columbia agreed to share his contract, and his first months were spent shuttling back and forth between the studios, Columbia in Poverty Row at the top of Gower Street, and the prosperous studio, Paramount, at the bottom, at Gower and Melrose. He appeared in a series of increasingly successful films.

It was while he was on location in Arizona for Columbia in the film, **Arizona**, that he married Brenda Marshall on July 13, 1941. At the time, Ardis, as she was known, was also under contract to Paramount.

When the United States entered World War II later that year, Holden was one of the first in the film colony to go. He entered the United States Army Air Corps as a private, and while he saw no action in either war zone, he came out a First Lieutenant from Officers Candidate School in 1945.

On his return to the industry later that year, Holden not only plunged into a series of important film roles, but also took an active part in the oligarchy's civic activities. He was on the board of the Veterans Affairs

Committee, working toward the placing of returning actor-veterans in various studio productions in order to get them started again.

He also became a member of the industry's Permanent Charities Committee, was a Screen Actors Guild delegate to American Federation of Labor conventions in San Francisco and in Houston. He also went on a variety of public relations tours for the film industry along with George Murphy, later a senator from California.

Although he was modest in his appraisal of his own work, Holden was always held in high esteem by his fellow actors for his obvious talent. In 1950, they nominated him for an Academy Award for his role opposite Gloria Swanson in **Sunset Boulevard**. Three years later, they awarded him the coveted statuette for his performance in **Stalag 17**.

Holden's presence also contributed greatly to the success of such pictures as **The Moon Is Blue, Sabrina, The Country Girl, Love Is a Many Splendored Thing, Picnic, The Bridge on the River Kwai** — one of the highest grossing films of all time — **and The World of Suzie Wong**. After a semi-retirement at his home in Switzerland, and the Mount Kenya Safari Club, Holden returned to Hollywood and gave a magnificent performance in **The Wild Bunch**.

Holden was an avid reader, had a literary taste ranging from his beloved travel books, to biography, novels and drama. His farflung business interests ran from a radio station to a restaurant, the Shorecliff Towers (where he died), an electronic company in Hong Kong, a luxury hotel, and the Mount Kenya operation. This last was his pet project and abiding love. This enabled him to engage in his other love: preserving endangered species of animals in Africa.

With all this going for him it is hard to believe that Holden so screwed up his life as a drunk and almost a derelict, albeit a rich one, toward the end of his life. He was only 63 that November afternoon when his body was discovered. He had everything to live for, and yet he had nothing to live for save the vodka and pill bottles. Nobody really knows the real reason he so destroyed his life, a brilliant and ongoing career, and wealth.

☆ ☆ ☆

His death was just as he predicted it would be — lonely and ugly. Three months before he died he said to Klassman that he had a premonition that he was going to die "an ugly death, all alone with no one there to even give a damn. It's not death — it's the thought of cashing in my life all by myself that keeps haunting me," he ruminated.

On November 16, 1981, that is exactly what did happen to William Holden, born William Beedle in the small town of O'Fallon, Illinois.

William Holden in a scene from **The Seventh Dawn**, a film made in his beloved Africa.
(Marvin Paige's Mot. Picture & TV Research Svc.)

☆   ☆   ☆

Another event in his life which kept haunting William Holden was having been charged with manslaughter in Lucca, Italy, in August, 1966, as the result of a tragic automobile accident. At the time, Holden was living in Switzerland but vacationing at Montecatini-Terme, a resort in Northern Italy. On July 26, 1966, he was entertaining at dinner the two daughters, Sara and Susan West, of a New York friend.

Cruising down the Firenze-Mare *autostrada* in his new silver-gray Ferrari, Holden and the two girls were en route to the West's summer home in Viareggio on the coast. The *strada* is one of those spectacular super highways of which the Italians are justly proud and which were started under the regime of dictator Benito Mussolini as military highways.

Wide, supposedly safe because of restricted ingress and egress, this one connects Florence with the beautiful Tyrrhenian Coast fifty miles distant.

Holden was driving very fast with his new toy on the no-speed-limit highway. The Ferrari's odometer registered 7,066 kilometers. Not too far ahead was a black Porsche and a tiny Fiat 500. The single occupant of the Fiat was on his way to Terre del Lago to meet his family for a short holiday.

The Ferrari passed the Porsche and then Holden caught sight of the mini-compact about 500 yards ahead. Holden's speedometer, according to investigators, read approximately 156 kph, or approximately 98.87 mph. Holden signaled the Fiat with his blinking headlights that he wished to pass. The mini-compact was driving the fast lane at about 105 kph, or 65.20 mph, also according to investigators.

The driver of the small Italian-built car did not move or accelerate — until the last second when Holden, instead, had already committed to passing on the right. In a matter of milli-seconds after the Fiat decided to move over, the left front of the Ferrari tore into the right rear quarter panel of the Fiat. It hurtled across the center strip and overturned in the wide median strip and ended up on its crushed roof.

The victim was rushed to the nearby town of Lucca with only the faintest hope he would reach the hospital alive. He did not survive for even that long. At the city limits of Lucca, Valerio Giorgio Novelli, forty-two years old, a textile salesman, married and the father of a thirteen-year-old son, became another traffic fatality in yet another incident on the *autostradas* of Italy. (*) Novelli succumbed to a multiple fracture of the skull.

Within hours, teletypes all over the world had flashed the news of the accident and that William Holden had caused it. Rumors started to fly that Holden was drunk, though he was not on that particular evening, as attested to by the *Carabinieri*, the Italian State police.

Holden's case eventually came to trial in Lucca one year later and he was charged with *omicidio colposo* — culpable manslaughter — according to Section 589 of the Italian Penal Code. He was found guilty *in absentia* and sentenced to a suspended sentence of eight months in prison. His lawyers telephoned Holden to tell him of the trial outcome but that the court did admit that there were "extenuating circumstances", that Nov-

---

(*) The Italian (and German) *autostradas* are deadly highways in spite of being touted as "safe" for highway speeds. In one terrifying trip we once undertook on the Rome-Naples link en route to Gaeta, we counted seven incidents of a serious nature in a 95-minute drive. Our driver was averaging over 145 kph (90 mph) in a heavy Mercedes 600 sedan. In spite of this, we were being passed by many smaller vehicles.

Holden with Grace Kelly (later Her Serene Highness, Princess Grace of Monaco, the daughter of a former Philadelphia bricklayer-turned-socialite, who felt Holden was not good enough for Kelly. (Marvin Paige's Mot. Picture & TV Research Svc.)

elli had failed to yield the right of way after Holden had signaled legally that he wanted to pass.

Novelli's widow received an $80,000 settlement, part of it from Holden's London insurance company, part of it from Holden personally. In addition, Holden sent another substantial check a few months later to educate the thirteen-year-old son of the victim.

☆   ☆   ☆

A year later, in December, 1968, another incident over which the actor was very upset was his involvement with the late oil man Ray Ryan.

In October, 1967, Holden and Ryan became partners in the famed Mount Kenya Safari Club in East Africa. But in 1968 Ryan was indicted on charges of conspiracy, obstruction of justice and income tax evasion — all stemming from Ryan's involvement in the Mount Kenya operation. Ryan — not Holden — was charged with destroying records showing that "gift memberships" in the club had been given to top Mafia and mobster chieftains. It was also rumored that Ryan was "in bed" with the mob.

Holden, much to his discomfort as a very shy and private person — except in front of a camera — was called as a witness. The hearing was closed to spectators and the press at the request of the Oscar winner's attorneys. However, it was leaked later that the government attempted to obtain records from Ryan and Holden of the Mount Kenya operation for a tax investigation of Ryan's income. The government also wanted to know about those "gift memberships." Holden was questioned as to his knowledge of the missing records, but his testimony, per se, was never revealed. It did come out that Ryan, Holden and Swiss banker Carl Hirschman were co-owners of the club, but that the latter two deferred to Ryan in the club's day-to-day operation. That aspect soon changed and Holden and Hirschman appointed a General Manager to run the club following the indictment of Ryan.

These two incidents, according to those who knew the actor well, had a lot to do with Holden's continual drinking and his constant wanderlust, trying to forget these unpleasant memories — unpleasant for a shy, sensitive and intensely private person: the incident on the *autostrada* and losing faith in a man he had trusted, Ray Ryan.

And, of course, Holden's broken romances with Hepburn and Kelly added to all this and preyed on his mind. It was the romance with Grace Kelly — later Her Serene Highness of Monaco — which almost destroyed him, as he was such a sensitive person. He admitted to Michael Klassman in the same interview that he and Kelly had talked seriously about marriage, but that the visit to her family in Philadelphia had turned Holden and Grace off to the idea. She knew she could never face her father again if she went against his wishes. John Kelly was now a millionaire who rose from being a common bricklayer to a respected position in Philadelphia society — and a social climber.

That crushing feeling over this and his many affairs and drinking, and his constant cheating on Ardis and who adored him, twice drove Holden to suicide attempts until they were divorced in the early seventies. Both attempts came in Europe during the 1960's while he was living and filming there. Neither one went very far, although the second was the more serious. He swallowed a great many pills and washed them down with a few healthy swigs of vodka. At the last moment, and just before he passed out, he called for help from the hotel bellman, was rushed to the hospital and had his stomach pumped out. (Why, one should ask, didn't he seek help when he fell against the nightstand in Santa Monica as he did on this attempted suicide, when a telephone was less than an arm's length away?)

Another incident which disturbed him greatly occurred during one of his furtive missions for the CIA. For the last twenty or so years of his life, Holden had very close ties to the intelligence organization and Ronald Reagan, as well as, going back even further, to Dwight Eisenhower and Richard Nixon.

His involvement with the CIA had long been rumored within the industry and hinted at in gossip columns of the day — including our own — in fan magazines. Holden met with Chinese and African leaders — the latter because of his close business and professional and personal ties to the vast African Continent. He was the unofficial Ambassador for these people, many believe. It was also well established that Holden delivered messages to other world leaders the government did not want delivered through formal diplomatic channels.

Holden was once taken to a place in the jungle in Africa where two rebel leaders — friends of his — were beheaded in front of him.

"Whenever he drank," said his psychotherapist, Klassman, "the image of their severed heads was ingrained in his memory."

Holden never forgot that horror — and neither could anyone else — and said he had recurring dreams of seeing those friends beheaded.

This event, too, contributed to his drinking and his downfall — and might even have contributed to his death in Santa Monica on November 16, 1981:

William Holden with the one great love of his life, Grace Kelly. It was Holden's ill-fated romance with Kelly that, many say, started him on his downward slide and which eventually led to his death. (Marvin Paige's Mot. Picture & TV Research Svc.)

- Was it possible that Holden's CIA involvement led to his death as the result of some mission no one is aware of?

- Could someone have gained entrance to his fourth floor apartment through the unlocked door of the balcony; perhaps lain in wait for him?

- There are many undetectable drugs on the market available to such people, which do not show up in autopsies. Could Holden have had such a drug placed in his vodka through the above method which disabled him, causing him to fall so heavily?

- Why did his maid suddenly choose to take a vacation when Holden was using the Shorecliff Towers apartment? Why did he — or she — not take the vacation during the other thirty-five or forty weeks when he was not?

- Why didn't the building manager become concerned about his tenant and part-owner of the building and go upstairs to check on Holden when his telephone was never answered? The manager knew Holden was "in residence" and had not told him he was leaving as was Holden's usual custom;

- It is not impossible for someone to have gained entrance to his apartment, possibly with a pass key, a lock pick, or some other means readily available to furtive types who carry out such affairs.

Like so many other deaths of famed filmland figures, there are too many unanswered questions about William Holden's death to draw any final conclusions in spite of Noguchi's "final report."

Whatever Holden knew from his CIA work, he never revealed to a soul; or did he? Perhaps he told someone he trusted something he should not have which caused his death.

Pat Stauffer, the woman he was to marry on New Year's Eve in Africa, said, "Bill was such a gentle, marvelous man. It would have been so much better to let him go with dignity and not to tell the world he had a blood alcohol content of point twenty-two or whatever. And now," she said, the day after Holden's body was discovered, "...there is talk that he was depressed about Stefanie Powers — which is ridiculous. He was depressed earlier this year (1981) about the death of a dear friend, Paddy Cheyefsky, sorry that he had lost touch with him. But he had snapped out of that and was looking forward to working on **That Championship Season** in May."

Stauffer also said that Holden's drinking problems had been the cause of their breakup ten years previously after they had been together for ten years. "He practically raised my daughter, Mindy," said Stauffer. "But, well ... it had gotten to the point in his life that he couldn't handle his drinking. And that's when Stefanie came into the picture."

Last year (1980) she said, Stefanie Powers was out of the picture, and "Bill and I were together again — and stayed together. Just two weeks ago (October, 1981) we rode motorcycles to the top of a mountain near Palm Springs at sunset. He told me how he had found peace of mind and wanted to start seeing more of his old friends, that we should plan a large party when we came back from Africa."

"He also told me" she continued, "that he felt he had fifteen good years left in him — and that he wanted us to spend them together."

Whether Holden's death was accidental, self-induced, or caused by a person or persons unknown, as the saying goes, will never be known.

In his will, Holden left Stefanie Powers $250,000. She put it to use in Africa on animal preservation as a memorial to William Holden.

The death of William Beedle, otherwise known as William Holden, Oscar-winning film star, will forever remain just another of Hollywood's Unsolved Mysteries.

☆   ☆   ☆

TWO SUPER STARS DEAD WITHIN TWO WEEKS - BUT THE IRONIES LIVE ON

• She had no known history of heavy alcohol use.

• At the height of his fame, he was a quart-of-vodka a day man and frequently talked about and acknowledged his drinking "habits."

• She was known as one of the happily married women in Hollywood, a woman who liked being a wife and a mother.

• He was a loner, a dreamer, some say even a drifter; albeit a rich one.

• Two superstars - Natalie Wood and William Holden - whose bodies were found within two weeks of each other.

• The Coroner's office said each one had been drinking; he to excess; she merely "under the influence." His alcohol blood level was at .22; hers at .14, just four tenths of a point over the legal intoxication level.

• He had tripped - they say - over a throw rug in his Santa Monica apartment, his refuge when he visited Los Angeles.

• She had slipped - they say - on the swim step at the stern of the 60-foot yacht - Splendour.

• As she fell into the water, she scraped her left cheek against a hard surface - perhaps the yacht or the dinghy - and she suffered a bruise.

• He began bleeding profusely. Then he passed out.

• She may have gone into shock. She may have been rendered unconscious.

• He never picked up the telephone to call for help.

• She may have tried to yell for help but may have swallowed water after her first try and been unable to cry out very loudly.

• He died from a loss of blood.

- Her death was due to accidental drowning - at least according to the Coroner's report.

- It was not unusual when his friends did not hear from him for long periods of time. He lay dead in his apartment for four or five days before he was found.

- She had been with friends. After her husband discovered she was missing and determined she would not return, he finally radioed for help.

- Her body was found floating in the water several hours later.

- There was no evidence of foul play in either cases, the Coroner surmised.

- Holden had a long-standing relationship with Stefanie Powers, the female star of the TV series, Hart to Hart.

- Wood was married to Robert Wagner, "RJ," the male star of **Hart to Hart.**

- Wagner and Wood were an "idyllic couple," said Lionel Stander the actor who played the Hart's chauffeur on the series. "The relationship between RJ and Stefanie in **Hart to Hart** is a reflection of the real-life relationship he had with Natalie," said the 81-year-old Stander.

Roy Radin a few months before his murder in Los Angeles. Producer Robert Evans has always been a suspect in the case according to a Los Angeles Deputy District Attorney. (Wide World.)

"I know it is more agreeable to walk upon carpets than to lie upon dungeon floors; I know it is pleasant to have all the comforts and luxuries of civilization; but he who cares only for these things is worth no more than a butterfly contented and thoughtless upon a morning flower;and whoever thought of rearing a tombstone to a last summer's butterfly ...?"

— *Henry Ward Beecher*
1813-1887
American Clergyman

5 ... Roy Radin:
"The Day of the Locust Revisited"

New York-born entrepreneur Roy Radin came to Hollywood on Friday, May 13, 1983, with an ambition to be a player and to produce major motion pictures. Approximately twelve hours after he arrived he was dead; murdered.

Someone had "escorted" the self-made millionaire New York Promoter to the rugged foothills of Los Angeles near Gorman on Interstate 5 and pulled the trigger. It had been pulled many times, as though Radin's executioner were using his body for target practice. Radin's corpse was then left to rot in his $1,000 three-piece suit, San Remo Italian loafers and Pierre Cardin tie. Roy Radin was dealing with someone who took his contracts seriously.

Now over six years later, the reason for Radin's murder is still basically unknown. However, police in Los Angeles, Miami, Florida, and Maryland believe they know who pulled the trigger(s) and who ordered the "hit" on Roy Radin, thanks to an informant. Two of the suspects are in jail in Los Angeles facing a trial for murder; one in Maryland, and the other returned from Miami after waiving extradition proceedings.

☆ ☆ ☆

Roy Radin wasn't the sort of person you could miss. He was young, 33, and weighed 275 pounds, down from the 300 pounds he had once weighed. And he was very rich for his age. Radin owned a Long Island mansion in Southampton and had show business connections that ran back to his speakeasy, and later night club owning father, "Broadway Al" Radin.

Radin, Jr., made his millions before he was 30 by managing, promoting, booking and traveling with a modern-day vaudeville show. He put his first acts together when he was 17 and then took them on the road, featuring at least one veteran of the boards, George Jessel. He also had such acts as J. Fred Muggs, the chimpanzee from the **Today** show; a midget saxophonist; and a drag queen magician. Jessel was the star attraction, and Radin once told a New York *Times* interviewer, "It wasn't one of my most notable shows, but Jessel taught me a lot. He went on the tour as a gamble. He knew I was only 17 and didn't have any money!"

Radin's fourteen years of promoting such shows reached a peak in the late 1970's when his shows included the likes of The Ink Spots, crooner Johnnie Ray, Milton Berle, Donald O'Connor, Godfrey Cambridge, Eddie Fisher and Red Buttons. These touring "minstrel shows," as they were dubbed in the Borscht Belt and *Weekly Variety*, were reportedly grossing Radin over $50,000 per week. Most of the performances were billed as "fund-raisers" for some 150 Police Benevolent Associations along the East Coast with whom Radin would "split the take."

One New York Attorney General questioned the way the money was divvied up. He charged that Radin raised $684,443 in performance revenue for three Long Island PBA's over the two years prior to 1975, but the PBA treasuries allegedly received only 27 percent of that figure. To Roy Radin's way of thinking, it was an equitable split. That way of "thinking" is what may have had him murdered 8 years later.

It was Roy Radin's close association with PBA's, particularly on Long Island, that led one of the servants in Radin's Southampton mansion to tell a reporter, "He just about owns the Southampton police department. He uses it as a private security force."

As a matter of fact, Roy Radin had himself a mini-empire — replete with servants, classic cars, and even a private plane — all the trappings of Long Island's *nouveau riche*. With all the other signs of wealth came the usual entourage of leeches and hangers-on. His estate bordering the Atlantic Ocean at the eastern tip of Long Island soon became the talk of the Southampton elite. To the old rich, the goings on behind the big iron gates were nothing short of legendary.

Radin — at that time 300 pounds — had an insatiable appetite for refined cocaine and unrefined women. He used no discretion in taking as much of the fast lane as he could buy.

In April, 1980, that fast Long Island life caught up with Roy Radin. It happened during a party at the mansion on Meadow Lane. Robert

McKeage IV, a businessman friend of Radin's, had invited Melonie Haller, a young and aspiring actress, to spend the weekend with him at Radin's place. Any reluctance she may have had was outweighed by McKeage's suggestion that "my friend, Roy Radin" might help her get her first good role since she played one of the female "Sweathogs" on television's **Welcome Back, Kotter**.

Haller was a wise enough professional to know that she had to go where the action was if she was to survive. She was also smart enough to recognize it when things got out of hand during the weekend. There was some "sexual rough stuff" which went too far in Haller's opinion. She smashed some video equipment when she realized it had been trained on her during some bizarre sexual activity she had been engaged in. She told police she was then beaten and raped by two women and two men.

According to other reports, someone telephoned Haller's mother to tell her that her daughter was "incoherent." Her mother asked that she be placed in a limo and driven back to her Manhattan apartment. Instead, the 23-year-old Haller was driven to the Long Island Railroad Station in Southampton and dumped on a train. A conductor spotted her and called the railroad police.

By the time the police examination was completed, four people who had been present that night were charged with assault. Radin, himself, was charged additionally with possession of LSD and cocaine, and with illegal possession of a handgun in violation of New York law. He was also charged with menacing Haller. But, thanks to Radin's PBA connections, he was charged only with the weapons violation, to which he pleaded guilty and was placed on probation. McKeage, on the other hand, with no PBA connections, served 30 days in jail after pleading guilty to assaulting Haller.

This incident seemed to be a turning point of sorts for Roy Radin, not so much in his behavior, but in his aspirations. It was about that time, his former associates say, that Radin became determined to break into motion pictures. He started to neglect his vaudeville shows, the basis of his fortune, while he tried in vain to make TV and film deals — but without much success. By early 1983 he had sold the Long Island mansion in order to be closer to the New York show business scene. But the truth is he needed the money. Cocaine was taking quite a toll on his bank account and what cash flow he had left.

Those cash flow problems, the drugs, the aspirations, and probably a certain amount of desperation were, no doubt, all factors that led to Radin's decision to turn to Hollywood and what he felt would be a more salubrious climate for his dreams of becoming a motion picture producer.

Because of his striking resemblance to the late MGMogul, Irving Thalberg, Robert Evans was induced by Thalberg's widow, the late Norma Shearer, to portray her late husband in **Man of a Thousand Faces**, the story of the late Lon Chaney with James Cagney in the starring role. The picture on the right is Evans as a young man and as he appeared in the film in 1957. (Marvin Paige's Mot. Picture & TV Research SVC.)

And it is also safe to say that some of those factors played a part in his death.

Karen DeLayne (Lanie) Jacobs met the Golden Boy, successful producer Robert Evans, through Gary Keys, a chauffeur she used regularly whenever she went out in the evening. Keys worked for the Ascot Limousine Service, partially owned by Evans. Keys knew the flamboyant producer was seeking investors for **The Cotton Club** and he had asked Keys to keep his eyes and **ears** open among his limo clients for possible investors in the project.

He asked Jacobs if she would be interested. She was — and a match was made, a meeting arranged. Evans later told associates who inquired about Jacobs' background that he had slept with her and partied with her. He also admitted to investigators looking into Roy Radin's murder that he discovered later that she was a major drug dealer involved with the Medellin Colombian drug cartel. He also learned that she was the mistress of another drug dealer, Florida-based Milan Bellechesses of Miami.

Exactly when Evans learned that Jacobs was a dealer, given his conflicting statements and those of others, is still not clear. But a police informant, who went to jail in Louisiana for child molestation, indicated it was immediately after he met her. The informant, Talmadge Rogers, told sheriff's investigators that Jacobs had told him that Evans was interested in obtaining narcotics money to produce **The Cotton Club** and other films. The Golden Boy is also alleged to have told Jacobs that he knew of at least ten other producers who were also interested in such a deal, being financed by drug money as a form of money laundering.

Evans later denied this, but Jacobs did tell him she "had a friend" who wanted to invest as much as $50 million in a production company. He also said that Jacobs told him she had $5 million herself she wanted to invest. Evans said he tried to tell Jacobs the movie business was not for her unless she could afford to possibly lose the money, or have it tied up for several years. Instead, he suggested she consider investing in his Ascot limo company. But Lanie Jacobs was not interested in any investment so mundane.

Alternatively, Jacobs began trying to put together a movie-financing deal on other fronts. She tried unsuccessfully to raise money from Arabs through an attorney who spoke Arabic.

She also tried, again unsuccessfully, to persuade American Express — of all people! — to branch out into financing motion pictures. (Bellechesses helped her to apply for those funds!).

And then, as fate would have it, Lanie Jacobs met Roy Radin and introduced him to Robert Evans.

☆   ☆   ☆

Lanie Jacobs met Roy Radin at a dinner party on one of his numerous 1983 trips to Los Angeles and they hit it off immediately. On their first date they went to another party. And it lasted for three days.

133

Radin's secretary, Jonathan Lawson, told the Sheriff's investigators that his employer was a heavy user of cocaine who, during his trips to Los Angeles, purchased drugs from Jacobs, writing her checks for thousands of dollars at a time.

Roy Radin knew only one way to think — big!

When she finally introduced him to Evans in early March, Radin told Evans he could raise $50 million, the amount Evans said he needed. No problem, said Radin optimistically, but with all the authority his 275-pound bulk could muster.

Evans told the investigators looking into Radin's death that the New Yorker called him back the next day. There was still no problem, Radin reportedly told him. He simply "had to get hold of the Rothschilds!" Everyone who knew Roy Radin said they knew of no Roy Radin connection to "the Rothschilds."

Early the next month, Evans said, Radin contacted him again with good news: The Rothschilds were out — they wanted nothing to do with any industry in which the inmates ran the asylum — but Radin told Evans that the Puerto Rican Government was "in!"

☆   ☆   ☆

At a divorce party Radin threw to celebrate detachment from his second wife, Toni, Radin had become friends with a Puerto Rican banker, Jose Allegria. The Puerto Rican had agreed to become the go-between for Radin and his government. The idea was to bring new industry to the economically ailing island — a new movie studio would employ, possibly, at least 500 people and bring in additional dollars to the island for the goods and services required.

In exchange for ten percent of the profits of **The Cotton Club** and any future productions, the Puerto Ricans agreed to put up $35 million. The deal was discussed "enthusiastically" by Evans, Radin and Allegria at a meeting in New York. Then, according to insiders to the deal, two things happened in quick succession, one on either coast.

Talmadge Rogers — angry because Jacobs had "stiffed" him for a $300,000 drug-running fee, made off with 10 kilos of cocaine and around $270,000 from the floor safe in Jacobs' garage in Sherman Oaks in the San Fernando Valley. Lanie, frantic at the loss and what she would tell the murderous Colombians about it, got into an argument with Radin over who would get what cut of the profits.

According to investigators' reports, the deal as Radin understood it was to have been 45-45-10 with Radin and Evans getting 45 percent each;

the ten percent was a "finder's fee" for Jacobs. But Jacobs had always been under the impression she and Radin would be equal partners, and apparently so was Evans. He thought his sometime bed partner and coke supplier was a principal in the deal.

At a meeting in Robert Evans' Manhattan townhouse, Allegria told detectives, the sought after $35 million evaporated in a flash. Jacobs burst into tears; Evans sided with Jacobs; Radin stormed out the door. He was not giving up any part of his 45 percent and screen credit on any pictures produced.

Following this acrimonious meeting, a by now very desperate Robert Evans and Lanie Jacobs attempted to bypass Radin by going straight to the Puerto Rican government through a lawyer-intermediary they both knew. But Allegria, still in control, unilaterally refused to cut Radin out of the deal. According to his statements to investigators, he told Evans and Jacobs to work things out with Radin or there would be no money from the Puerto Rican Government.

Then, the coke-snorting duo offered to buy out Radin for $2 or $3 million — the exact amount is in dispute. Furious at the double cross, Radin said "no deal." It was, perhaps, the worst decision of his life. And he was beginning to learn how Hollywood — the oligarchical society — played the game with outsiders.

How could he give up on Hollywood so easily?

To paraphrase a cliche, Radin should have taken the money and run — as far away from Hollywood as he could.

Instead, after sober reflection, the New Yorker decided to return to California one more time to try to work out his difficulties with Jacobs and salvage the deal for all of their sakes.

☆   ☆   ☆

On the last night he was seen alive by those who cared for him, the high school drop-out from Long Island who had gotten rich promoting has-been comedians, saxophone-playing dwarfs and transvestite magicians, was seen stepping into a limo outside his West Hollywood hotel. Radin made this one last trip to Baghdad-on-the-Pacific to try to patch things up with Lanie Jacobs, and possibly, compromise his adamant refusal to lower his split. Jacobs asked him to have dinner with her.

Even though he had stopped seeing Jacobs socially, he was dating a close friend of hers, Ana Montenegro. When she heard that Radin was having dinner with Lanie, she begged Radin not to go. Radin's secretary recalls her saying, "Stay away from Elaine. She's dangerous!"

Robert Evans as a bullfighter. He had a small role as a matador in **The Sun Also Rises.**
(Marvin Paige's Mot. Picture & TV Research SVC.)

Montenegro later explained to a private detective, hired by Radin's family in an attempt to discover what happened to him, that Jacobs thought that Radin had engineered the theft of the cocaine and the cash from her garage safe, cash she owed the Cartel for her "supplies!" This was on her mind when she asked Radin to dinner, along with the busted financial deal for **The Cotton Club.**

Even though he ignored Montenegro's warning, Radin did take one precaution: he arranged to have a friend follow him when Jacobs picked him up in a limo around 8 p.m. That friend was actor Demond Wilson, best known for his role in the hit TV series **Sanford and Son.** Radin had been managing Wilson's career for several years. Wilson then recruited a friend for company, brought along his gun and, according to his companion's statement to the sheriff, "some cocaine... to pass the time."

Parked outside the hotel, Wilson and his passenger watched as Radin stepped into the black limo with darkened windows and a lady in a gold lame dress inside. They did not see two other furtive figures in the back seat.

As the limo headed west on Sunset Boulevard, Wilson later told authorities, a car managed to get in between his vehicle and the black limo during an unrelated police chase. The limo bearing Radin and Jacobs was then lost in traffic after it made a left turn on Doheney and disappeared down the hill. Wilson decided to head for La Scala, where the dinner was supposed to have taken place, to wait for his friend. Roy Radin never showed up.

A month later, Roy Radin was still missing in spite of the efforts of the Los Angeles County Sheriff, the private investigator and the many friends of Roy Radin It was then that a beekeeper, seeking a spot to deposit his hives, stumbled across Radin's partially decomposed body in a gully. He had been shot at least fifteen times in the head, which made him almost unrecognizable. The body was tagged "John Doe #94" in the L.A. County Morgue. The body was eventually identified through dental records.

☆　　☆　　☆

Hollywood, since the discovery of the contract murder of Roy Radin, has been running scared. It is one mess that cannot be deodorized, swept under the rug or hushed up as some others have been over the decades.

Robert Evans' fair-weather friends and cronies are staying out of the picture. One chronicler of the Hollywood scene made over 100 telephone calls to former Evans associates, employees and friends. Of those 100 calls, only six yielded call-backs. Those few all had the same response: "I can't talk about Robert Evans." Not "I won't," but "I can't!" It is as though the oligarchy had clamped a lid on everyone discussing the Robert Evans involvement, if any, in the murder or "hit" of Roy Radin. Either to protect Evans, or to invoke the code of Hollywood of PYOA (Protect Your Own Ass), no one has been able to figure out. The latter was probably the case.

While production head at Paramount Pictures, Evans had a string of hits for the Gulf + Western subsidiary including **Barefoot in the Park, Rosemary's Baby, The Odd Couple, Love Story, Paper Moon, The Godfather** series, **The Great Gatsby** and many, many others.

*There were also a few failures, most notably **The Day of the Locust**, the*

Nathaniel West story of a diverse group of Hollywood personalities whose aspirations lead them in the end to violence. The novel is an indictment of a society that neglects spiritual values in a frenzy of self-gratification.

This picture was an omen of Robert Evans' and Roy Radin's future.

Riding on his wave of successes, Evans decided to strike out on his own and pocket the profits instead of putting them in G + W's pockets and its stockholders'. He became an independent producer under the aegis of Paramount. **Chinatown** and **Marathon Man** both were hits, while **Black Sunday**, starring Bruce Dern, was only a mediocre success, just breaking even. This was followed by another flop, **Players**, about professional tennis, another Evans obsession — tennis, not the picture!

Evans was considered a "winner" by Hollywood standards but he had no personal life to speak of. He did admit at the time of his divorce from Ali McGraw — the star of yet another Evans hit while at Paramount, **Goodbye Columbus** that he was a "workaholic." He spent practically all night in the projection room at home, which friends referred to as his "screening womb." They also say he always appeared to be under a fog of nembutal and Valium. But he was still considered "a winner."

He liked to lampoon that infamous line from one of his biggest hits while at Paramount, **Love Story**: "Success means never having to admit you're unhappy!"

Then something happened to Bob Evans. It wasn't something odd; it was cocaine, nose candy. It was at the time the newest enthusiasm around the film industry. For a man who had already been compulsive about everything he undertook — from gambling to tennis and tanning — cocaine took hold.

The coke usage inevitably led him to a 1980 conviction for drug possession along with his brother Charles and brother-in-law Michael Shure. All three pleaded guilty of purchasing five ounces of the substance for $19,000 from a New York undercover officer. Evans was placed on probation and community service.

Cocaine also led Evans to the acquaintances who would tie him to the death of Roy Radin — and the great black bridge that connects the two events is a film called **The Cotton Club**.

In 1981, following a big hit with **Urban Cowboy**, and a flop with **Popeye**, Evans obtained the film rights to a non-fiction book, **The Cotton Club**. He was determined to make the film of the book; the history of the Harlem night spot, a favorite of New York's cafe society in the 1920's, fascinated him.

A string of failed financing deals for the film followed Evans' acquisition of the rights prior to the Puerto Rican caper with Lanie Jacobs and Radin.

- Money was promised by the now defrocked "billionaire," Adnan Kashoggi, but then fell through;

- Al Pacino, who starred for Evans in **The Godfather(s)**, turned down the starring role which would have helped Evans with legitimate financing. At that time, Pacino was "bankable;"

- Sly Stallone accepted the role, then bowed out. Some say because of Evans' cocaine problems and at the urging of his oligarchy establishment associates;

- A group of Texas oilmen arrived in Hollywood promising cash, and departed, never to be heard from again;

- Los Angeles Lakers owner Jerry Buss was in — then out.

The offers of deals came and went. They led to two Las Vegas casino owners, Fred and Edward Doumani. They had cash, lots of it; they wanted in on the deal. Francis Coppola was signed to do a rewrite, then to direct—a job that Evans himself once had hoped to have. Richard Gere and Gregory Hines, hardly two of the most sought after or bankable stars, were set for the leading roles.

The rest is a well-known disaster. The one saving grace of the film was the performance by Britain's brilliant character actor Bob Hoskins (who starred in 1988's **Who Framed Roger Rabbit?**) for his role of a 1920's era gangster. The film ended up costing over $47 million, and, by its release date late in 1984, no one involved in the project was on speaking terms and almost everyone was involved in litigation over control of the project.

Evans mortgaged his house for $3 million to put more cash into a losing cause. Practically every critic in the U.S. dubbed the project a bomb, a disaster, a failure. Many, however, singled out the work of Hoskins as "brilliant!"

Behind the scenes, according to court documents filed in 1988, there was a brutal reality; the contract murder of Roy Radin which some person or persons paid a great deal of money to have carried out. Instead of the story of **The Cotton Club**, this is the story which should have been on the screen.

In October, 1988, three alleged "hit men," William Maloney Mentzer, Alex Lamota Marti and Robert Ulmer Lowe, were arrested for carrying out the murder of Roy Radin. But suspected of ordering the hit, and paying for it, some say with the help of Evans, was Karen DeLayne Jacobs. She was arrested in Florida and said she would fight extradition. She later dropped those plans. The court documents, and the interviews with suspects and witnesses they contain, do NOT link Robert Evans directly to Radin's murder. But they place him very close to the action.

The Los Angeles County Sheriff's Department homicide unit had all but ended its probe into the Radin killing. The unit took up the case again in mid-1988 for reasons that were not made clear until late October. The homicide investigators met William Rider, the brother-in-law of, and one time body-guard and security chief for, Hustler magazine publisher and Los Angeles lowlife, Larry Flynt.

Rider had once been the supervisor of Mentzer, who had also worked as a bodyguard at one time to Flynt. He also lived with Lanie Jacobs in Palm Springs following the untimely demise of Roy Radin. During a poker game, according to Rider, Mentzer and another former Flynt bodyguard, Alex Marti, admitted shooting Radin to death. Rider also told detectives that Mentzer told him that Lanie alone did not order the hit.

Rider told the Sheriff's Department that on the night the Long Island playboy was killed, Marti "just went crazy and started shooting Radin," he said, quoting a conversation he had with Mentzer at the poker game.

Rider added that Mentzer admitted to contributing one of the fifteen shots pumped into Radin's body, "sort of a *coup de grace*," according to the report. It also noted that Marti and Mentzer tried to sell him Radin's ring and Rolex watch.

Following these startling revelations, sheriff's investigators sent Rider undercover at the risk of his life, for more. His hotel room, car and body were "wired for sound." In the resulting tapes, the report says, Lowe was the limo driver on Radin's "Last Ride."

Mentzer also told Rider that Lowe was driving the limo when Jacobs picked up Radin for the dinner meeting, ostensibly to be held at La Scala. According to Mentzer's account, Radin was stuck in the back seat of the limo, trapped with the two burly bodyguards. Jacobs was in a jump seat facing the unholy trio. As they drove west on Sunset, a police siren spooked the group, Marti hit the floor, stuck his gun into Radin's genitals and told him, "If you don't want to lose everything, keep quiet." The police car, apparently, is what caused Demond Wilson to lose the limo in the resulting traffic snarl. Everything went wrong for Roy Radin that fateful night. The police car turned out to be chasing a speeder down the Sunset Strip — not the limo.

In another taped conversation, Lowe told Rider that he received $17,000 and a black Cadillac Seville; that the "hit" was paid for by Jacobs and Evans and that the weapons used that night were taken to Florida in the Seville and thrown into the Florida Everglades.

Armed with Rider's information, authorities started to close in on Jacobs in Miami. Officials there were also interested in Jacobs because of yet another mysterious death — that of her husband, Larry Greenberger, who was blown away in September, 1988, by a gunshot blast to the face. Jacobs called it "suicide." Others believe Marti and Mentzer "assisted" Greenberger in his "suicide!"

☆   ☆   ☆

The reports filed by the Sheriff's investigators, who pursued the Radin case with dogged and professional determination until the Rider breakthrough, sketch the only version — official version — of what is believed to have happened to Roy Radin. High-priced defense lawyers for Jacobs are sure to dispute the official reports. They tell a story as decadent as **The Cotton Club** during its 1920's heyday of bootleg liquor, hoods, dishwater blondes.

Most controversial are the allegations that ex-Golden Boy Robert Evans WAS involved with Jacobs in commissioning the "hit" on Radin. It is believed that Jacobs and Evans would have done anything to salvage the Puerto Rican deal; but it could not be salvaged with Roy Radin, as intractable as he was over his 45% share.

In his own statement to investigators, Evans said he was only *casually* acquainted with the reputed cocaine wholesaler, Karen DeLayne Jacobs. But in the same report, Jacobs' associates insist she was Evans' drug supplier, sometime lover and friend, as well as a would-be investor in **The Cotton Club**. Prosecutors are convinced that Jacobs insisted Radin be eliminated because he refused to surrender any part of his 45% to her; she wanted an equal share with Radin — 22 1/2% of his agreed-upon share with Evans and Allegria.

Moreover, according to investigators, Evans' associates are quoted as telling detectives that Evans knew she had Radin killed and feared at one point for his own life. Ten days before Radin's body was discovered, Evans talked to Fred Doumani, the Las Vegas casino operator, one of the three original investors in the film and one of its ultimate financiers.

Doumani had seemed to be disenchanted with Evans and the entire project because of the problems involved in the financing and the negative publicity already surrounding the project in the press and in the trade papers. This prompted Evans to seek the alternative financing.

Their falling out, from the court documents, cost Evans a great deal. The producer is supposed to have told Doumani, according to the latter's statement: "You let me down regarding **The Cotton Club** and now I've got myself in some kind of trouble."

Then, Doumani told detectives, Evans recounted the blow-up of Evans' alternative financing with Radin and Jacobs, describing Jacobs as a player in the international dope trade, how Evans had been partying and sleeping with her. Now, Evans told Doumani, Jacobs was going to have Evans killed, and Evans needed some protection.

Doumani says he asked Evans, "Why do you believe Radin is dead? He could just be missing!"

Believe me, he's dead," Evans insisted, according to Doumani. "The bitch had him killed and I'm next."

Evans, when talking to investigators, denies ever having had any such conversation with Doumani.

Getting in deeper, according to the Sheriff's reports, Evans denies having had anything to do with Radin's death, and he also denies using cocaine since his conviction in New York or soliciting drug money to make movies. Other witnesses interviewed by Sgt. William Stoner, retired Det. Charles Guenther, and the late Det. Willie Anh along with Sgt. Carlos Avila, have alleged that the opposite is true with regard to The Golden Boy.

So who is, or who is not, telling the truth?

Is someone lying in an attempt to save his own skin? It is rather obvious that this is the case.

Until Jacobs and the three other accused low-life contract killers are brought to trial in Los Angeles, the unsolved mystery as to **why** Radin was killed will never be discovered. It is unlikely anyone will talk — unless the gas chamber stares them in the face. In fact, even during any murder trial which will ensue, the real reason for the death of Radin, the high-living playboy who wanted to live, play and work in Hollywood's fast lane, will probably never be known.

But what IS fascinating, and typical of Hollywood, is the eventual fate of Robert Evans. He once had it all: a marriage to actress-cum-overnight-star for **Goodbye Columbus**, Ali McGraw, and another marriage to a former Miss America and television personality Phyllis George. He was also one of the most powerful men in Hollywood, in charge of Paramount Pictures production schedule, and later an independent producer of some renown.

But cocaine became his bride, his mentor, his guiding light; and his downfall.

Hollywood isn't calling him anymore. The Oligarchy, which in recent years has shown itself willing to forgive liars, cheats, embezzlers, convicted drug pushers and users, crooks and even child molesters, has not yet shown itself willing to forgive Robert Evans, no matter what his part in the Radin case may turn out to be.

The Oligarchy also hands out high-paying, powerful jobs to those former embezzlers, forgers and their unsavory characters, and rehires convicted and jailed drug users, so why has Robert Evans been singled out for a fast ride into the abyss?

☆   ☆   ☆

- Is it because Evans' **Cotton Club** shenanigans became common knowledge and let the public in behind the scenes as to how films are *really* financed outside the usual scheme of things?

- Is it because Robert Evans became far too public with his problems?

The answers are not available — except behind closed doors.

Nevertheless, many former and current cocaine users, and one in particular who served a nine-month jail sentence in England for cocaine smuggling, is and are working regularly.

Possibly it is because Robert Evans trod on a few toes during his ten years at Paramount and later as an independent, as have many executives in high-profile positions.

The oligarchy at the top wants only mediocrity beneath them. Anything over and above that level of talent worries those in the penthouse suites. They fear they may lose their own jobs, their power, and their six- and seven-figure salaries to those below them who are judged "talented" and/or able.

When a Hollywood columnist was hired to write the "Coast To Coast" column for *The Hollywood Reporter* many years ago, he was greeted his

first day on the job by the paper's lead columnist, Hank Grant, with:
"Just remember, kiddo, all they want around here is mediocrity."

I told Grant I could tell that was true by just reading his column every day for several years. Grant regularly wished "Happy Birthday" to stars on a daily basis, some of whom had been dead for several years. Some of his "exclusives" had been printed in the New York **and** Los Angeles papers days or even weeks before Grant used them as lead items.

That just about sums up "life at the top" in the oligarchical society in two sentences.

But Robert Evans was never mediocre. Perhaps that also explains some of his current problems. At one time he was a high-rolling winner. His unfortunate involvement — perhaps obsession would be a better word — with **The Cotton Club**, ultimately may have cost him everything; even, perhaps, his liberty.

Why this obsession so overtook The Golden Boy will always remain one of the most controversial of Hollywood's Unsolved Mysteries.(*)

☆　　☆　　☆

(*)UPDATE — May, 1989: Robert Evans was subpoenaed to appear as a witness in the preliminary hearing for Jacobs, Mentzer, Martin and Lowe in "The Cotton Club Murder" of Roy Radin.

Los Angeles Deputy District Attorney David Conn, on the eve of the hearing in Los Angeles Superior Court, said he had NOT ruled out Evans as a suspect in the murder. But Conn added that Evan's role may be clarified — he emphasized "may be" — at the hearing. "We'll just have to put him on the stand and see what he'll say," said Conn immediately prior to the publication of **Hollywood's Unsolved Mysteries.**

The subpoena was not unexpected but news of it spread like a prairie fire throughout the oligarchy and threw a chill over Evans' production of **The Two Jakes**, the sequel to the Evans-produced box office smash **Chinatown**. Production began two weeks prior to the subpoena being served on Evans. Jack Nicholson is starring and directing in **The Two Jakes** which is entirely under the actor's control along with screen writer Robert Towne.

But even the Deputy District Attorney (Conn) was taken aback on May 12, when Evans appeared in answer to the subpoena in Municipal Court Judge Patti Jo McKay's courtroom.

The producer immediately invoked his Fifth Amendment privilege against "self-incrimination!" McKay thereupon warned the former head of Paramount Pictures: "Mr. Evans, this court can hold you in contempt and can order you incarcerated if you do not answer the questions. Do you understand that, sir?"

Evans answered "Yes" in a hoarse whisper. His lawyer said later that his client refused to answer any questions, because the prosecution refused, and still does, to clear Evans as a suspect in the murder of Roy Radin.

A few days later, however, following a weekend recess, Judge McKay ruled that as Evans' life had been threatened if he testified, he "properly invoked" the Fifth Amendment and, therefore, was "excused from testifying."

Conn continues to refuse to grant Evans immunity from prosecution, or absolve him of any connection with Radin's death.

ROY RADIN CHECKED RESTAURANT SECURITY ARRANGEMENTS AND MADE 'GOODBYE' TELEPHONE CALLS THE NIGHT OF HIS DEATH

Not only did Roy Radin ask his client and friend Demond Wilson to follow him as a precaution, Radin also called several restaurants in Beverly Hills to ask about their security arrangements. He finally settled on the posh La Scala when he was told there were security guards around the premises and that it had no "on site" parking lot. The only parking available was by valet and the nearest parking was a block away.

About 6 p.m on the night of his Last Ride, Radin telephoned his mother, Renee Radin Dorr, in New York. A family member said Radin's mother felt the tension in her son's voice immediately.

"What's the matter, baby?" she is reported to have asked her son. The same source said Radin sounded scared and upset, and that he told his mother that no matter what happened to him he still loved all of them; then he added, " ... I mean in case of a 'plane crash!'"

Radin also telephoned his ex-wife, Toni Fillet, whom he had recently divorced. In the middle of that conversation, he broke it off: "I have to go now, the limosine is here!"

That was the last conversation Roy Radin was known to have had with anyone other than Elaine Jacobs and the two friendly neighborhood goons in the back of the limo waiting for Radin at the curb.

He never made it to La Scala.

Lanie Jacobs disappeared the next day; her house in Sherman Oaks was cleaned out of everything.

Jacobs Defended by
Carlos Lehder's Counsel

Before agreeing to return to Los Angeles voluntarily to face charges in Roy Radin's contract murder, Elaine Jacobs was defended by the same Miami lawyer who defended Carlos Lehder, the Colombian cocaine kingpin.

In 1988, Lehder was sentenced to life in prison without possibility of parole.

Sinful and Forbidden Pleasures

Bob Crane and Inger Wegge in a studio shot from **Hogan's Heroes,** his hit TV series.
(Marvin Paige's Mot. Picture & TV Research Svc.)

Bob (Colonel Hogan) Crane. Crane's murder in a Scottsdale, Arizona apartment is unsolved to this day. However, the Scottsdale police say they have had a suspect for years but not enough evidence to indict the perpetrator. (Wide World)

"Let us not say, Every man is the architect of his own fortune; but let us say, Every man is the architect of his own character."

— George Dana Boardman
1828-1903
American Pastor

6 ... "Colonel Hogan's" Unsolved Murder

Bob Crane was on the verge of a reconciliation with his wife, at least on the surface, and of a dramatic television comeback. The star of television's **Hogan's Heroes**, the brash, wisecracking prisoner of war in Hitler's Germany, had met with no success in seeking a new television show except for one which was cancelled after one season.

Crane also thought he was in a shaky financial position and it was the main reason he kept on working in dinner theatres across the country. In this way he could earn upwards of $200,000 per year for about 30 weeks a year.

The reconciliation with his wife, Patricia, and the new television show were not to be. And he was in a shaky financial condition — but not of his own doing. He did not live long enough to find out why. Before these things could be resolved or discovered, Crane was killed by two severe blows to the head, which caused massive skull fractures and brain damage. The blows were inflicted by a blunt instrument such as a tire iron, a lug wrench from an automobile, or a piece of iron pipe. For the *coup de grace* the killer tied a length of cord from a video camera in the room around Crane's neck to make sure the actor was dead.

The Maricopa County Medical Examiner, Dr. Heinz Karnitschnig, said Crane was struck on the left side of the head as he slept, "and never knew what hit him." His death was placed "in the early morning" of June 29, 1978. It occurred in the Winfield Apartment-Hotel in an apartment leased by the Windmill Theatre (where Crane was appearing) for visiting performers. Karnitschnig said he felt, on a cursory examination, that it was a well-planned murder and not a crime of passion.

The Medical Examiner added later that the killer was "probably a man and not a woman." A track of blood spots on the ceiling was missing. According to Karnitschnig, the killer's first blow laid open Crane's scalp, covering the weapon in blood. The second blow was delivered with a short arc, slinging only a couple of droplets onto the ceiling and table lamp near the bed.

Investigators theorized that if the killer had been a woman, she would have had to swing the heavy weapon with a wider arc, which would have thrown more blood onto the ceiling. The wounds, according to the M.E., were deep, and the skull was crushed, indicating a very strong person. The killer, the police felt at the time, was probably a man who knew Crane, and he took his time. There were no signs of haste or frenzy. He even took the time to wipe the blood off his weapon on the bed sheet and take it with him. Apart from the cord around his neck — which did not kill Crane — the weapon was never found, in spite of an exhaustive search around the Winfield.

☆   ☆   ☆

According to Bob Crane's biography, published by CBS-TV while he was starring in **Hogan's Heroes**, he was born in Waterbury, Connecticut, on July 13, 1937. While in high school, from which he dropped out, Crane's ambition was to be a drummer in one of the big bands of the post-war era. Ultimately, he drummed his way to a seat with the Connecticut Symphony Orchestra.

A relic of this phase of Crane's career always sat on or near the set of the World War II comedy at the Desilu Studios in Hollywood — a set of drums which he had owned since his high school days.

In 1959, Crane put aside the sticks because he married his high school sweetheart, Ann Terzian. When they had one child, with another on the way. Crane felt that life on the road was no life for a married man with children. Instead, he turned to radio announcing and became a popular disc jockey. He started on WLEA in Hornell, New York, then WBIS in Bristol, Connecticut. Crane's big break came when he signed on with WICC in Bridgeport and remained there for six years. Word of his brashness, acumen with a mike and quick wit, reached the ears of the program director of KNX, the CBS Radio owned and operated station in Los Angeles. When the station was searching for a strong entry for the morning drive time show to combat the popularity of Dick Whittinghill on the Gene Autry-owned KMPC down the street on Sunset Boulevard,

It reached into Bridgeport and signed Crane. Word of mouth had reached Los Angeles about his popularity — just what KNX needed. After one year, the gamble paid off in the ratings for KNX and Crane soon became the number one disc jockey in Los Angeles in morning drive time listening.

It was his fast wit and timing at the mike that led him into television acting. Many of Crane's guests who were interviewed by him — which was a shrewd and calculated move on his part — were so delighted at his comedy talent they made him acting offers. In time he felt he was ready and accepted the role of Donna Reed's next-door neighbor, Dr. Dave Kelsey, on **The Donna Reed Show**. He managed, all the time he was appearing on the series, to continue his radio work on KNX from 5 a.m. to 9 a.m. five days a week. He was earning over $150,000 per year.

Guest appearances on **The Tonight Show** followed, as well as **Your First Impression, The Dick Van Dyke Show** and **The Alfred Hitchcock Hour**. His motion picture credits included **Return to Peyton Place** and **Man Trap**, all bit parts, but good experience for the tyro. When he landed the starring role on **Hogan's Heroes**, it finally forced him to leave KNX and devote full time to his acting.

Crane and Ann, who eventually had three children together — Robert, now 36, Deborah, 29, and Karen, 26 — were divorced in 1970. The pressures of his work, the hours, just were not conducive to a happy marriage for a housewife used to the routine of suburban Connecticut.

Following the cancellation of **Hogan's Heroes** after six years — and it is still being shown in over 75 countries — network officials wanted to cash in on Crane's well-known face and TVQ rating — the scale which advertisers and networks use to judge the popularity and recognizability of television personalities, even though the networks deny using it as a criteria.

Crane turned down over a score of offers. Sarcastically he told us, in an interview over brunch at the rooftop restaurant of The Holiday Inn in Brentwood, California, "one series was for me to be head of stewardess training for a swinging airline. I read the script and said, `This is Robert Cummings, circa 1953'."

Another script he rejected was about a sheriff in a small country town. "Andy Griffith had already done it," he told the producers through his agent. "Then," he said, "there was one about a bachelor who runs a babysitting service. Who would believe a 40-year-old running a babysitting service? Bob Denver, maybe," referring to the popular star of **Gilligan's Island**.

Finally Crane accepted a series which would not last very long.

☆   ☆   ☆

Actress Victoria Berry, who was appearing with Crane at The Windmill, wondered why the actor had not appeared for a cast luncheon for their farce, **Beginner's Luck**. Berry also had an appointment with Crane at 2:30 p.m. that day to re-tape the soundtrack on a videotape of a scene from their play. Crane, she said, was helping her with the videotape so that her agent could submit it to casting directors to get her future work in Hollywood.

Berry entered the apartment through the unlocked door. This was strange to her, because she knew Crane always double locked it when he was in the apartment alone or sleeping. She was also surprised to see that it was so dark inside. The curtains were drawn. She also noticed a half-empty bottle of Scotch and a bottle of vodka on a table. To Berry this was also strange. She knew Crane drank very little, and that when he did, he drank only one vodka and orange juice, generally in the evening.

When Berry entered the bedroom after receiving no answer to her calls to Crane, she saw the blood but didn't recognize the figure hunched up on the bed because of the misshapen features. At first she thought it was a woman whose hair was standing on end. She again shouted Crane's name; then she realized it was Crane; she recognized his wristwatch, and then screamed. This alerted neighbors, who called the authorities.

Though upset, Victoria Berry noticed other details. Crane, a methodical man accustomed to "living on the road," had hung his trousers neatly over a chair in the living room, his shirt on a hanger. His keys and his billfold were on the kitchen table. The apartment key of bright blue metal was still on the key ring. Sometimes he would remove the key from the ring and give it to Berry so that she could use the swimming pool at the Winfield during the sweltering 115 degree heat of a Scottsdale summer.

Then there was the "Little Black Bag!" Berry described it as "an 'equipment bag' with several zippers." When found, she said, it was almost empty and on the bed beside Crane. Police confirmed that it wasn't completely empty, but contained "miscellaneous personal effects" about which they would not be more specific.

Since Crane's door key was on the key ring and he usually locked the door, police theorized that he knew his killer and let them in the apartment before he went to bed. But this theory didn't hold water. Crane would hardly go to sleep with a guest in the house. The theory which holds the most water is that Crane DID have a visitor who eventually left. When leaving he or she could have made sure the door was unlocked and waited for Crane to go to sleep and re-entered; or else while they were in the apartment, they could have slipped a lock on a window — the apartment was on the ground floor — and then climbed back in and killed him as soon as he went to sleep.

One of the problems with the investigation, police said at the time — an investigation which was eventually called "very inept" by other law enforcement officials, and by the neighboring Phoenix Police Department — was the victim himself.

Bob Crane, they said, had "a great many girl friends, or acquaintances, in and out of the apartment." The police said there were literally close to 50 video tapes of a sexual nature with Crane in various sex acts with many different females.

In the bathroom, he had an elaborate photographic lab including an enlarger. Police said they found a strip of negatives in the enlarger showing a woman clothed, then nude. As the negatives were in the enlarger, it is possible the killer took some black and white prints from the area, overlooking the negatives.

However, Crane, friends said, never forced his photographic "interests" on his women friends. His models consented to be photographed in various stages of undress and in sexual activity.

☆   ☆   ☆

Following his death, people who knew Bob Crane well talked a little about the strange offscreen life of the talented, witty actor. To the public at large, he was a funny, likable professional who performed brilliantly, whether in his long-running television series or on the stage at dinner theatres. He once told us that he could earn a great deal of money in these gigs — up to $250,000 a year — but got sick and tired of the traveling and living out of a suitcase.

Behind the scenes, they said, there was a complex, difficult to understand, and often bitter personality. The bitterness seemed to come through the several times we talked to and interviewed him over the years.

When his second wife, Patricia, filed her divorce action in West Los Angeles six months before his death, she alleged that:

- Crane had harassed and slapped her, and had screamed obscenities at her;

- He threw open the windows of their West Los Angeles home and yelled that she was "crazy";

Actor Felice Orlando, Bob Crane and Sigrid Valdis in **Hogan's Heroes.** (Marvin Paige's Mot. Picture & TV Research Svc.)

- He refused to take their six-year-old son, Scott, to the hospital after Scott had broken his arm;

- He often tried to show "adult" films to Scott, and she was sick of his pornographic collection.

A week before his death, however, Patricia Olson Crane visited him in Scottsdale so that Crane could visit with their young son before she left for Seattle to appear in a stage play. She was taking Scott with her for his summer vacation treat.

"They seemed amicable when they were together, and Bob was even talking about a reconciliation. But I doubt that would have happened," one member of the cast told the media following Crane's death.

"Patti had made some pretty hardhitting allegations in her divorce petition and Bob never really got over them," said another.

Until just a few weeks before his death, Crane, who was very popular with millions of fans through **Hogan's Heroes**, and who liked to visit and talk to fans in a coffee shop early each morning after his theatre performance, was a tormented man. He hid his heartbreak with a smile — like all clowns — and Bob Crane was, in reality, a clown, always seeking a laugh with a wise crack, *a bon mot*, a smile, a wink.

After the breakup of his marriage with Patti, who had appeared with him in **Hogan's Heroes** as the German fraulein love interest, he was very morbid, according to Victoria Berry. His wife had actually kicked him out of the house and he had spent hours rationalizing about the breakup of his second go-round.

In the divorce petition, Patti also alleged that he owned a "large collection of pornographic films, including one with (Respondent) in it."

The charge of negligence toward his son, Scott, hurt the most, according to those around him at The Windmill. In the days before his death, Crane was trying hard to be a better father. Said Faye Wilson of the Windmill Theatre staff, "He talked about how he had been seeing a psychiatrist because of his wife's complaint that he wasn't fit to be a father! He was seeing him so that he *could* be a better father," she said.

☆   ☆   ☆

If Bob Crane was trying to learn how to be a better father, why did he insist on pursuing his "hobby" of taking porno videotapes and still pictures of himself engaged in sex acts with his multitude of women friends?

An album of what were supposed to be "pornographic" stills in an album could have led police to the killer — if it had been located. Detectives searched for the album, described by Victoria Berry as "very graphic," for several months following Crane's murder.

Apparently, the album was taken from his apartment," said Scottsdale Chief of Police Walter Nemetz. "The album was full of porno stills," he said, according to witnesses who had been questioned, and by those who had seen it. Dozens of videotapes, however, were found in the apartment showing Crane with women in various stages of undress and in various sexual positions with and without Crane. All were explicit.

"There (were) lots of motives for the murder," said Nemetz. "Mr. Crane developed a lot of strange acquaintances because of his ...er...er...hobby, or what appeared to be a hobby. His very peculiar activities off stage could lead to many motives among his friends and acquaintances."

"These," continued the chief, "could include cuckolded husbands who heard about them and, possibly, one of them went to the apartment in an attempt to retrieve a tape or tapes with (his) wife or (girl friend) in starring roles."

Crane's life-long friend from Connecticut, John Carpenter, who had since migrated to the West Coast, was out with Crane until about 2:30 a.m. the day of the murder.

Carpenter told the Scottsdale police that he last saw his friend outside a Scottsdale coffee shop, The Safari, part of the hotel of the same name on Scottsdale Road. Before leaving for the Safari, Crane had stopped by his apartment to drop off a few things from the theatre. While he and Carpenter were in the apartment, Crane received a telephone call from Patti from Seattle. According to Carpenter, this eventually developed into a shouting match between them. "The sweetness and light visit of a week or so before..." certainly had fallen apart by that time.

Instead, said Carpenter, Crane made the decision not to reconcile with Patti because of a newly formed relationship with a Phoenix woman described as young, blonde and pretty. Most of Crane's friends tended to be a little wacky, according to his friend Carpenter. "But this one is a little different," Crane told him. "He said he had dated her three or four times and said he really liked her."

☆   ☆   ☆

When we last interviewed Crane about two years before his death, he was still downhearted over the failure of **The Bob Crane Show** — which had begun network life as **Second Chance**. Bob said he had held high hopes for the show when it began. "It was a fun show," he said, " and I like the character I played. The idea was to present a nice, warm human comedy about a middle-aged guy who throws away a successful business career to go to medical school to become a doctor.

"But I was apprehensive about the changes they kept making in it, worrying because it then sounded too much like **The Donna Reed Show** all over again. But, there you are — that's what the network wanted, and they were proven wrong. I did all I could to have the changes cancelled and if we had, I really believe we had a chance of making it a success. I was happy to get the name changed to **The Bob Crane Show**. **Second Chance** worried me," he said. "I wondered at the time if it wasn't `The Last Chance!'

"So, we got bumped off the air. It was over, practically, before it had begun. I felt good doing it. I had recently had success with a Disney movie, **A Son In Law For Charlie MacCready**. (*)

I felt good about it and getting back to a regular series. I thought at the time I could do both — make films and do TV, and everything seemed to be going along fine. Then, the balloon burst and it ended."

"What," he asked thoughtfully, "keeps us moving back? Is it habit or money or what? Well, for some of us it's just that we get kinda homesick for the sets, the smell of the sound stages, the order to cut and for action by a director. Of course, the money is another reason. I'm not that rich, so I can do with whatever money I can get."

Crane explained that "it" for him was a combination of being eager to keep working and being just as eager to make money at it. He said he was the type who has to keep doing "...something!" When other actors rested up during a break, Crane said he couldn't. "The first day I'm up pacing around the house. To be idle drives me up a wall!"

But hadn't he been idle during the demise of each of his television series and **Super Dad**?

"No," he replied. "I had an extremely hectic time. I was all over the place. I did some specials, I hosted some local TV shows. I was master of ceremonies for top events, like beauty pageants, and picked up good money doing it. I flew to New Zealand for a convention of prisoners of war because of the other series. I taped radio shows and took part in sports events. I did some stage work and came back to Hollywood to do some pilot shows for series that never made it to air."

There were some rumors at the time of **Super Dad** that the Disney Studios had some misgivings after signing him for the film because of

---

(*) In some areas of the U.S. and overseas it was called **Super Dad**. We will refer to it by its shorter title.

Crane's un-Disneylike offscreen image.

"Yeah, yeah," he replied in a brush-off sort of way, "I read about that, too. But nobody at the studio really said anything. I mean, not officially. They didn't know about my hobby of playing the drums in topless-bottomless bars around town!"

Very un-Disneylike behavior, to say the least.

"But," he continued, "what was wrong with that? I loved sitting in with small groups to play the drums and naturally I like looking at those naked ladies. I'm a normal, red-blooded guy and I was only looking," he emphasized, "at those ladies. I wasn't doing anything with them. It happened that they were at the places where I could play drums."

☆ ☆ ☆

A month following the murder, law enforcement officials in other agencies expressed private concern about the Scottsdale Police Department and its ability to handle the high-profile and complex murder investigation of such a prominent person. The city, it should be pointed out, because of its size, did not have a "central" homicide bureau, or detective squad. The same detectives who investigated burglaries, robberies and other crimes, also investigated the few murders that were committed in the retirement city.

One private investigator voiced an opinion that Crane's killing could have been a "murder for hire" by a cuckolded husband. Because noise was a factor, as in the Vicki Morgan killing, a bludgeon-type of weapon was used. But the PI could not come up with a motive with the exception of the "cuckold syndrome" which a lot of people had come up with when the news of the videotapes and still pictures came out.

The Scottsdale police were bombarded with "theories" but came no closer to solving the murder of Bob Crane. A man of Crane's prominence, involved as he was with sex and porno films, invited conjecture about jealous husbands and lovers.

Such stuff, said the police, was the grist for tabloids, not serious police work. Theories were also advanced from Hollywood that the husband or boy friend of one of Crane's paramours who possibly "starred" on one of the tapes, "ordered" the hit and then managed to have it hushed up in the Arizona city. The oligarchy tentacles had been known to reach that far — and farther.

Crane's life-long friend, John Carpenter was, for a time, the number one suspect in the killing. While the Maricopa County District Attorney would not confirm — at least for the record — that the Los Angeles businessman was the "prime suspect," other sources confirmed at the time that he was.

When Carpenter was reached at his Los Angeles office, he was speechless when told the news by a reporter. "I'm shocked. Completely shocked," he said. Carpenter declined any further comment until he had consulted with a lawyer.

Carpenter had volunteered the information to the police that he was probably the last person to see the actor alive or talk to him the day (or early morning) he was killed.

Crane, said Carpenter, finished his Wednesday evening performance, as usual, around 10:30 p.m. As was his custom, he hung around the lobby for several minutes chatting with fans, something he liked to do, and signing autographs.

Friends say he was tired. Very tired. It wasn't a large crowd that night. In fact, the play, which was owned by Crane, had not drawn more than half a house for three weeks. The theatre management told Crane that it was cutting his five week run short by a week.

This did not upset Crane, and he was looking forward to a week off. His friend, Carpenter, had flown in a few days earlier on business, and to visit Crane. He was staying at the Sunburst Hotel, not far from the Winfield Apartments.

When he left the theatre Wednesday night, Crane told a theatre employee he was going to go home, even though a woman and her girl friend were at the performance that night at Crane's invitation.

Carpenter said that Crane did return to the Winfield and received a call from his wife. As the conversation was rancorous and loud, neighbors in the apartment complex heard the ruckus and parts of the conversation.

Crane and Carpenter then went to an East Phoenix bar with the two women whom they had arranged to meet (after stopping off at Crane's apartment). At 2 a.m. all went to the Safari, where Carpenter said he had last seen his friend around 2:30 a.m. before leaving for his hotel to pack and catch an early morning flight to Los Angeles. Carpenter said he also telephoned Crane when he got back to the hotel. The subject of the call was not disclosed, except that the major reason was to say goodbye.

Carpenter checked out of the Sunburst Hotel "very hurriedly" early the next morning, said a hotel employee. He seemed nervous and demanded a limousine to take him to the Sky Valley Airport in Phoenix. None was available so the desk called him a cab.

About 2:30 p.m. from Los Angeles on Thursday afternoon, Carpenter called the theatre and asked for Crane. An employee told Carpenter she didn't know where Crane was and suggested he call the theatre's other office. The girl said as the call was long distance, she would check for him. Carpenter held on and in a few minutes was told Crane was not there. The employee then checked with the Winfield and learned the news from Victoria Berry who told her what had happened. The employee relayed this information to Carpenter who hung up aghast at the news.

☆　　☆　　☆

The police investigation stumbled along at The Windmill. Employees said the police were not even aware of the theatres' "second office" referred to in Carpenter's call to the theatre. They were never even told of Carpenter's inquiries until much later in the investigation.

Also, the police only made a cursory inspection of Crane's dressing room at the Windmill and one of the employees was entrusted to pick up Crane's personal belongings.

On Thursday evening, Crane's eldest son, Robert, and Lloyd Vaughan, Crane's business manager, *the man who handled all of Crane's business and financial affairs*, arrived in Scottsdale and talked to the police about the situation. Vaughan, the police said, appeared to be very nervous and preoccupied and just going through the motions of tending to business. He put it down to being very upset over his client's death.

☆　　☆　　☆

According to Vaughan, the next day police took them to Crane's living quarters at the Winfield. They gave Vaughan and Robert a bottle of wine and some beer from the refrigerator which, to anyone's knowledge, were never checked for fingerprints. (At least no one noticed any "dusting powder" on the bottles). They allowed the two men to pack all of Crane's belongings in suitcases that were already in the apartment.

Sources both inside and outside the Scottsdale Police Department say none of the items were checked for fingerprints and the murder weapon was never found. This could not be confirmed and the police may be withholding information on prints in case the murderer is ever caught. The trunks of rental cars at the airport should have been checked for missing or bloody lug wrenches. One rental car was checked at the Phoenix airport but the results were never made known. We understand that they did lead to a suspect, however, who did not hold up.

All in all, everyone connected with the case agreed that the police bungled it and conducted a very inept investigation. Most outsiders feel a suspect should have been arrested within forty-eight hours of the murder.

None of the following questions have ever been satisfactorily answered:

- How did the murderer gain entrance to the apartment? There were many keys given out over the years to various performers. Was a window left unlatched, a door unlocked from an earlier visitor? Crane always double-locked the door when he went to bed;

- Why did the police not try to track down the bottle of Scotch found in the apartment? Why was it not "dusted" for fingerprints. (If it was "dusted," then the Police are not saying what they found);

- It was a well-known fact that Crane never kept any spirits in the apartment. He seldom drank anything except an occasional beer and orange juice and vodka. If this is the case, who brought the Scotch to the Winfield? Did the police check the drinking preferences of Crane's close friends — or visitors?

- Were all the "players" in the video-tapes showing Crane having sex with many different women ever checked out AND their husbands and/or boy-friends for possible motives?

- What was in Crane's "Little Black Bag" with all the zippers that was so important to the murderer that he took it out of the closet where it was always kept and rummaged through it on the bed next to Crane's lifeless body?

All the Scottsdale Police would say about the "black bag" was that when they found it on the bed, all it contained was "a few personal items." Otherwise, it was almost empty.

On June 11, 1981, officials of the Maricopa County attorney's office and the Scottsdale Police confirmed what the unseated County Attorney, Charles Hyder, had maintained all along:

> *"There was simply not enough evidence to charge anyone*
> *with the crime!"*

As part of his successful campaign platform to unseat Hyder at the previous November election, County Attorney Tom Collins promised Scottsdale that he would take another look at "the Bob Crane murder case."

Some Scottsdale Police officers who investigated the 1978 homicide were disgruntled and threw their election support to Collins because of this campaign pledge. They were disgruntled because charges were not filed by Hyder and his staff against a man they suspected in the killing.

A County Attorney's investigator and the Police completed "another look" at Crane's killing on June 11, 1981.

Major Dave Townsend of the Scottsdale Police Department said that the review added another "key suspect" to the case, a woman. He would not reveal her identity.

"However," said Townsend, "both offices (Police and County Attorney) agree there is not enough evidence to file any charges. I am," he concluded, very satisfied with the present County Attorney's attempts to help in this investigation."

Townsend concluded his remarks that the investigation will never be closed until someone is charged with Crane's murder. It would appear at this late date that it will be a cold summer day in Scottsdale before this occurs.

Today, the killer of Bob Crane still walks free — probably on the streets of Beverly Hills or Los Angeles. Crane is, many believe, the victim of a husband or boyfriend of a wife or a girlfriend who was "featured" in one of the sex tapes discovered in the apartment — and that a particular tape was stashed in the little black bag.

Or ...

"The killer will never be free from the guilt of that act," said Gary Maschner of the Scottsdale Police Department. And Maschner hopes that "someday that guilt will one day break open the murder case," he said in June, 1984, the sixth anniversary.

"The killer has got to live with it," said Maschner "knowing what I do about random murderers or first time killers — it preys on his mind every time he thinks about it."

Maschner also says he thinks the killer has tried to contend with the guilt by confessing to somebody. "People like to talk; people need to talk."

But until the Scottsdale Police get some new information, their investigation of the case will remain stymied.

"As for now," said County Attorney Collins, "there's nothing new."

Collins said that new "leads" come in every week, but none of them lead anywhere but to a dead end. "Just a couple of weeks ago," he laughed, "someone `confessed' to the murder, but we later proved they couldn't be the murderer because of some evidence we have held back from the press and public," he said.

What the police do know to date is this — and it is all the information they will release:

- Crane was last seen alive on the morning of June 29, 1978, at 2:45 a.m. by patrons in the Safari Coffee Shop in Scottsdale, and by John Carpenter.

- Crane's body was found at 2:20 p.m. the following afternoon in the Winfield Apartments, which are now the Winfield Place Condominiums at 740 East Chaparral Road, Scottsdale.

- There was no sign of a forced entry and the front door was unlocked when Victoria Berry arrived at 2:20 p.m. There were no signs of a struggle.

- The police have always been drawn to one suspect in Crane's murder, and they still lean towards that suspect, the last known person to see Crane alive and talk to him.

- The police have never had enough conclusive evidence to convince the County Attorney's office that the suspect should be indicted.

The Scottsdale Police probably did bungle the investigation at the start as many people and outside law enforcement agencies say.

But there is also the possibility that Bob Crane "entertained" the wife or girlfriend of some powerful figure in the oligarchy. Many in Scottsdale believe this may be the case and, therefore, the police department AND the County Attorney have "backed off" filing any charges.

On the other hand, Scottsdale, Arizona, is a very closely knit retirement community in the Arizona desert. It is a wealthy area and it is highly possible that Crane could have also "entertained," and featured in living color on a videotape, the wife and/or girlfriend of one of Scottsdale's leading citizens, with access to many sources of information and the seat of power in Scottsdale.

Nevertheless, it would appear that now, over ten years after his murder, the killer of Bob Crane will never be brought to justice — unless the killer confesses, or gives himself absolution on his death-bed by confessing to the crime. Either of the latter two options seems highly unlikely.

But as the American theologian Tyron Edwards wrote in the 19th Century:

> *"Sinful and forbidden pleasures are like poisoned bread;*
> *they may satisfy appetite for the moment, but there is*
> *death in them in the end...."*

It may well have been "poisoned bread and forbidden pleasures" that were the catalysts which precipitated the murder of Bob Crane.

But Hollywood and television are the losers for the loss of the witty, brash and personable high school drop-out from Waterbury, Connecticut. His murder, and who did it, might always be considered another of Hollywood's Unsolved Mysteries.

HIS BUSINESS MANAGER SENTENCED TO JAIL/PROBATION THREE YEAR'S AFTER ACTOR'S DEATH

One of the more compelling reasons which kept Bob Crane "on the road" working dinner theatres was his believing his business manager who told Crane he had "cash flow problems" and was not in a very sound financial position.

Unbeknownst to Crane before he was murdered, the problem was created by his own business manager, the then 36-year-old Beverly Hills attorney, Lloyd Vaughan. Vaughan was ordered to stand trial in Los Angeles Superior Court following a preliminary hearing on the indictment.

A. Lee Blackman, representing Crane's widow, testified at the hearing for Vaughan: "It's a really depressing story. Vaughan called my office and said he wanted a private meeting with me.

"He said he had embezzled the money because he had gotten in over his head financially," he testified.

Crane's widow, Patricia, testified that Vaughan told Blackman that more than $102,000 restitution would be made to the Crane estate.

The Los Angeles District Attorney's office did not know of the embezzlement until December, 1979, when Patricia Olson Crane complained that Vaughan had not paid a promised $75,000.

In March, 1981, Vaughan pleaded *nolo contendere* in a plea bargain that included a promise he would not be sent to State prison. He also agreed to pay the Crane estate a total of $108,000 in restitution, $75,000 of which was delivered before the criminal charges were filed against him.

Vaughan was sentenced to one year in jail and five years probation for embezzling $75,707 from the estate. The balance was for legal fees and interest.

It was Vaughan, along with Crane's son, Robert, who rushed to Phoenix-Scottsdale on hearing the news of his client's death.

Too Beautiful To Grow Old

Publicity portrait of Natalie Wood taken during the filming of **Meteor**, one of her last films. (Marvin Paige's Mot. Picture & TV Research Svc.)

"Pleasure is to a woman what the sun is to the flower; if moderately enjoyed, it beautifies, refreshes and improves; but if immoderately, it withers, deteriorates and destroys."
— *Caleb Colton*
1780-1832

7 ... Natalie Wood's Mystery Death

A Thanksgiving weekend yachting trip and a break from filming for Natalie Wood and her husband, Robert Wagner, turned into a lonely and very mysterious death for Natalie. The cause of her death is still being debated and will be debated for a long time to come. There were no witnesses, no hard evidence as to how, why or when.

The star's body was found at 7:44 a.m. on Sunday morning, November 29, 1981. Natalie Wood was floating face down below the surface of the water, about 200 yards from Blue Cavern Point on the remote northern end of Santa Catalina Island, 26 miles off the coast of Southern California. When the body was sighted, it was approximately one mile from the Wagner's yacht, Splendour.

The inexplicable manner of Natalie Wood's death by drowning still leaves many unanswered questions. It stunned the oligarchy of which Natalie and her husband were popular members.

What happened that Saturday night/Sunday morning of November 28 and 29 remains a mystery to this day to most of those involved in the investigation and to the family of Natalie Wood. Her death was officially recorded as "accidental drowning."

Coroner Thomas Noguchi, who investigated the drowning and made the determination her death was "accidental" in conjunction with the Los Angeles County Sheriff, issued a later call of another public inquiry into the mystery of her death. This was brought about by sensationalized new theories and versions, including that of the Captain of the Splendour and unofficial bodyguard for Natalie, Dennis Davern.

Robert Wagner and Natalie Wood during their first marriage at a Foreign Press Association Golden Globe Award banquet in 1961. (Marvin Paige's Mot. Pic. & TV Research Svc.)

Noguchi, who later lost his job because of his outspoken doubts about the *cause* of Natalie Wood's death and his desire to develop a "Psychological Profile," said, a few years following her death, that he would urge that the case be re-opened. It never has been re-opened, nor ever will be, because of pressure "downtown" brought about by the oligarchy.

A private investigator, who has also published two books about the unsolved mystery of Marilyn Monroe's death, gadfly Milo Speriglio, probed Natalie's death extensively with the resources of the Nick Harris Detective Agency of Los Angeles, of which he is president.

Said Speriglio, "In my professional opinion, the closest Natalie Wood's death gets to "accidental drowning" is "accidental homicide."

"I don't buy a lot of that stuff that's been said about her "accidental drowning." I suspect there's a possibility it may have been a homicide. But I don't think it was *deliberate* homicide, which would be considered by the courts as first degree murder."

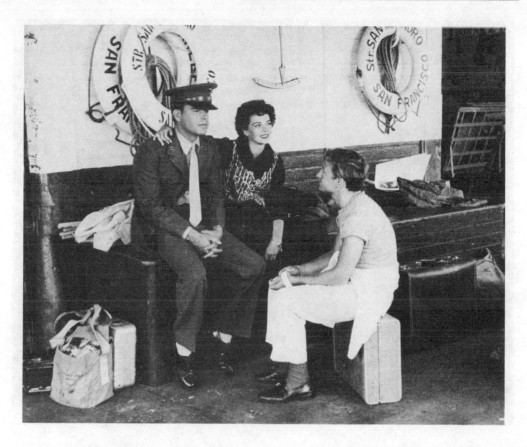

Natalie Wood and Robert Wagner during their first marriage, on the set of **Love and War** at Warner Brothers Pictures. They are shown with their "friend" Nick Adams, the star of **The Rebel** TV series. Adams was Natalie's first lover at the age of 14 at the urging of Natalie's mother "to teach her the ways of the world." Adams also accompanied the Wagner's on their honeymoon! (John Austin Collection)

"But," continued the gadfly, "...I do suspect that there is a lot more to this case than meets the eye. Family members have told me they feel exactly the same way."

At the center of the controversy surrounding Natalie Wood's death were several stories and rumors which are still circulating after almost a decade that Natalie was involved in a "Love Triangle." These sparked the rumors of jealousy, recrimination, drunken rages and finally, panic, during the hours leading up to her death in the cold, murky waters off Catalina Island.

Lionel Stander, Stefanie Powers and Robert Wagner in **Hart To Hart**. Natalie flirted with Christopher Walken during the filming of **Brainstorm**, her last film. Natalie heard rumors that Wagner might have been consoling Stefanie Powers following the death of the latter's longtime intimate friend, William Holden. (Marvin Paige's Mot. Picture & TV Research Svc.)

It took Davern, the yacht's skipper, over six years to speak out about the bizarre events which preceded the tragedy. Many of his claims have been backed up by an author who wrote about the events of that weekend but drew no positive conclusions.

The claims made by all the amateur Johnny-come-latelies question the *official* story that Natalie Wood fell into the water while trying to climb into the yacht's dinghy to avoid an argument with her husband and Christopher Walken.

Walken was the cause of the rumors swirling around Natalie. He was her co-star in **Brainstorm**, which had been on location for several weeks in North Carolina. Walken was invited by Natalie to go along on the weekend cruise. It was the first time, in anyone's memory, that the Wagners had asked only a *single guest* to accompany them on such a jaunt. Usually, it was a couple, or two or three people of both sexes.

The rumors running rampant around the watering holes and in the gossip columns of the day were that Wood and Walken, a young, good-looking actor, had been having an affair on the North Carolina location.

Davern, the skipper, claims:

- A jealous and yelling Wagner smashed a bottle of wine as he accused Walken of "trying to seduce my wife in front of me..."

- Wood flirted openly with Walken and, at one point, the two disappeared below decks for a half hour;

- Wagner wouldn't let Davern search for Wood after they discovered she was not aboard the Splendour;

- Instead of worrying about his missing wife, Wagner drank with the skipper until Wood's body was found by the U.S. Coast Guard;

- There was a mysterious half hour during which Wagner disappeared after telling Davern he was going to check on Wood below decks.

As the Captain of the Splendour, Davern said that by the time they reached Catalina from the yacht's Marina del Rey berth, he was so concerned about mounting tensions between the three principals that he distributed what he calls "bootleg quaalude" pills in an effort to calm everyone down.

"The vibes were all bad," he said. "Natalie was intrigued by Walken. He was a young, good-looking guy and she played it up with him."

The Splendour arrived off Catalina on the Friday after Thanksgiving Day. After an afternoon of shopping and sightseeing, the strain on shipboard was heightened that night. According to Davern's account, "Natalie was playing up to Walken and he was just going along with it."

The trio of Wagner, his wife and Walken, along with Davern, had dinner and drinks at El Galleon restaurant in the island's capital of Avalon on Friday night, November 27. Natalie, according to a witness, started with a beer, then switched to Margaritas, a strong mixed drink with a (Mexican) Tequila base — two or three and you can't find your feet. Later that evening in the restaurant, the three actors got into an argument at their table, according to the same witness.

A rainstorm was blowing up and RJ (Wagner's nickname) wanted to go back to the yacht and move it to Isthmus Cove, a more sheltered anchorage. But Natalie and Walken — who won the coveted Oscar for his role in **The Deer Hunter** — wanted to stay in Avalon and keep on partying. Wood and Walken claimed they had had a tough eight weeks in North Carolina and in the studio on **Brainstorm** and they wanted to unwind.

According to the same witness, RJ said "O.K., I'm going. You guys can stay but you'll have to find your own way back to the yacht by yourselves. I'm taking the dinghy."

Davern got up to leave as well but Wagner told him to stay. After his departure, Walken, Natalie and Davern hung around the restaurant and bar and Natalie, according to other witnesses, got "...roaring drunk."

Shortly after midnight, not wanting to make their way back by water taxi to the Splendour because of the windy and rainy weather, the trio checked into two rooms at The Pavillion Lodge in town. Natalie took both rooms under her name.

An hour later, Walken and Natalie were seen together in her room by hotel security guard Gary Piper.

"She (Natalie) was having trouble with the heater in the room and I was called in to light it for her," the guard said.

"When I went into the room, she was sitting on the bed and Walken was on the floor. They were engaged in an intense discussion."

The next morning, the trio caught a ride via water taxi to Isthmus Cove where Wagner had moved the Splendour by himself overnight. They rejoined him on the yacht to a cool reception.

The drinking and arguing started again later that afternoon, the fateful day of November 28.

A native of San Francisco, Natasha Gurdin, a child of Russian and French parents, was spotted by director Irving Pichel while he was shooting **Happy Land** on locations in and around Santa Rosa, California — a town about 30 miles north of the Bay City — when Natasha was just four years old. Pichel, a veteran director, was so smitten with her beauty he gave her a job as a bit player in the film.

Natalie with another of her early lovers, Warren Beatty. Their romance broke up when Beatty walked out on Natalie at Chasen's Restaurant in favor of the hat check girl at the famed watering hole of the oligarchy. Natalie was stuck with the dinner checks. (John Austin Collection.)

Two years later, Pichel remembered little Natasha Gurdin and cast her as the daughter of Claudette Colbert and Orson Welles in **Tomorrow Is Forever**. Welles was to say later that Natalie, in that film, "...performed like someone who had been acting for years. If ever there was a natural actress," said Welles, "this six year-old was it."

Then came her break through the film, **Miracle on 34th Street**, in which she played a nine-year-old girl — which she was at the time — who doesn't believe in Santa Claus. Kris Kringle, played by the late Edmund Gwenn, convinces the child that Santa does indeed exist. Natalie Wood — as she was known by then — gave a warm and touching performance.

Following **Miracle on 34th Street** Natalie appeared in a slew of films with such major stars as James Stewart, Fred McMurray and John Wayne.

We remember once riding with Natalie in a bus en route to a movie preview junket promoting **Here Comes the Groom**, which starred Bing Crosby and Jane Wyman, in 1951 or 1952. We were on our way to Lake Arrowhead and I remarked that she seemed a lot older than the twelve years of age she was at the time. "It's because I work around adults most of the time," she replied, nonchalantly.

Four years later, Natalie's big break came in what has come to be known as her "breakthrough" film which put her in the top rank of rising stars. She played the late James Dean's sweetheart in **Rebel Without a Cause** in 1955. This film is still a cult picture among young people, not only in the U.S. but around the world, not only for Natalie, but for Dean as well. Natalie, in fact, received her first Oscar nomination for **Rebel**, and it all seemed to come together for her with that film: maturity, talent, and a growing popularity.

Most of her fans, and fan magazines, assume her "love diary" *per se*, and her worldly wise ways began with this film and her dating of the bisexual Dean. But, in fact, Natalie's first sexual encounter was three years earlier, when she was just fourteen. And, incredibly, it was her mother who arranged it with Nick Adams, then 23, and a close friend of the family. Shortly before his tragic death thirteen years later, Adams told a fan magazine interviewer that he had been Natalie's first lover.

Adams said, "Natalie's mother told me to teach Natalie `the ways of the world'." According to Adams, the matchmaking mother explained to Adams, "She's going to be doing it anyway, and I'd rather it be with you. I know I can trust you!"

But Natalie's mother couldn't trust everyone in the love-filled world of Natalie Wood. Many ex-employees on the 20th Century-Fox studio lot said Natalie was already making eyes at older men when she was just ten years old. "She seemed far too mature for her age," said one publicist who knew Natalie well.

Natalie with one of "my buddies." In print, Hedda Hopper asked Natalie: "Is Tab Hunter *really* your type, Natalie?" What Hopper was referring to in her own inimitable bitchy style was the alleged bisexuality of Natalie and Tab at the time. (Marvin Paige's Mot. Picture & TV Research Svc.)

Natalie with James Dean in **Rebel Without a Cause**, another of her early lovers. (Marvin Paige's Mot. Picture & TV Research Svc.)

Adams wasn't Natalie's lover for long. "Soon there were guys a lot older than she was, or even me, taking her out," he revealed. "When she was 16 (before **Rebel**) the great love of her life — at that tender age — was director Nicholas Ray, who directed **Rebel Without a Cause**. He was in his forties at the time," said Adams.

That, according to Adams, sparked friction with her Russian-born mother, Maria Gurdin. "Every night Natalie would come home from a date and there'd be screaming by Maria. Nat would run out of the house crying," said Adams who was a constant visitor to the Gurdins.

"I guess there wasn't much they could do about it," he said. "She was, after all, practically supporting the family with her film work, including her sister Lana."

After losing James Dean in that tragic car accident in Northern California and while their affair was still hot and heavy, even though Dean was known to be bi-sexual, Natalie formed the first of her seemingly endless "sexless" relationships with Hollywood "bachelors." The public read about her making the rounds to night spots and restaurants with Tab Hunter and Raymond Burr who, at 39, was old enough to be her father. There were rumors as well that Natalie had also formed a sexual relationship with several women.

Dates with Tab Hunter, in particular, prompted the bitchy columnist Hedda Hopper to ask Natalie pointedly in print: "Is Tab *really* your type, Natalie?"

The actress answered cryptically, "There's no romance. My boy friends may come and go, but my buddies always stay." Nobody heard about the "buddies," as Natalie described them to Hopper, but there were plenty of "boy friends" coming and going.

In rapid order, Natalie had flings with Elvis Presley, hotel heir Nicky Hilton, theatre tycoon Arthur Loew, Jr., Venezuelan shoe magnate Ladislav Blatnik, David Niven, Jr., the late Woolworth heir Lance Reventlow, and actors Stuart Whitman, Perry Lopez, and Dennis Hopper.

☆　　☆　　☆

Then, suddenly, Natalie Wood, who was known to be playing her greatest love scenes off camera, was ready for something new — marriage. Her real love, "idyllic love" she was to say at the time, hit her in the person of Robert J. Wagner, also under contract to 20th Century-Fox. Like Natalie, Wagner was also a teen-aged idol. They married in 1957 and became known to the society of the oligarchy as "Nat and RJ". They were inseparable on the Hollywood scene along with, strangely enough,

Natalie's first lover, Nick Adams. This caused a few titters among the "in crowd," particularly when Adams accompanied them on their honeymoon to Arizona. Everyone in the know knew what the score was with Natalie and Nick Adams.

Then, on June 20, 1961, the once "perfect marriage" ended with a divorce announcement. It even stunned Liz Taylor, then married to Eddie Fisher; they were close friends of "Nat and RJ." Said Liz at the time, "We had dinner with them the other night and they acted as happy as ever."

No one has ever been able to pinpoint the breakup of the marriage. Some say it was Natalie's working with Mr. Stud, Lover Boy Warren Beatty, in **Splendor in the Grass**. According to those in the know, with Beatty and Natalie it was Splendor in the Bedroom. It was obvious to everyone within the oligarchy that Wagner had been replaced by Beatty. Her marriage to Wagner ended in a blistering set-side fight witnessed by Wagner's new love interest, Joan Collins, also under contract to 20th Century-Fox. Natalie stormed off the set — just as she would many years later on the night she died when she could no longer stand an argument involving her husband and Christopher Walken.

Many others, however, feel the real reason for the first breakup of the Wagner's was a combination of things, in particular a horrible film the Wagners made together called **All The Young Cannibals**, which was finished in 1960, but not released until 1961. There is an old saying in the oligarchical society that a marriage between an actress and an actor can survive everything but a bad picture starring both which bombs at the box office. Also, just about the same time as **Cannibals** was being shelled by the critics, the Wagners decided to remodel their Southern style mansion into a Roman Palazzo *a la* early Liberace.

The remodeling job cost $150,000 or thereabouts, a princely sum in those days. RJ didn't really mind the cost, but he did object to ceiling plaster falling into his morning cereal, and wall plaster falling into the bathtub when he was relaxing in the hot water.

Whatever the cause, "Hollywood's perfect couple" broke up and Natalie started dating Beatty openly. They went together for a long time, but Beatty never was — or is — the marrying kind. Natalie was, because of her upbringing by her Russian and French parents and the European tradition: she wanted to be a wife AND a mother.

One night, Warren took Natalie to Chasen's for dinner. At the stylish restaurant, the hat check girl was a busty, pretty young blonde: the operative words for Beatty were busty, young and blonde. After ordering dinner, Beatty excused himself from Natalie, walked to the check stand opposite the front door, and then talked the "busty young blonde" into leaving with him for a three day "vacation." Natalie was stuck with the check for both dinners.

Soon, however, Natalie was off to other beaux. One particularly ardent admirer was Arthur Loew, Jr., scion of the theatre and MGM fortune. When Arthur gifted Natalie with a $10,000 sable coat one night at the La Scala restaurant, the magazine and gossip columnists went berserk trying to concoct stories about the duo. Many had them marrying, and Natalie already *enceinte*.

If all this makes Natalie sound like a night-life type of girl, forget it. Like all the great stars from Clark Gable and Humphrey Bogart to Bette Davis and Carole Lombard, Natalie played hard — very hard — but worked hard, too. She was always on time the next morning, knew her lines, and could find her marks, hung over or not.

In front of the cameras, Natalie Wood was always the ultimate Hollywood professional. And she could act; she was a natural and took very few lessons during her career. She received three Academy Award nominations for **Rebel Without a Cause, Splendor in the Grass** — after which the Wagner's yacht was named — and **Love With the Proper Stranger**. Natalie, in everyone's opinion, was also a knockout as "Maria" in **West Side Story** even though she was neither a singer nor dancer. And in **Gypsy**, she played stripper Gypsy Rose Lee as a sexpot although Natalie, herself, would be the first to say she wasn't one.

The general consensus was that Natalie never gave a bad performance in anything she ever did no matter how horrible the film and that includes **All The Young Cannibals**.

☆   ☆   ☆

In 1969, after "playing the field" since her divorce from RJ, Natalie was ready for marriage again. She married an English producer and agent, Richard Gregson, by whom she had a daughter, Natasha. Wagner, meanwhile, married Marion Marshall, the ex-wife of director Stanley Donen. Most onlookers said even though both re-married, they just went through the motions because they were still in love with each other. Nevertheless, both marriages were your typical, incestuous Hollywood-related arrangements.

Then, the old love which everyone suspected between Natalie and RJ was rekindled. Natalie came home unexpectedly one day and found Gregson *in flagrante delicto* with his secretary and it was the end of the marriage for Natalie and the Brit.

Natalie Wood with second husband British agent Richard Gregson. After divorcing Wagner, she married Gregson, by whom she had a child. (John Austin Collection.)

Natalie Gurdin Wood Wagner Gregson remarried Robert J. Wagner in 1972. From that (re)-union came their daughter Courtney. Following their second marriage Natalie agreed to work only when she felt like it. She enjoyed being a wife and mother after what seemed a lifetime (she started, remember, at four years of age) of working before the cameras all over the world.

For their second marriage, Natalie Wood and Robert Wagner chose a spot where it would start again and, tragically, in the end, finish. They were married on a yacht in a quiet cove off the Catalina coast. The isolated coves, especially spots like the Isthmus where tourists seldom visit, long held a special fascination for Hollywood stars, a romantic place far from the "madding crowds" on the mainland. Humphrey Bogart, Erroll Flynn, and John Barrymore all were weekend regulars there. John Wayne loved its rugged bays and clear blue waters.

But none, ironically, were more entranced by Catalina's magic than Robert Wagner and Natalie Wood. Naturally, it never dawned on either of them or the wedding party that nine years later a search party would discover Natalie's body almost in the very spot where the yacht was moored for the ceremony.

What goes around must come around.

☆　　☆　　☆

Late in the afternoon of Saturday, November 28, 1981, all four went ashore to Doug's Harbor Reef and Saloon. There, the quartet spent two hours drinking at the bar before sitting down to dinner at 7 p.m., said one of the island denizens not long after the fact.

After settling down in a corner booth, Wagner and Wood decided they didn't like the wine list the inland bistro had to offer. Davern and Walken volunteered to return to the yacht in the dinghy to fetch a couple of bottles from the Wagners' private cellar, in a manner of speaking. During the trip, Davern admits, he and Walken smoked some pot.

When they returned to Doug's, the two bottles were polished off very quickly by the four; customers could see that there was a lot of tension at the table and that the vibes "were not too good." Because of this, two patrons sent two bottles of champagne to the table hoping it would lighten up the mood. After all, Catalina Island was a place to relax and have fun — not arguments. But the atmosphere again turned ugly, according to those present.

Wagner grew "upset" because he felt Natalie "...was flirting with Walken in front of him," said a source close to the authorities conducting the investigation the next day.

Natalie Wood and Gregory Peck at the Golden Globes in January, 1964. Natalie accepted the Globe for Sophia Loren, named "World's Most Popular Female Star." Peck presented the award to Wood. Loren, filming in Europe, could not attend. (Marvin Paige's Mot. Picture & TV Research Svc.)

Studio portrait of Natalie during the filming of **Meteor**. (John Austin Collection.)

The night manager of Doug's, who had known the Wagners for a long time, and Davern, confirmed:

"Natalie was drunk and she was definitely being flirtatious with Chris Walken. She was giving him suggestive looks, snuggling close, and caressing his shoulder at the table. None of this was lost on Wagner," he told investigators.

Around 10 p.m., the investigators learned, the Wagners started to fight. "Robert Wagner wanted to leave. He told his wife, `I'm tired. I want to sleep!' But Natalie wanted to stay and party,"

Witnesses to the Wagners' behavior, and the passivity of Walken and Davern, said all four were drunk. Finally, Wagner told his wife, "I'm leaving now" and Natalie told him, "Good! Leave! I'm going to stay at the bar."

Wagner, according to more witnesses, became red-in-the-face angry, and stared at Natalie very coldly. He grabbed her by the arm, pulled her aside and they talked for almost fifteen minutes, then all four left together, but Natalie was obviously "steamed."

According to Davern's account to investigators, and in interviews, it was around 11 p.m. when they returned to the Splendour and went to the Salon for more drinks — wine. "All four of us were pretty drunk by this time," he admitted. "Natalie again was nestled close to Walken on the settee as she was at Doug's."

"Then," said Davern, "RJ suddenly picked up a half empty bottle of wine, and exploded. Wagner smashed the bottle down on the table and yelled at Walken: `What are you trying to do, seduce my wife?'" "Glass and wine," related Davern, "flew all over the place."

Natalie in a pensive mood in a portraitsitting for **Meteor,** one of her last films. (Marvin Paige's Mot. Picture & TV Research Svc.)

" I really thought there was going to be a brawl between Walken and Wagner," said the skipper, "But Chris wisely scrambled off the couch and went outside, as if for a breath of fresh air. By that time, we all needed one. Natalie then screamed at RJ: `I'm just not going to stand for this.'"

Wagner then stomped up to the wheelhouse above the salon, clutching another bottle of wine. Walken, meanwhile, went below decks to his cabin. Davern then went topside to talk to RJ because he was anxious to defuse the situation as much as possible. According to the skipper, Wagner talked a little, but not too much. "He drank a lot and spent a lot of time staring out over the cove. About a half hour passed." Then Davern dropped his bombshell. "It is possible," he said in his account of that night several years later, "that Walken and Wood met below decks" — the area is not visible from the wheelhouse where RJ and Davern were situated.

Sometime after midnight, Wagner told Davern he'd better check on Natalie. He went below, presumably into their master stateroom in the stern.

Wagner, said Davern, was absent from the wheelhouse for a full half hour, he estimated, although a complete check of the boat from bilge to wheelhouse would only require about five minutes. When Wagner returned to the wheelhouse, said Davern, he calmly said that both Natalie and the dinghy were missing. Davern only had Wagner's word for this. He did not go back and check for himself as he should have done as the titular "Captain of the Vessel" responsible for the yacht and its passenger's safety.

According to Davern, Wagner started drinking again and didn't "look worried at all. If it had been my wife," he said, "I would have been frantic."

Davern told Wagner that they should summon the U.S. Coast Guard and start looking for her. Davern said he even went so far as to fire up the engines to turn on the searchlights and to scan the immediate area for the dinghy and/or Natalie. Wagner told him to turn them off, that it would cause too much commotion and result in unnecessary publicity.

☆   ☆   ☆

Reports from Catalina on Sunday the 29th said that a woman who was a guest on a yacht moored about 200 yards away thought she heard screams coming from the Splendour the night Natalie drowned.

The woman says she and a friend heard a woman repeatedly calling for help and believes the sound was clear enough for other people to also have heard it, regardless of the intermittent rain squalls.

The woman, Marilyn Wayne, a Los Angeles commodities broker, told investigators, according to a story in the Los Angeles *Times*, "my friend woke me up on the boat around 11:45 and said, `Do you hear a woman calling for help?'   I listened through the porthole and I could hear someone saying, `*Help me, somebody. Please help me*'!"

Wayne said the cries stopped about 12:10 or 12:15 a.m. Clyde French of the Los Angeles County Sheriff's office, which has jurisdiction over the Island , said that, "sometime after midnight, Robert Wagner discovered that his wife was missing. However, the time of Mrs. Wagner's disappearance from the Splendour was never *firmly established*.

Marilyn Wayne said later that she thought the screams were coming from the vicinity of the Splendour but said that they could see no one, nor the searchlights which Davern had turned on momentarily until ordered to turn them off by Wagner.

Wayne added that she and her friend did not go to the woman's aid because they thought she might have been with people who were having a loud party on another nearby yacht. Wayne added that she and her friend heard *those* people call out: "We're coming to get you," several times.

The commodities broker concluded that she felt there wasn't a person in the Cove who couldn't have heard those screams, she said. The sound was clear and it had stopped squalling. The woman, said Wayne, did not sound drunk and was perfectly coherent in her cries for help.

Another strange incident for Wayne was around 6 a.m. the next morning. She and her friend talked to the Catalina Harbor Patrol, which was asking boaters if they had seen or heard anything the night before.

"We asked if a woman was missing," said Wayne. "And they said, 'Yeah! They're looking for her now.' We told the Patrol what we had heard, but they didn't seem interested."

Why?

☆   ☆   ☆

Meanwhile, in the wheelhouse atop the Splendour, and during the time Wayne heard the screams, Wagner kept repeating to Davern, who had sobered up, that he was sure Natalie had returned to the restaurant. It turned out to be wishful thinking.

At around 1:30 a.m., Wagner called the restaurant on the ship's telephone and determined that she wasn't there. Davern, he says, then searched the boat on his own — except for Walken's cabin. "I didn't want to mention to RJ the possibility of Natalie being in that stateroom with Chris," he said.

Davern said it never occurred to him, or, as far as he knows, Wagner, to wake Walken up to see if he knew where Natalie was, or even if the actor was in the cabin assigned to him.

Wagner made that call on Radio Channel 16 "around 1:30 a.m." according to Don Whiting, the manager of the restaurant. The actor told Whiting he was worried about his wife since both she and the dinghy were missing, according to Whiting's recollection of the conversation. Whiting said he then asked Wagner if he wanted to launch a full scale search.

Wagner replied that he *did not yet feel the situation called for alerting the authorities such as the Harbor Patrol and the U.S. Coast Guard.* For the time being, Whiting said, Wagner asked if people in the harbor could check to see if Natalie was at the dock, the saloon, or the telephones at the end of the dock. Whiting added to investigator Sgt. Duane Rasure that Wagner told him it was not unusual *for his wife to go ashore in the dinghy alone.*

This conflicts with statements made later to Noguchi that Natalie *was not in the habit of taking the dinghy out alone, and that she was afraid of the water, especially at night.*

Isthmus Cove resident Paul Wintler heard the call and after conferring with Whiting, made a sweep of the shoreline and moorings. He found nothing.

At about 2:30 a.m., Wintler made a more thorough search of the shoreline.

Again, nothing.

About this time, Whiting woke up Harbor Master Doug Oduin. They and another harbor worker then went to the Splendour shortly before 3 a.m. to confer with Wagner. They told him Wood was nowhere to be found in Isthmus Cove. Wagner then requested the men contact the Coast Guard for help.

Oduin recorded in his log that the Coast Guard at San Pedro, 26 miles away on the mainland, was notified at 3:26 a.m. Almost four hours had elapsed since Wagner and Davern realized that Natalie and the dinghy were missing. Four hours in which Natalie might have been saved with a full-scale search during a lot of that time.

Around 5:15 a.m., as the search continued, Whiting's spotlight played across the dinghy in a little cave in a high granite cliff at Blue Cavern point. It was drifting near the shore with its engine and ignition in "off", the gear shift in neutral, and the oars in their stays.

At 7:44 a.m. Sunday morning, November 29, a Search and Rescue helicopter from the L.A. County Sheriff's Squadron spotted a body floating about a mile from the anchored yacht. It was, on its recovery, the bloated corpse of Natalie Wood, age 43, actress and film star, the wife of Robert J. Wagner.

When Wagner was finally notified, Davern observed, he wept on the skipper's shoulder and cried, "She's gone! She's gone!" After what had happened the previous two days, Wagner should have been very remorseful — and he was.

About this same time, Walken emerged from his cabin and asked what was going on! After telling him, Wagner and Walken decided to flee the area. They both knew the press would descend on the island as soon as the news of Natalie's death was put on the Sheriff's teletype to all the newsrooms. They boarded a hastily chartered helicopter and headed for the mainland. Davern was left to make an official identification of the body and to later return the Splendour to the mainland as soon as the Sheriff released it as a possible crime scene.

Author Warren Harris supports Davern's story of a love triangle between the couple and Walken, but with a twist. "In the course of my research," he says, "I spoke to several people about what *really* happened that day, and what it amounted to was this: Natalie had been flirting with Walken the entire weekend, particularly on the Saturday on shore. This was not because she particularly desired him as a lover, but in retaliation for the rumors which had reached her in North Carolina on location for **Brainstorm,** that RJ and his **Hart to Hart** co-star Stefanie Powers had become `romantically' involved.'

"It was just after William Holden had died — about two weeks, and RJ had been very attentive to Stefanie because she was shaken up pretty bad about how Holden had died. Word then had begun to circulate throughout the industry, reaching some columnists, that the pair were having an affair. When the `whispers' got back to Natalie from her close friends, she was furious. It was then she started to flirt up a storm with Walken in North Carolina."

"In the end, both he and RJ told Natalie to cut it out, to cool it, and according to some sources, that's when a distressed Natalie started to drink a little heavier than normal. This resulted in the .14 alcohol content of her blood. It is also when she decided to leave the yacht and head for the hotel on shore," said Harris.

But the latter statement is a little hard to believe:

- Natalie was dressed only in a nightgown, a red down jacket and knee-length socks. This was hardly the attire to check into a hotel in, or go ashore;

- The question has also been asked many, many times, why should Marilyn Wayne have heard what she reported as being "a woman's voice" coming from the direction of the moored Splendour about 200 yards away when Davern and Wagner, standing on the deck of the wheelhouse, could not hear it?

- Why did Wagner not ask to have the Coast Guard called earlier than 3:26 a.m. so long after he first realized that Natalie and the dinghy were missing? This was around 1 a.m. Why, also, did Wagner prevent Davern from conducting a sweep of the area with the Splendour's searchlights of the surrounding area?

- Wagner's entire night was spent drinking and brooding with Davern in the wheelhouse while the search was being conducted for his wife.

Another puzzling aspect of the entire tragedy is a statement made by a close friend of the Wagners, and a question which cannot, has not, nor will ever be, answered. A year or two following Natalie's tragic death, the friend said he flatly does not believe the official story (of Coroner Noguchi and Sheriff's investigators) that Natalie tried to climb into the dinghy alone. "She was deathly afraid of the water, so much so that she had recurring nightmares about drowning," the friend said.

"If it was anyone else, I would believe the theory that this is what happened and that she missed her footing and fell into the channel."

"But not Natalie," he said, shaking his head. "Something terribly wrong happened that night!"

Following the tragedy, only Robert Wagner and Christopher Walken know what *really* went on between the three of them that tragic night of November 28-29, 1981. Both have always refused to discuss the case except the statements they made to the Sheriff's investigators at the time and immediately following the tragedy. Those reports are sealed in the Los Angeles County Sheriff's office in the ancient Hall of Justice in Los Angeles.

☆   ☆   ☆

There are still many of those people in Hollywood who believe that Natalie was having an affair with Walken; a torrid affair. "There were rumors that Natalie and Walken were going at it hot and heavy — in her trailer and at the hotel on the location," said one set insider who worked on **Brainstorm**.

Robert Wagner traveled to the east coast to see Natalie once or twice on the location and she supposedly then cooled it with Walken while he was around. "But as soon as RJ left," said another member of the location unit, "they resumed their `close' relationship."

Noguchi says he still stands by his final report of an "Accidental Drowning." But he is the only one who does.

Gadfly Speriglio still insists it should be called an "Accidental Homicide."

But Noguchi, in his book, **Coroner**, can't understand *why Natalie left the boat in the first place.* "There's a lot of room left," says Noguchi, "for further investigation on that point alone."

Also, one might ask, why didn't Marilyn Wayne call the Harbor Patrol or the Coast Guard when she heard the cries for help?

Noguchi, again, poses another question: "What *really puzzles me*," he asks, "Why did nobody come to her rescue? This is even a more important question when one considers the report of Ms. Wayne," said the deposed Coroner.

Now, almost a decade following the tragedy of Natalie Wood, people are still puzzled about her death.

- Just why did Natalie attempt to, or leave the yacht that night?

- If she wanted to get away from the arguing of her husband and Walken, all she had to do was retire to her stateroom and lock the door; Given the wind and other conditions of that November night, she couldn't have heard what was going on topside;

- Why did not Marilyn Wayne, who heard the screams make some further attempt to find out what was going on?

One further point, because the Wagners invited only Walken to go along on that weekend trip when the normal complement was two or three people, it lends credence to the fact that Natalie wanted to be with Walken to infuriate RJ because of the rumors that RJ and Stefanie Powers were having an affair behind her back. The old cliche of "Hell hath no fury," etc., might be applicable here.

The lonely watery death of Natalie Wood will always remain a very poignant reminder as another of Hollywood's Unsolved Mysteries.

NATALIE WOOD WAS ANOTHER VICTIM OF 'THE CURSE' WHICH TOOK CO-STARS, THE DIRECTOR AND THE PRODUCER

Natalie Wood's tragic and untimely death was the lst of a series of violent, accidental or premature deaths which cursed the actors, director and the producer of the 1955 film **Rebel Without a Cause**.

The film's stars, James Dean, Sal Mineo, Nick Adams, the director, and Natalie Wood, each met with bizarre and untimely deaths.

When the film opened, it was an instant myth maker — its stars seemed to have nothing but fabulous futures before them. But almost immediately, what seems to be "The Curse of Rebel Without A Cause" struck.

On September 30, 1955 James Dean was driving to a racing event in Northern California in his silver Porsche Speedster when he crashed at 86 mph. He died immediately, his head almost severed from his body. He was just 24 years old, and a brilliant, but undisciplined actor.

Sal Mineo was 17 when he played Dean's rich but neurotic buddy in the film. Mineo went on to become a renowned actor, winning Academy Award nominations for both **Rebel** and **Exodus**. He was assured of a bright future.

But his later career was less promising than it was expected to be. Producers would not hire him because he had become "type cast." Mineo was reduced to playing an ape in **Planet of the Apes**.

On February 12, 1976, at the age of 37, Mineo was stabbed to death by a robber outside his West Hollywood apartment.

Nick Adams went on from **Rebel Without a Cause** to star in TV's **The Rebel** series — that word again — as "Johnny Yuma," a Roman bounty hunter. He was also Oscar-nominated for his performance in **Twilight of Honor.**

But Adams, then 36, had apparently been depressed over marital difficulties with a very vindictive, neurotic and troublesome wife. He died a mysterious death which is still considered one of the strangest of Hollywood's Unsolved Mysteries. Adams' death was put down as a possible suicide after the actor swallowed 30cc of paraldehyde, a powerful tranquilizer for extreme nervousness. The drug had been prescribed for Nick because of his depression. There was no method of ingestion anywhere, and a telephone was within two feet of him. There were no notes — at least none found by the police or Coroner.

The director of the jinxed film, Nicholas Ray, died of lung cancer in 1979. He was one of Natalie's early lovers.

The film's producer for Warner Brothers Pictures, David Weisbart, died of a mysterious and unannounced illness at the age of 44.

Christopher Walken ... A Shadowy Figure

The center of the controversy and the rumored "love triangle" which surrounded Natalie Wood's last days, was Christopher Walken, the co-star of Natalie's uncompleted last film **Brainstorm**.

Walken, who was awarded the Oscar for his role as a suicidal Vietnam vet in **The Deer Hunter**, was known to be a shadowy figure off screen and when away from Hollywood or on a film location. His private life was then, and still is, shrouded in secrecy.

His wife, Georgianne, an ex-Broadway chorus girl, remained in the Walkens' Connecticut home while Walken pursued his film career all over the world.

Walken once said, "There is something about me that's very unpredictable. I do things that are impulsive and I don't understand why."

Obviously, neither did Robert Wagner or Natalie Wood.

Crying Out For Help!

Freddie Prinze in a publicity portrait during the filming of **Chico and the Man**. (Marvin Paige's Mot. Picture and TV Research Svc.)

"All the world's a stage, and all the men and women merely players. They have their exits and their entrances; and one man in his time plays many parts."

— *William Shakespeare*
"As You Like It"

8 ... Freddie Prinze:
Was A Coroner Proven Wrong?

Everyone, including the Los Angeles County Coroner, said at the time that there was no doubt that comedian Freddie Prinze shot himself to death by putting a gun to his temple — a la Russian Roulette — and pulling the trigger, and that it was a clear-cut case of suicide.

Was it?

☆   ☆   ☆

At 3 a.m. or thereabouts on January 27, 1977, the telephone rang in the Marina del Rey apartment of Martin (Dusty) Snyder, Prinze's business manager. It was the comedian, and Snyder told police later that his client sounded strange and wanted to talk. Because of this, Snyder hastily dressed and drove to Prinze's apartment in the Wilshire-Comstock complex in West Los Angeles near Beverly Hills.

Snyder had been worried about Freddie Prinze for several weeks; Prinze had become addicted to Quaaludes, a dangerous drug often implicated in suicides. Addiction can lead to such symptoms as loss of memory, inability to concentrate, tremors and finally depression. Quaaludes — the brand name for methaqualone hydrochloride — was, at the time, much in demand by many drug addicts. Prinze's supply had been prescribed by his internist, Dr. Edward Albon, and those prescriptions would be the catalyst for a civil law suit following Prinze's death.

When Snyder arrived at the Prinze apartment, the comedian was dressed in his favorite "karate" pants. After opening the door, he returned to the couch on which he had been sitting, and Snyder sat opposite him on a love seat, a large coffee table separating them. Snyder said later that when he arrived, his client "didn't seem too disturbed."

As soon as Snyder sat down, Prinze wrote something on a piece of paper, then pushed it across the coffee table to him saying, "Is this legible?"

On the paper were written the words, "I cannot go on any longer." Before Snyder could reply, Prinze picked up the telephone beside him and called his estranged wife, Kathy Cochran Prinze. In that conversation, Snyder overheard him telling her that he was going to "end it all."

Immediately, Snyder slipped out of the room to telephone Prinze's psychiatrist, Dr. William S. Kroger, and ask what he should do to defuse the situation. Kroger had been with Prinze until 2 a.m., as had Prinze's secretary, Carol Novak.

Reportedly, Dr. Kroger replied, "He's been behaving this way all week. He's just crying out for attention and help, but I'm not concerned with him doing any harm to himself."

When Snyder returned to the living room, Prinze was on the telephone to Carol Novak, according to the police reconstruction of the events which took place that night.

By the end of that call, said Snyder, the actor seemed to be relaxed, quietly bending over the coffee table and adding more words to the note he had written earlier. When he finished writing — and the additional words were never released to press or public — Prinze suddenly pulled out a pistol from beneath the sofa cushions. Instinctively, Snyder reached out to grab the weapon but Prinze gestured with the gun for Snyder to sit back. Snyder talked desperately to Prinze and reminded him of his mother and baby. *He also told Prinze that his insurance policy for $200,000 had a suicide clause, which meant they wouldn't get the money.*

Prinze listened, but then suddenly, without saying another word, pressed the muzzle of the weapon against his right temple and squeezed the trigger. The close contact muted the sound of the gun and the bullet's impact but the results in the luxury apartment were catastrophic. Blood had spattered everywhere, the bullet came out of the left side of Prinze's head and lodged in the opposite wall. The 22-year-old talented Freddie Prinze, toppled sideways onto the sofa cushions.

On the face of it, Prinze's death was one of the most obvious cases of suicide in Noguchi's experience.

But it worried Noguchi and he felt there "might be trouble later on!"

The biography of Freddie Prinze, issued by the National Broadcasting Company, said that he was born on June 22, 1954. At the time, his family lived on West 157th Street in the Spanish-speaking area of Washington Heights bordering on Harlem in upper Manhattan.

It was NBC which first catapulted Prinze to national fame as the happy-go-lucky, wise-cracking Chicano (*) in **Chico and the Man**.

The series, an instant hit, also starred veteran character actor Jack Albertson as the bigoted, hard-drinking old garage owner in East Los Angeles in a neighborhood dominated by Mexican-Americans and their "Chivvies," Chevrolets. Prinze played Albertson's mechanic, always beating his boss in business deals and screw ups, and gradually weaning him from his bigotry.

At one time, Prinze described his birthplace of Washington Heights as "...a slum with trees." He had also developed somewhat of an identity problem in the neighborhood of mainly pure Latinos from Puerto Rico and other Caribbean nations. His father was a Hungarian Jew of gypsy parentage; his mother a Puerto Rican.

Prinze also recalled in some of his later stand-up routines that he was "a fat kid, poor at athletics, and that I had asthma. I also studied piano and ballet, which tended to blow my credibility as a tough guy!"

Prinze — who changed his name from Preutzel for professional reasons later on — also learned to play the drums and guitar and perform in his close-knit family's musicales. By the time he was four years old, he was doing an imitation of his amateur comic father.

Later, he amused his friends with comic imitations of television's variety show host, and ex-Broadway columnist, Ed Sullivan, as well as other TV personalities of the day. But Prinze insisted on telling interviewers later that his principal interest was in drama and ballet. To lend credence to this, Prinze was once offered a scholarship to Joffrey's American Ballet Center.

At New York's High School of the Performing Arts, the school dramatized in the feature and television film, **Fame**, the direction of his ambitions changed to comedy when he made a big hit with a comic role in the play **Barefoot in the Park** during his Junior year. He was to drop out of school later the same year, but not before he was "discovered" by a talent agent and booked on Jack Paar's television show.

Prinze also played in small clubs and resorts, perfecting his stand-up routines and trying out new material — all of which he wrote himself from, generally, real life experiences. Then came the breakthrough. In December, 1973, he appeared on the **Tonight Show** starring Johnny

(*) A first generation Mexican-American born of Mexican parentage.

Carson. It was on this show that **Chico and the Man** creator James Komack first saw him. Komack at the time was auditioning performers for Chico and unhesitatingly signed Prinze for the role of the young Chicano.

The series premiered on NBC in the fall of 1974 to mixed reviews by the critics. But it was an instant hit with the public — "critics be damned," he said later. In its second week it knocked CBS' **Rhoda** out of first place in the ratings and then settled into a solid fifth place every week. During its first season, an average of 40 million people watched **Chico and the Man**.

The series looked set for at least a five-year run — or more. But it was not to be.

☆   ☆   ☆

As soon as Snyder realized what had happened to his client, lying in a rapidly expanding pool of blood on the sofa, he called the paramedics. But one look at his client told him there was not much hope for him. Prinze was rushed to the UCLA Medical Center about five miles to the west off Wilshire Boulevard. He arrived at the Center at 4.06 a.m. and a 'round-the-clock struggle began to save Prinze's life; but it was hopeless from the start.

Doctors said later that the .32 slug passed completely through his head from right to left in the temporal area. Prinze underwent two hours of surgery at 10:30 a.m. later that morning, about seven hours after he had pulled the trigger.

Richard Greene, administrator of the medical center, said "Mr. Prinze tolerated the surgery well." But, he added, "...because his brain tissue was severely damaged, it would be very premature to offer a prediction as to the chances of survival or disability. It might be several more days before doctors can make a prognosis," he concluded for the assembled media.

The struggle to save Freddie Prinze's life ended at 1 p.m. the next day, Saturday, January 29, 1977. A respirator which had been handling his life functions since he entered the hospital was turned off when Prinze's brain could no longer function due to the extensive tissue damage. In the room with him when he died were his mother, Mary Preutzel, singing and television star Tony Orlando, and his estranged wife, Kathy. Orlando took a long time to recover from the loss of his best friend and did not work for two or three years following Prinze's death. He felt responsible and that perhaps he could have prevented his friend's death with more diligent attention to his mental state, and heavy drug usage.

The body was taken to the Los Angeles County Forensic Science Center in downtown Los Angeles for the autopsy as required by California State law.

A week later, Noguchi studied the final report and told an aide: "I'm worried about this one!" He did not explain himself but did call in Dr. Robert Litman, the suicide psychology expert of Los Angeles County. After going over the autopsy findings, both Noguchi and Litman agreed that it was "Death By Suicide." That was the official verdict.

As it turned out, 6 years later, both "experts" were judged to have been wrong — *or were they*?

☆   ☆   ☆

The success of **Chico and the Man** pushed Prinze into the front ranks of television stardom. He finished taping the final show of his first season in April, 1975, and promptly launched his big time night club career, opening at Caesar's Palace in Las Vegas. That same summer he also recorded his first comedy album, **Looking Good**, a catch phrase of Chicanos at that time, and used extensively in the dialogue of the television series.

Just prior to taping that final show of the season, Prinze met Kathy Cochran. Six months later they were married, on September 13, 1975, and very much in love. It appeared that Freddie Prinze, a "Hungo-Rican" from the upper west side of Manhattan, would settle down.

But that, too, was not to be for Freddie Prinze, the brash young comic. Kathy Cochran Prinze broke her self-imposed silence about Prinze's death a year or so later. She said she was determined to tell "...the whole truth about our life. There have been too many falsehoods told by too many people who claimed they knew Freddie and/or myself. Most of them knew us for only two or three minutes, but they told newspapers and magazines they knew Freddie or me very well," she said, "...and concocted fabrications about him."

Cochran admitted that her late husband, who had filed for divorce on December 13, 1976, was a drug addict and pill popper. He took pills, she said, the way other people take coffee, and cocaine the way average people drink cocktails.

"I'd have to check on Freddie four or five times a night to see if he was still breathing. I'd have to flip him from his back to his stomach so that he wouldn't vomit and choke to death," she explained in a sad tone of voice. "And when he did get sick, I'd have to hold his head up. *He also had a flair for the dramatic and he loved to play practical jokes*," she said. In the

Star Freddie Prinze, actor Ronnie Graham and Jack Albertson in a scene from **Chico and the Man.** (Marvin Paige's Mot. Picture & TV Research Svc.)

end, she believes, it was his morbid sense of drug-induced humor that cost him his life, and cost their son a loving father.

When Prinze and Kathy Cochran first met, they were always together. "Freddie wasn't filming **Chico** at the time. We played together, he told me about his work, he was always reading scripts, or parts of scripts to me. We listened to all his favorite music. He wanted me to know everything that he loved," she said.

Prinze, in turn, also gave Kathy a world of romance, a Hollywood Hills home with the *de rigueur* swimming pool, a lot of affection and eventually, Freddie, Jr., the sunshine of their lives. But by the time of his death, all the good things had fallen apart. The sunshine had slowly vanished into the dark of night. Ugly nights.

Once, while in Lake Tahoe for a night club engagement, Kathy had seen him use cocaine, the white, iniquitous powder that is destroying the moral fiber of the United States. "I didn't like the idea," she related, "...but I didn't know it was an everyday occurrence with him."

Living with him, she found out differently. She recalled one night in particular when "...a lowlife friend came over to the house. I went into the bedroom because I couldn't bear to see what was going on. When I came out later, Freddie was already in the falling down and stumbling stages."

He went to the front door to say goodbye to his friend and I thought I saw something pass between them. Freddie then went immediately into the bathroom, and I knew why," she explained, sadly.

"When he came out, he had cocaine all over his mustache and he had Quaaludes in his mouth. He was like a little boy then, all apologetic. But it was getting to be too late for apologies."

Freddie, she said, just couldn't stop. Although, she admitted, he *did try*. While appearing at Cherry Hills, New Jersey, he was given a "rock" of cocaine. Filled with guilt, he flushed it down the toilet.

When Freddie was not stoned, and not off in his private, drug-induced world as a result, he tried passionately to be a loving father and husband.

In between bouts of pills and coke he was just those things, according to Kathy.

Freddie Prinze, she said, was a desperate man calling out for help. Nobody at the time realized it. "They say he was just seeking attention from everyone around him." She did not elaborate on the "they" until a few years later.

Freddie Prinze in a pensive mood. (Marvin Paige's Mot. Picture and TV Research Svc.)

One of his last writings, said Kathy Cochran Prinze, was found in a secret diary he kept, reading:

> "All I see is lawyers for the last two years is lawyers, lawyers. I'm starting to get fed up. I just want peace, my wife, my kid and my work.
> "I need a rest. Thank God my old lady's [Kathy] by my side. This is the turning point. I will be the greatest."

"I am sure he did not know what he was doing," she said, "about pulling the trigger on that pistol. His death was an accident, not a suicide. He should never have been allowed to have that gun." (This latter statement was brought out very forcefully as the crux of litigation a few years later.)

"I am sure," she said in conclusion, "that Freddie did not know what he was doing when he pulled that trigger."

☆　　☆　　☆

Noguchi and Litman continued to stand behind their "final Autopsy Report" — that Freddie Prinze's death *was* a suicide. They took all the facts into consideration, including the telephone calls to Kathy, his secretary and his parents at around 3 in the morning. They also considered other circumstantial evidence.

But Noguchi, with his analytical mind, was still puzzled and had qualms about the "Death By Suicide" verdict he had rendered and signed. A witness had been present, he pointed out. In his book, **Coroner at Large**, he writes: "In my long and sad experience with suicides, victims almost always perform the act in solitude. Prinze had committed suicide in front of a witness, a friend."

"Why?"

Noguchi's earlier concerns proved to be accurate. An attorney for Freddie Prinze's mother called the Coroner and said the family would claim in a civil suit that Prinze's death was an accident, *not* a suicide, the verdict to which the Coroner had attested.

"I wasn't surprised," wrote Noguchi. "As insurance money was involved, I felt there might be another aspect to the Prinze case about which I was not aware of or thought much about.

"I asked the attorney how he intended to prove that it was not suicide."

Noguchi must have been taken aback with the attorney's reply because he had not been informed of all the facts during the investigation

207

into Prinze's death. If he had been, it is possible the Coroner's verdict might have been very different.

Besides the comedian's marital problems with Kathy, which had been brought about by his cocaine use and pill popping — the latter being prescribed in horrendous doses — and nothing else, he also had his share of legal problems. This often befalls naive young talent who hit the big time — and the big money. Litigants always seem to come out of the woodwork like termites fleeing the exterminator. Lawyers wring their hands in glee and start visiting BMW showrooms as soon as they latch on to such a client.

One year prior to his death, Prinze lost a court fight to break a contract with the New York talent agent who had signed him up while he was still attending the High School of Performing Arts. Prinze argued that since he signed the document at the age of 19 and technically was not an adult, and before he made it big on television, he should be allowed to nullify the document.

This was a pretty flimsy reason for trying to break a contract with a man who got him started on the **Tonight Show**. It was sort of like locking the barn door after the horse had escaped.

In November, 1976, Prinze was arrested by the California Highway Patrol and charged with driving under the influence of drugs, a misdemeanor under California law. The arresting officer said he found a prescription bottle of methaqualone, (Quaaludes) in Prinze's shirt pocket. Prinze pleaded innocent to the charge and was scheduled to appear in Los Angeles Superior Court one month to the day after his death.

Prinze's attorney in that case, Donald Wager, said that Prinze had been despondent for quite a while over the breakup of his marriage to Kathy. "I think he loved her very much," said Wager. "He was despondent because the marriage was breaking up, not over the drug arrest. He was confident he would `beat the rap' on the drug case as the drugs had been prescribed for him."

This, too, would have repercussions a few years later.

Prinze's death was a tremendous shock to veteran actor Jack Albertson, the co-star of **Chico and the Man**. "Freddie was very close to me in many ways," he said the day following Prinze's death.

"I can't see any reason, except there seems to be a pattern among young people who achieve success so early that there's a destructive thing on their part, a death wish."

Albertson added that Prinze was always "...very closed mouth about his activities and problems," but that he did know of Prinze's marital difficulties. They had been all over the gossip columns. "They were preying on his mind," said the actor.

Albertson, who died several years later, said he had never heard Prinze discuss suicide. "But," he said in a later radio interview, "...at the very beginning of the series he told me he did not expect to live past the age of 30!" he recalled.

"The kid had everything to live for, regardless of his problems. The only thing we can do now is say a kind word for him, a prayer, that's all we can do!" Albertson reflected, plaintively.

James Komack, the creator-producer of **Chico and the Man**, said Prinze stopped by his office on the Thursday before the shooting, but had given no indication how deeply troubled he was. Komack added, "...he didn't leave my office in a suicidal or self-destructive frame of mind."

Komack did add, however, "I believe Freddie could have been playing out some strange dramatic scene, or it could have been just a plain old accident. Maybe he thought the gun wasn't loaded. Who knows how these things happen?"

☆   ☆   ☆

In a long discussion with Noguchi, the attorney for Prinze's mother, Mary Preutzel, who had recently moved to California to be near Freddie, told the Coroner what might have changed his and Litman's mind if he had been aware of it.

"Earlier that day," said the lawyer, "Prinze, while high on 'ludes' had waved the same gun in front of his secretary Carol Novak, and pulled the trigger. He then collapsed on the floor. When Novak rushed to his side in horror, the actor sat up laughing."

According to both Novak and Prinze's psychiatrist, Prinze had been "...fooling around with the gun for some time, showing off," as Dr. Kroger, the psychiatrist, described Prinze's antics.

The family, continued the lawyer, was going to stress in court that Prinze's death was not a suicide, but an accident that had occurred while Prinze, under the influence of Quaaludes, was playing another of his well-known pranks, and forgot that the safety was off, or didn't check to see.

On January 20, 1983, the family's claim was upheld by a jury, six years almost to the day of his death, that Freddie Prinze's death was an *accident*.

Two hundred thousand dollars in life insurance proceeds, which had a "No Suicide" clause, was paid. Following the trial, the Preutzel's attorney said: "It has been his mother's feeling all along that Freddie did not intend to commit suicide. He had too much to live for. That if it had not been for the (prescribed) drugs and cocaine, he would not have done what he did."

But that was not the end of it.

Many of Prinze's friends and others who knew him well feel Freddie Prinze might have committed suicide, but did it in such a way in front of a witness so that his family and child could collect on his insurance. He had been told by Snyder several times that his life insurance contained a "No Suicide" clause and that if he did take his own life, no one would get a dime except the insurance company in forfeited premiums.

- Is it possible that this was Prinze's idea...?

- That he asked Snyder to come over that early morning just so he could carry out his fiendishly developed last grandstand play? That he really "could not take it any longer," as the note said?

- That in spite of his overwhelming success, he fully intended to take his own life in front of a witness, a credible witness?

- That Freddie Prinze pulled that fake attempt in front of Carol Novak as a "rehearsal," in a manner of speaking. Or to lend credence, on the other hand, to what could have been a diabolical scheme to collect on insurance policies. His estate at the time was only in the region of $75,000, not enough to provide for his child;

- Prinze was also NOT in the habit of calling his parents, his secretary and others, nor is any rational person, at 2 or 3 o'clock in the morning; and why did he make those calls in front of Snyder? These calls could have been his way of saying goodbye but

lending a legitimate air to his death being an accident, not a suicide, and hoping the "accidental death"
verdict would be returned by the Coroner?

- Prinze made out and signed a new will on December
  21, just eight days after he had filed suit for divorce
  from Kathy. He left three fourths of his estate to his
  mother, and the remaining one fourth in trust for his
  son. This will left nothing to his estranged wife, or
  to his father, Karl. Why, at Prinze's age, was he so
  insistent on making out a will?

☆　　☆　　☆

Prinze and Kathy had separated several months prior to that will
being drawn. This, and all other indications, point to the fact that Freddie
Prinze's death, in spite of the Jury's findings, was a suicide as first called
by Noguchi and concurred in by Dr. Litman.

Prior to the lawsuit over the "accidental death" theory, Prinze's widow
and son won almost $1 million, settlements of malpractice suits against
Dr. Kroger, the psychiatrist, and Prinze's internist, Dr. Edward Albon.

Those suits, settled in 1981 and 1982, which might also have influenced the jury in the insurance claim and its accidental death ruling,
claimed that Kroger had "improperly allowed Prinze access to the gun he
used to kill himself" after once taking it away from his client. Against Dr.
Albon, the claim was that he had over-prescribed Quaaludes for Freddie
Prinze, a large quantity of which were found in Prinze's blood-stream
during the autopsy.

In the eyes of the law — albeit "Jury Law" — Freddie Prinze, who had
shot himself in front of an eyewitness, turned out *not to* be suicide.

Because of the law suit(s), the actual cause of death, whether by
suicide or by accident, was a drug.

Quaalude ....

In reality, therefore, Freddie Prinze did not die by his own hand — in
spite of appearances.

He died in one last tragic attempt to get a laugh. Whatever the reason,
the demise of Freddie Prinze, who had a brilliant career ahead of him, has
to be one of the more poignant of Hollywood's Unsolved Mysteries.

PRINZE EULOGIZED AT HIS FUNERAL

A crowd of fans and friends of close to 1,000 heard the 22-year-old star of Chico and the Man eulogized as one whose captivating smile and winning ways belied inner turmoil and pain.

"He was a genius and that was the beginning of the pain," said James Komack, producer-creator of the show that made a star of Freddie Prinze — in less than three years.

"Why could he not accept the joys and happiness we enjoy?" Komack asked of those assembled at The Old North Church at Forest Lawn Memorial Park-Hollywood Hills. "We forgot he was special and couldn't fit into our preset molds."

Singer Tony Orlando, who went into a deep depression for several years following the death of his closest friend, said he wanted to "...clear his (Prinze's) record forever," referring to Prinze's unfortunate use of controlled substances.

"This man was in turmoil. He was in great pain but his audience never knew. It was not his marriage," said Orlando. "We all have problems in our marriage. His problem was so complicated that no one should even try to figure it out.

"Freddie Prinze is today exactly where he wants to be," the singer said with a breaking voice.

"Rejoice in his heavenly breath ... "

Prinze's co-star in **Chico and the Man**, the veteran actor Jack Albertson, his voice choking with emotion, said:

"Millions of people, captivated by his smile...fell in love. Freddie was one who brings to others those two most precious commodities — love and laughter." But Albertson said, with great emotion, " ... None of us knew the extent of his true despondency."

Kathy Prinze's Last Word ...

Prinze's widow, Kathy Cochran Prinze, said, "He didn't know what he was doing. He was so stoned he had no idea the gun was loaded. **His death was an accident, not suicide ... "**

Gig Young in his favorite role and picture, **Teacher's Pet**, for which he received an Oscar nomination. He lost, but later won the Best Supporting Actor Award for **They Shoot Horses, Don't They**, his greatest performance. (Marvin Paige's Mot. Picture & TV Research Svc.)

"We mount to Heaven mostly on the ruins of our cherished schemes, finding our failures were successes."

—*Amos Bronson Alcott*
1799-1888
Early American Educator

9 ... Kim & Gig Young: Was It A Pact ... ?

The New York Police Department investigators said it was a murder-suicide pact between actor Gig Young and his 31-year-old bride of less than three weeks, Kim Schmidt. The police report said that Oscar-winning Young shot his wife, and then took his own life in the bedroom of their luxury mid-town Manhattan apartment on October 19, 1978.

Young, who would have been 61 the following November 4, was found dead clutching a .38 revolver, with the body of his beautiful young wife sprawled beside him. She had on full makeup, a green velour blouse and gray slacks. She was bejeweled with numerous rings and necklaces and lay face up. There was a single bullet hole through her head. The same type of wound killed Young.

The couple had been dead for about five hours when discovered by the building manager, who said he heard noises like gunshots earlier in the day. He had not, he said, become suspicious until he noticed groceries still standing outside the apartment door, groceries which had been delivered much earlier that day.

A diary on the bedroom desk was open to the September 27 entry: "We got married today!" On a shelf in the adjoining den, a small, converted bedroom, stood Young's Oscar for his portrayal of the sleazy marathon dance pitchman of the depression era of the 1930's in **They Shoot Horses, Don't They?** His last appearance was in a Canadian summer stock production. He was scheduled for an upcoming theatre run in Florida in November.

Shocked friends said Young had been in good spirits, had no financial problems or any other kind to their knowledge. He had once been an alcoholic and admitted it. He overcame the problem and had not taken a drink of any kind in years. There were no notes of any kind as to what

A Real Life
`Game of Death'

Gig Young, and his wife, Kim. (AP Photo.)

might have set off the deaths. According to the Medical Examiner, this was highly unusual in a case of murder-suicide.

☆　　☆　　☆

"Whenever you play a second lead and lose the girl," Gig Young told a reporter in 1966, "you have to make your part interesting, yet not compete with the leading man. There are few, very few great second leads in this business. I have been told by producers that I am one of them; in other words, I have been typecast throughout most of my career."

It was probably not a role Gig Young courted, but in 55 films in a 37-year career, several Broadway plays — for one of them he received a Tony Award to add to his Oscar — and numerous television appearances, Young certainly was one of the great second bananas in Hollywood history — and on Broadway, according to his peers. Even though many of Young's films were second-rate, he never was. He nearly always portrayed the handsome sophisticate who usually lost the girl at the final fade-out.

On a New York City talk show several weeks before his death, Young revealed that his all-time favorite role was playing second fiddle to Clark Gable in the 1958 film, **Teacher's Pet** Of course, in the end it was Clark Gable who snatched Doris Day away from Gig Young. But Young did receive an Oscar nomination as Best Supporting Actor for the role. He received yet another nomination in the same category for **Come Fill The Cup** in 1952. The nominations finally bore fruit for Gig Young with his Oscar for **They Shoot Horses** in 1969. His Hollywood peers all respected him and considered him an "actor's actor."

Young's only television series was **The Rogues** in the 1964 season, which ran for two more after that. He co-starred with David Niven and Charles Boyer. The latter died of a heart attack in 1978.

Throughout Young's career, he was his own harshest critic. "There are not more than five (roles) that were any good, or any good for me," he once said of this picture work.

Oddly enough, earlier in 1978 in yet another interview with a syndicated columnist, Young said he considered himself a "loser!" He admitted that he made an excellent living over the years playing his "second fiddle" roles and the guy who always lost the girl in the end. "But it had taken," he said, "a toll on my personal happiness." He went on to say that it was probably the reason his other three marriages (before Kim Schmidt) all failed.

"You lose self-confidence in the **real** life as opposed to the **reel** life.

Even though this may not make sense to many people, you play a loser long enough, and you end up a loser — at least you are convinced you're a loser."

☆ ☆ ☆

The mother of Kim Schmidt Young — Gig's bride of less than three weeks — and speaking from her home in Melbourne, Australia, a few weeks after her daughter's death, was certain then, and still is certain, that Kim and her husband, "were murdered."

"I do not believe what they are saying," she said, naturally heartbroken over the death of her 31-year-old daughter. "I am certain Kim was not killed by her husband, but that they were shot by someone else," said Mrs. Schmidt through heavy sobs.

"My husband and I believe someone killed them and so do all their close friends in America from the letters I have received," she added.

Mrs. Schmidt said both her daughter and Young had many loyal friends in America who would do everything possible to discover the truth about their deaths and to try to prove they were not the result of a murder-suicide pact.

"These are loyal friends of Kim and Gig of some standing who would like to know the truth about my daughter's early death and that of her husband," she said. Many times she repeated that the findings of the New York Police Department were not the truth.

☆ ☆ ☆

Kim Schmidt first met Young in Hong Kong early in 1977 while filming an ending to Bruce Lee's final film, ironically titled **Game of Death** (*)

Kim was a script supervisor and had a small role in the film.

Her real name was Ruth Hannelore Schmidt and she was born in East Germany. Her mother emigrated to Australia following WWII when Kim was about five years old, according to available information. Her immediate past before she married Young seems to be clouded in mystery and very little was known about her. She worked in Hong Kong frequently as a script supervisor and in small parts in Kung Fu films for the many producers turning out martial arts pictures for Hong Kong,

---

(*) Lee died halfway through this karate thriller. Six years later, director Robert Clouse re-assembled the surviving actors, including Young and, with the use of a double for Lee, completed the picture. The last half hour of **Game of Death** is incredible when Lee goes one-on-one with each of the villians in some of the most explosive fight scenes ever filmed. Lee had completed them prior to his death. Some say the exertion contributed to his demise.

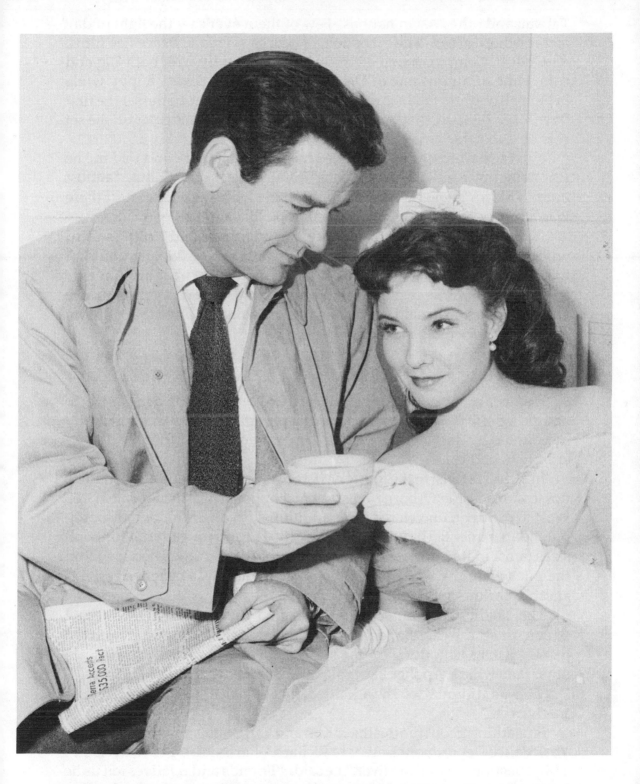

Gig Young and Janice Rule in **Days Before Lent** for MGM. (Marvin Paige's Mot. Picture & TV Research Svc.)

Taiwan and other Asian nations. Few of them ever saw the light of day outside those areas. The exception, of course, were the Bruce Lee films.

Colleen Camp, a young actress who was friendly with both Gig and Kim while filming **Game of Death**, recalls: "Gig was very happy while in Hong Kong and fell in love with Kim when they met on the set the first day. From then on, they were always together. Even his chair on the set was next to hers."

"Just a few months ago he called me from New York and told me he was bringing Kim over from Hong Kong. It is," said Camp, "almost impossible for me to picture Gig with a gun. It almost sounds as if there was a robbery and somebody made it look like a murder-suicide."

Elaine Young, a Beverly Hills real estate broker and Young's third wife, and the mother of his daughter, Jennifer, now 25, also couldn't imagine Young with a gun in his hand. "I can't even imagine him ever having one in his apartment," said Mrs. Young. "And as for that story about the diary," she said, referring to the open date book on the bedroom desk, "that's incredible. Gig never even wrote letters."

☆   ☆   ☆

Elaine Young's opinion about her ex-husband not being able to handle a firearm, or even having one in his apartment, was supposedly discounted by the New York Police Department a week after the discovery of the bodies.

In a bizarre twist to the mystery, detectives going through the Young's possessions at the Osborne Apartments, opposite Carnegie Hall at 205 West 57th Street, uncovered three additional revolvers hidden throughout the apartment. They also discovered 350 rounds of ammunition of all sizes, most of it in dresser drawers. The police never revealed to whom the guns were registered. Why that information was never released is another curious twist to the tragedy.

The Medical Examiner who performed the autopsy, Dr. Michael Baden, ruled the cause of death in both cases as a single gun shot to the head. "There is nothing on the surface," he emphasized, "to indicate other than what the police have ruled — a homicide-suicide," Baden said. But he was still puzzled, he admitted, by the lack of any kind of note or motive.

Something about the deaths of Kim and Gig Young also troubled New York Police Department Detective Richard Chartrand. "The `why' is still a big question we can't answer," he said. "Friends and relatives tell us he looked fine. They thought he was happy, was financially comfortable and never was at a loss for work whenever he wanted to, either on the stage, TV or in films."

"Nobody," continued Chartrand, "has been able to shed any light on this case. I'm stumped. *Not only that, they had a dinner party at a local restaurant scheduled for 8 p.m. that evening to celebrate their marriage."*

"It appeared that Mrs. Young had dressed to go out, although Young himself was dressed in just a plaid shirt and gray slacks."

He added that the couple's last few days, as far as he could ascertain, seemed to be ordinary, but they had not left their apartment at all on the day of their deaths. They had telephoned an order for groceries to be "delivered before noon" that morning. "This does not point to the fact that their demise was premeditated. When a murder-suicide like this is perpetrated, it usually is planned well ahead. There is just no motive which we can come up with." Then what was the reason?

☆　　☆　　☆

A close friend of Gig Young's, former New York columnist Earl Wilson, spoke to Young several times before and after his marriage to Kim.

"He seemed very afraid of this marriage," Wilson wrote. "When I spoke to him, he seemed nervous and fearful that the marriage would not take place at all."

"He said, `We're supposed to get married the day after tomorrow'," Wilson wrote on the 26th, " 'but don't print it yet because it would be embarrassing if we didn't.' "

Wilson did write it because of a newspaper strike in New York and he knew the column would not appear in Manhattan.

The day following their marriage in a judge's chambers, Young called Wilson and said, "Okay, Earl, we did it!" Then, perhaps ominously, "I don't want any big party this time," Wilson quoted him as saying. It was Wilson's feeling that his friend seemed very reticent even to discuss it at all.

Young did tell Wilson that he and Kim had quarreled quite seriously once in Hong Kong *over something about Kim's past* which had come up in a conversation. They decided at that time, according to Wilson's recollection not to get married. But when Kim came to New York about a month after the wrap of **Game of Death**, they became engaged at the Stage Deli in December, 1977.

Wilson did remark in his column, however, that not even their close friends could understand why the couple were missing from such haunts as La Scala, Sardi's, and Bill Hong's, their favorite watering hole, in the three weeks following their marriage. That riddle was never solved. As a friend told Wilson later, "It was like they were hiding from something, somebody!"

☆   ☆   ☆

If it was, indeed, a murder-suicide pact, it could have had something to do, said these same friends, with Young's long-standing relationship — ten years — with Harriet Vine Douglas, a former actress and dancer. Douglas said following his death, "I was the lady in his life for ten of the last eleven years."

It was also Douglas who claimed Young's body for burial at the request of Young's sister, Genevieve, from her home in St. Cloud, Minnesota. Young was born Byron Barr in St. Cloud in 1918. It was Jack Warner, when he placed Young under contract, who changed his name to Gig Young, the name of a character he played in his first film for Warner Brothers.

Kim Schmidt was known to be jealous of Harriet Douglas and her past relationship with Young. But she also realized that Gig had had a long-standing relationship with her. In fact, said Douglas, she had spoken to Young six or seven days prior to his death. In that conversation, Young told her he had refused to sign a document prepared by his business manager in which Douglas would disavow any future claim to his property or to his estate. Douglas also said that, "Gig left a will signed with me in it, and another will without me in it which was *not* signed."

These two facts could have caused problems between the Youngs.

In late 1977, she drove Young to the Holiday Inn at Los Angeles International Airport where he was to meet Kim, who was arriving from Hong Kong to join him. They planned to live in New York at the Osborne, in the apartment Young had owned for several years.

Mrs. Douglas said she advised her friend — probably out of envy or jealousy — not to get married to Kim but "go to New York and live with her."

She said that Gig told her then, "Don't let any crazy things I do spoil our relationship!"

After an idyllic month or two in New York together, Gig decided to marry Kim and they became engaged. It was then that Young decided to sever permanent ties with Los Angeles because of a slight skin cancer he had developed from the California sun. He asked Harriet Douglas to sell his condominium, which they had shared. She did, for $350,000, a profit of $188,000 over the purchase price. Quarrels developed when they began dividing up the furniture.

There was rancor between the three of them, according to Douglas. "Kim was so jealous she didn't even want an ash tray from me," she said. "They (Kim and Gig) quarreled over some lamps and Gig snapped at her 'I didn't know all the lamps were yours!"

"I also warned Gig not to telephone me behind Kim's back, but to keep everything out in the open. I also suggested to Kim that she not let him take a drink or take any pills."

In her last conversations with her former lover, Douglas said they were at first "testy" but the last time she spoke to him, six or seven days before he died, the crispness of the previous conversations had disappeared from his voice. She said he was "sweet" and she asked him, "You coming home, baby?"

Harriet Vine Douglas was confident that the man for whom she had divorced her husband, Broadway actor Bob Douglas, would be coming back to her "in time" but, she admitted, she sometimes played "hard to get!"

☆   ☆   ☆

A few weeks after their bodies were discovered, the deaths of Kim and Gig Young still troubled many people, including the New York Police Department, but the file was closed with the original theory.

- Why did the Youngs leave no note as in 95% of such deaths?

- Why would they arrange to host a dinner party if they planned such an act?

- Is it possible that Kim told Young she was going to leave him because of previous or ongoing quarrels? Was this the reason they hadn't been seen in public since their marriage? Did Young shoot Kim because she told him of her plan and because he still considered himself a loser because of yet another failed marriage and couldn't accept it?

- Why was Kim dressed more or less formally, as though to go out and Young in a plaid shirt and slacks?

- Was Kim Schmidt, nee Ruth Hannelore Schmidt, jealous of Gig's relationship with Harriet Douglas and gave this as a reason for (possibly) leaving him?

- Could they have been killed by someone else who arranged it to look like a murder-suicide pact?

- If none of the above, then what was the motive?

The New York Police Department still has no answers to these or any other questions except their own theory that it was a homicide-suicide pact agreed to by Kim. No signs of a struggle or fight were evident in the neat and tidy apartment at the Osborne.

Following the memorial service in Beverly Hills arranged by Harriet Vine Douglas, Gig's friends would not let the questions die, or Gig rest in peace. We received calls for several days following the death by friends of Gig's who say there is no way the actor could ever pull a trigger on a gun. He was a non-violent type and too gun-shy. Even in the few western films he appeared in, they said, he was afraid to fire a gun, even with blanks.

But they could not reconcile their statements with the three other revolvers found in the apartment. Could they have been Kim's weapons, purchased since she arrived in the U.S. or brought in with her from Hong Kong in checked baggage. The latter would not have had to go through airport security checks or X-ray machines in those days.

Another theory Young's friends put forth was that Gig and his East German-born bride were murdered because of *something in her past which Gig knew nothing about*. This is a wild theory put forth in their moment(s) of grief. They say it could have been done by someone they knew who was admitted to the apartment. But, with no signs of any kind of a struggle, this theory can almost be eliminated. However, "hit" or "contract killers" *have been known* to fulfill their "contract" to make them look like murder and suicide.

New York Police Department experts say that a shot to the head is the favorite spot for such people. Amateurs can seldom pinpoint the spot in the head which will cause instant death, as in those which entered the craniums of Kim and Gig Young. The police never did say whether or not there were any powder burns on Young's hand, which there would have had to be if he had fired the pistol which killed them.

Those friends who came up with the "wild theories" based it on the then unpublished fact (in the New York papers) that the couple were to host a small dinner party that evening in an uptown restaurant. It was known to the investigators, but they withheld the information from the press.

☆   ☆   ☆

The deaths of Kim and Gig Young exemplify one of those mystifying riddles that will go down in Hollywood lore of the future along with those concerning Thomas H. Ince, Thelma Todd and William Desmond Taylor.

Even though the deaths of Kim and Gig Young occurred in Manhattan, Gig Young was still considered a dues-paying member of the oligarchy.

Therefore, the deaths of Gig and his bride of less than three weeks will have to go down as another of Hollywood's Unsolved Mysteries.

☆   ☆   ☆

GIG YOUNG'S DAUGHTER SAYS 'DON'T ENVY HOLLYWOOD KIDS!'

Fourteen years after her father's death, Jennifer Young, the daughter of Gig Young and his third wife, Elaine, a successful Beverly Hills realtor, said her father was a failure as a parent.

"He walked out on us when I was four years old and I never saw him in person again ...

"I never even heard from him on my birthday, Christmas or any other holiday," she said plaintively in an interview when she was eighteen years old in 1981.

Jennifer Young claimed she cried herself to sleep many nights and if she ever saw her father on TV, she'd slap the screen in anger and scream, "How could you leave me? I still love you!"

Jennifer lamented that only a "Hollywood Child" can know how heartbreaking it is to see their father in newspapers and magazines, and on television or the big screen, yet never see him in person. "Most of my girl friends with show business parents are children of Hollywood divorces — not just one divorce and remarriage, but many!"

Jennifer Young claimed in that interview that she saved herself from self-destruction and heartbreak because her mother was a strong force in her life. "She was strict yet loving — and always there for me." she said.

But most children of star parents aren't that lucky, she claims.

"They are victims of their famous parents' success."

A Dream of Kings

Inger Stevens during a promotional tour for the film **A Dream of Kings** in which she co-starred with Anthony Quinn. The pair dated for several months following the film. Quinn blamed "...the false values of achievement in Hollywood" for Stevens' death. "She should have stayed in Sweden, married a truck driver and had babies," said Quinn. (Marvin Paige's Mot. Picture and TV Research Svc.)

"Alas! the love of women! it is known to be a lovely and fearful thing; for all of theirs upon that die is thrown: and if 'tis lost, life has no more to bring to them but mockeries of the past alone..."

— *Lord Byron*
1788-1824

10 ... Inger Stevens:
Accident .. Suicide .. Or ...?

Was Inger Stevens murdered, did she commit suicide, or was her death an accident?

Dr. Thomas Noguchi, the Los Angeles County Coroner, attributed the death of television's "Farmer's Daughter" to "acute barbiturate poisoning." Inger Stevens was discovered on the kitchen floor of her secluded home at 8000 Woodrow Wilson Drive in the Hollywood Hills by her sometime roommate and companion, Lola McNally, on April 30, 1970. Stevens was clad in a flimsy, golden brown negligee almost matching her California tan.

McNally claims that when she called her name, Inger opened her eyes, lifted her head and tried to speak. She was unable to make any sound. McNally told police that she had spoken to Inger the previous night and she had sounded fine.

The paramedics were called, but Inger Stevens died in the ambulance en route to the hospital. On arrival, medics removed a small bandage from her chin which revealed a slight amount of what appeared to be fresh blood oozing from the cut. Doctors were unable to say how long it had been there, but that it appeared to be fairly recent, less than a few hours old.

At the time of her death, there were three people who could help Noguchi in assembling a "Psychological Profile" of Inger Stevens to discover whether or not her death was a suicide.(*)

(*) It was these "Psychological Profiles" which were later to get Dr. Noguchi in trouble with the Hollywood community and fired as the L.A. County Coroner.

Those three people were:

- Lola McNally, who sometimes shared Inger's house as her secretary and companion;

- Actor Burt Reynolds with whom Inger was intimate in the last days before her death;

and ...

- Isaac L. (Ike) Jones, a black, former football player from UCLA and, at the time, a convalescent home operator.

It was Jones who threw a monkey wrench into the autopsy and into Noguchi's attempt to discover what really happened to the beautiful Swedish-born star. Not only had Inger Stevens starred in **The Farmer's Daughter** series, but in over fifteen feature and television films during her career. It was a career that was taking off and which had the aura of major stardom.

Jones filed suit in Los Angeles Superior Court several weeks following Inger's death claiming that he was the actress' husband. He produced an affidavit signed in 1962 by himself and Inger. In that affidavit, a contract between them, they both agreed to keep their marriage secret from the world.

Jones' suit claimed that they were married in Tijuana, Baja California, in November, 1961, and honeymooned in Mexico City. On their return to Los Angeles, according to Jones, they maintained separate residences as Inger was told "..by certain people..." that the mixed marriage could harm her career and earning capacity as it had those of Sammy Davis, Jr., after his entanglement with another Swedish actress, Mai Britt, several years before. Jones asked Judge Joseph Sprankle for Letters of Administration for the estate as her legal husband. At the time, Inger's estate was valued at $175,000, but did not include substantial future residuals from her television work, her 25% ownership of seventy-five segments of **The Farmer's Daughter** in which she had starred for three seasons in the title role.

Testifying against Jones, and denying his claim of a valid marriage to the chronically unhappy star, was McNally, her closest friend and confidante. She denied that there ever was such a marriage and that if there had been, Inger would surely have confided in her. Instead, she testified to the fact that she did know of a long-time *relationship* between Inger and Jones, and that they had lived together in a rented home in Malibu for a time. But she was sure there was no marriage. Jones could not produce a marriage certificate, saying it had been lost when his "wife" moved into the Woodrow Wilson Drive house.

As evidence of the "marriage", Jones' attorney produced "legal documents," *purportedly* signed by Miss Stevens, which recognized the marriage and said all property in the actress' name was to be considered "community property." A strange document, to say the least.

Under cross-examination by the lawyer for the Los Angeles County Public Administrator, Jones admitted having no real or personal property in his own name. He also admitted filing Federal and State income tax forms as a *single* man during the purported eight-year marriage. Jones did admit that they separated soon after March 17 of 1970.

Further testimony by Lola McNally verified this and added that Inger wanted to divest herself of Jones "...once and for all" so that she could marry her new love, Reynolds. She had dined with the actor three nights before her death.

Producer Aaron Spelling (**Love Boat, Charlie's Angels,** *ad nauseum*) backed up McNally's testimony. "They were wrapped up in each other," he testified. Judge Sprankle denied Jones' application. Jones, however, appealed several months later with "new evidence" and testimony from Inger's brother, Ola.

What Inger Stevens was trying to tell her friend when she raised up her head and tried to speak, no one will ever know. Nor will it ever be known how, from whom, and where she received that cut on her chin not too long before her limp form was discovered by McNally.

Medics and the coroner wondered:

- Was she struck by someone?

- Was there a bitter argument which preceded her death?

- Did she fight with Reynolds about Jones?

- Did she fight with Jones about Reynolds?

Neither the police nor the Coroner ruled out any possibility, even suicide, so soon after discovery of the body.

☆   ☆   ☆

Vivacious and sparkling, Inger Stevens was born Inger Stensland in Stockholm, Sweden, on October 18, 1934. She learned what to her was the magic of the theatre from her father, Per Stensland, a professor in the Swedish school system. He was fond of directing school plays and appearing in amateur productions as an actor. Inger's mother was also a teacher, but did not share her husband's interest in the theatre.

Inger's introduction to the stage came at the age of six when she was taken to see her father portray the role of *Scrooge*. His transformation from a man with abundant dark hair to one with a scraggly white mane enchanted the wide-eyed Inger. It was then and there that she decided to become an actress. It wasn't until years later, however, that she was able to realize her goal — her dream of someday becoming a movie star.

Her mother abandoned the family to marry another man when Inger was an impressionable six-year- old. The two Stensland children, Inger and her younger brother, Ola, were sent to live for a time with an aunt and uncle, while her father continued his academic studies in America, having earned a Fulbright scholarship. The aunt and uncle were kindly people, Inger was to say later, and she often referred to their generosity to her and Ola in most interviews she granted during her career.

Inger's known loneliness began, apparently, at that stage of her life, being away from her natural parents; she adored her father. She tried to understand why her father and mother didn't want to be together anymore.

When Inger was thirteen, she and her brother left Stockholm to come and live with their father in New York. Their parents had completed their divorce by mail and Per had remarried. He was working on his thesis on labor relations at Harvard, and was unable to meet the two frightened teenagers when the boat docked in New Orleans. Instead, he made arrangements through Traveler's Aid with the Salvation Army to escort the two to New York.

Inger said many years later that she never really got over her fear of feeling stranded and alone and unwanted, as she had at that stage of her life. She wore a tag around her neck with her name on it, as did her brother. She hated the tag because people pointed at it and she was immediately singled out as "a foreigner."

"We came over on a freighter carrying Swedish matches," she told me in an interview at 20th Century-Fox many, many years later while Inger was co-starring with Walter Matthau in **A Guide For The Married Man**. "We were on the ocean for nine weeks and landed at New Orleans. All we knew of the English language when we got here was 'Yes' and 'No'," she explained.

This was the start, many friends believe, of Inger's insecurity and feelings of rejection, which plagued her for the next twenty years or so until her death.

What Inger and her brother discovered was an ambivalent household with her father and stepmother totally wrapped up in their teaching careers and themselves. Per was at Columbia University, the stepmother in the New York school system.

Luckily, like many Scandinavians, Inger had an ear for languages and picked up English very quickly by listening to the radio and to television in its then infancy. Further, a parental decision was made to speak only English in the home to help both children learn the language quickly. Inger Stensland, a Swedish immigrant to America, eventually learned to speak English without the slightest trace of an accent. Many years later by an odd quirk of fate, she had to learn a Swedish accent for her role on **The Farmer's Daughter**.

In a *Saturday Evening Post* interview with Richard Warren Lewis, she said later, "I witnessed an awful lot of arguments in my family. Because of this, I kept things to myself and never really said what was on my mind. I was always afraid of hurting somebody!"

In 1949, when Inger was fifteen, her family moved to Manhattan, Kansas, a far cry from the sophistication of New York's Manhattan. Her father had received an appointment to teach at the University of Kansas. The trouble between Inger and her stepmother, whose side her father was always taking, was getting worse by the day.

Inger decided to leave home.

Under the name of Kay Palmer, the first names of two school friends, she worked at a burlesque house in Kansas City. She had seen an ad, she told friends later, in the Kansas City paper reading, "Candy Girl Required — $35 per week." She applied for and got the job. She was, however, eventually asked to dance. She refused to take her clothes off, but she considered it a teen-aged lark to dance in burlesque and she did, eventually earning $60 per week. Her stern Swedish father eventually located her and returned Inger to their home in Manhattan.

In high school, she was more determined than ever to become an actress. She worked hard, too, at school plays, and amateur theatricals, winning several contests. In order to finance her ballet lessons (she felt she needed to learn how to walk properly as an actress), she taught social dancing at the college. She also took on a collection of odd jobs at the J.C. Penney and other local stores in Manhattan. Inger Stensland had one goal in mind — to save enough money to get her to New York and into the theatre.

Soon after her graduation, her father moved to Lubbock, Texas, to another teaching position. Inger, just before her eighteenth birthday, migrated to New York with her savings and a burning ambition. She found a walk-up apartment over a candy store on 91st Street near Madison Avenue. To support herself when her savings started to run low, she took on whatever jobs were offered to her: as a model for Seventh Avenue garment houses, and as an usher at a movie theatre. For three months she worked in the chorus of the Latin Quarter night club at $75 per week for thirteen shows a week. Lou Walters, the owner, and father of television personality Barbara Walters, took a liking to her. Inger always wore white gloves to auditions to look more sophisticated, and Walters always called her "White Gloves," even after she became well known.

With the security of the Latin Quarter job, Inger decided she was ready to audition for the Actor's Studio run by Lee Strasberg — Marilyn Monroe's left wing nemesis — and Elia Kazan. Out of the 150-odd who auditioned, only 20 were selected. Inger was one of the twenty.

She got her first job in television, that of a tired housewife in a com-

mercial. More commercials followed, and an aggressive talent agent, Anthony Soglio, spotted her and became her manager, her agent and her lover. Eventually, in a move she came to regret, they were married. Soglio had already changed her name for professional reasons.

Inger began appearing regularly on **Studio One, Kraft Music Hall, The Robert Montgomery Show, Armstrong Circle Theatre**, all the magical shows from the early days of live television.

Inger Stevens as **The Farmer's Daughter.** (Marvin Paige's Mot. Picture & TV Research Svc.)

Inger Stevens at Metro-Goldwyn-Mayer during the filming of **Man on Fire** in which she starred with Bing Crosby. During the film, and for several months afterward, Stevens and Crosby were lovers until Crosby remarried. (Marvin Paige's Mot. Picture & TV Research Svc.)

Inger learned to perfect her technique, her love affair with the camera(s). She always knew her lines, and she could find her marks without looking down at the floor. She was rapidly becoming a professional.

The marriage to Soglio, which took place on July 5, 1955, in Greenwich, Connecticut, lasted just six months. They were finally divorced six months later. However, Inger paid dearly for the union, and was required to pay Soglio five percent of her earnings through 1960. It was a high price to pay for six months and a constant source of irritation to her.

In the Richard Warren Lewis interview in the *Saturday Evening Post*, Inger lamented, "That (wedding day) was the worst day of my life. I wanted to be any place but where I was. I married Anthony for all the wrong reasons. I had been dating him for about eight months and he was the only person I knew on a social basis. For me, the whole affair was an expensive nightmare."

In February, 1956, came Inger's big break. She appeared at the Holi-

Inger in Washington for shooting of several segments of **The Farmer's Daughter.** The series is still being shown in re-run in the U.S. and in several foreign countries. (Marvin Paige's Mot. Picture & TV Research Svc.)

day Theatre in the comedy **Debut** with Tom Helmore. Critics panned the show and it closed after only four performances. Several critics, however, singled Inger out for a brief word of praise. She had also been noticed by Hollywood scouts and was summoned to California by producer-director Albert McCreery. She was immediately signed for several **Matinee Theatre** and **Alfred Hitchcock Presents** segments.

She then came to the attention of 20th Century-Fox, who placed her under a studio player contract but dropped her after three months. When Inger appeared on **"Eloise,"** a **Playhouse 90** segment, producers William Perlberg and Bill Seaton spotted her and immediately tested her for the feminine lead in **Tin Star**, a feature to star Henry Fonda. But Anthony Mann, the director, felt Inger was "too young" for the part. Nevertheless, after seeing her test, Paramount Pictures placed Inger under long-term contract.

About this period of her career, Inger once said, "It was the most difficult time of my life. Running away as a teenager, I survived without scars because I didn't realize the dangers. But when I came to Hollywood, I was old enough to know and I was lonely and confused.

"At first I had no friends, no one really to care what happened to me. I was very naive about people and things. Everybody's interest in Hollywood isn't in you as a person, but how they can use you to get what they want. I felt it very keenly after living here a few weeks. I had never worked in films before, and it was rather a startling transformation for me to undergo."

Inger was learning the hard way about the callousness of Hollywood and its inmates. It and the people would eventually destroy her.

Metro-Goldwyn-Mayer borrowed Inger from Paramount for **Man of Fire**, starring Bing Crosby. Inger played the role of a new girl in Crosby's life while Bing appeared as a man involved in a bitter custody battle with his ex-wife.

"I never thought I would ever get such a role opposite a top star like Bing," she recalled. "But I went in there and just did it. It scared the hell out of me."

When Inger was carried off the set with an appendicitis attack, Crosby visited the hospital every day bearing flowers, books and goodies. They soon became attracted off stage as well as on. Gossip columnists soon got word of the romance between the up-and-coming Swedish-born actress and the millionaire widower. Since his first wife, Dixie Lee, had died five years earlier, Crosby had been linked with Joan Caulfield, Mona Freeman, Kathryn Grant and dancer Betty Hutton.

"I thought Bing loved me," Inger told a columnist afterwards. And she kept thinking that until the very day it was announced that Crosby had married Kathryn Grant. They had previously dated for a year, but Bing broke it off to date Inger. She never knew that Crosby — callous bastard that he was known to be in his private life — had still been

The tragic Inger Stevens (far right) in two scenes (one on following page) from **Man on Fire** in which she co-starred with the man she thought would marry her, Bing Crosby. Crosby, a very callous man in his private life, sent Inger to decorate "their" Palm Springs house while he courted another woman behind Inger's back. She learned of his marriage on the radio. (Marvin Paige's Mot. Picture & TV Research Svc.)

secretly dating Kathryn behind her back. He even sent Inger to his Palm Springs house to get her out of town.

"One day," Inger recalled, "he called me up and told me to go and buy drapes and curtains for his Palm Springs house. He said he wanted me to decorate it to my taste. *He even told me it was going to be my house so I had better fix it up the way I liked it.*

"It may not have been a marriage proposal, but it sure sounded like one. Believe it or not, I was at the Palm Springs house, had the radio on while working with the drapery man, and heard the announcement. I went into a state of shock and it took me months to recover. I became sick from all the stress that man caused me."

Inger was learning the ways of the oligarchical society and the way it treated people.

(See description on page 238.)

After several more pictures, and a sixteen-city, cross-country promotional tour for **The World, The Flesh, and the Devil**, in which she co-starred, and still devastated over the break up with Crosby, in December, 1959, she decided to move back to New York.

After a New Year's Eve party, Inger returned alone to the new apartment she had recently leased at 24 Gramercy Park West, still cluttered with crates and boxes which had only just arrived from her Hollywood house.

She then proceeded, for reasons unknown to anyone, to take 24 sleeping pills and swallow half a bottle of ammonia. Three days later, her unconscious form was discovered by the building superintendent. Dave Tebet, an NBC executive and a close friend from Inger's early television days, tried over and over to reach her for a dinner engagement they had made. After failing for three days, he summoned the super to break in.

It was a miracle, according to the doctors at Columbia Hospital, one block away, that she was still alive. There were blood clots under her left lung, she developed phlebitis in her legs. But somehow she made it through the morning. It was also discovered that she was blind. That condition only lasted two weeks, when she gradually began to regain her vision.

The only visitors allowed were Tebet and her brother, Ola. "I was feeling lonely, very withdrawn," she confessed later. "I'd been in love (with Crosby) and it ended. I tried to end it, but it solves nothing." (*)

Many people recalled that Inger was in love with Crosby because she tended to prefer older men because of the influence of her father on her life. Many of Crosby's friends, and one of his sons, later told me that it would have been a very good thing if it had worked out between them. The only problem was that Crosby was a devout Catholic, and Inger was not.

All during this time, Inger underwent a three-year long battle with Paramount Pictures. All studio contract players were treated as serfs and she was constantly turning down roles she knew were not suited to her talents. She faced suspension several times and guest-starred on such television shows as **Hong Kong, Twilight Zone, Adventures in Paradise, Follow the Sun,** and many others.

In 1961, she decided to vacation in Europe. But returning to Los Angeles in June of that year, she was the last passenger to leap from a burning jet which had crash-landed at Lisbon. The plane exploded, according to newspaper reports, less than one minute after Inger had leapt to safety.

On her return to Hollywood following that tragedy, she signed on as star of **The Farmer's Daughter** for ABC-TV. Overnight she became television's Golden Girl, "...honest...believable...and capturing the spirit of the outspoken farm girl from Minnesota," read one review.

Inger received the TV Guide award as Favorite Female Personality of the year, and the Hollywood Foreign Press Association honored her with a Golden Globe as Best Actress on television. Inger owned 25% of the series and it lasted three years in the Top Ten in the Nielsen Ratings.

Inger, it seemed at the time, had it made.

Following the cancellation of the series, she went on to co-star in 10 more feature films, and to buy the home on Woodrow Wilson Drive. She hosted her own special, **Inger Stevens in Sweden**. She had a hectic schedule of eight films in two years from 1969 to 1970, icluding **A Guide**

(*) It was this statement which later caused Dr. Noguchi to call into question Inger's suicide theory and to develop a Psychological Profile of the actress. Noguchi could not understand why, if it was a suicide, Inger left no notes behind. That aspect is still a mystery.

for the Married Man, A Time for Killing, The Long Ride Home, and Fire Creek starring James Stewart and Henry Fonda. At Universal, she appeared in **Madigan**, again with Henry Fonda, with Richard Widmark as its star.

She also co-starred in **Five Card Stud** for producer Hal Wallis which starred Dean Martin and Robert Mitchum. Inger Stevens' professional career never looked so promising.

She was also being considered for three more films.

☆ ☆ ☆

Inger once told me in an interview for a fan magazine while she was working at 20th Century-Fox, "The thing I miss most is having someone to share things with. I come home hurting to unburden myself of the things that happened during the day, but there is no one to tell them to."

"Yes," she said, philosophically, "I have dates, but this isn't the same. I hope someday to find a man who will love me and whom I can love and respect. Until then, I have to find other means of curing my loneliness."

Was this a prophetic statement? A statement people should have paid attention to? Her doctors? Her managers?

Many say yes.

We met up again with Inger in 1968 while she was in Rome to star for Universal in **House of Cards** with George Peppard. The film was an abysmal failure because of a bad script.

Inger, we discovered, was still lonely and it again illustrated for us the type of lives film personalities have to endure. It is not the glamorous peel-me-a-grape kind of existence many people think it is.

Inger was living in a rented duplex in an old *palazzo* which looked like it had been built during the last days of the Holy Roman Empire. "Oh, the noise," she sighed. She was not the country-girl type, "but the sounds and cacophony which is Rome can kill," she laughed.

"I live in this old Palace and when you run the vacuum cleaner you have to disconnect the refrigerator or you blow a fuse and everything in the building goes out," she laughed.

"At 5:30 every morning, the bells in the church next door start clanging, the Italians start gunning their engines on the sports cars. I cook myself a steak and go to work."

Almost twelve hours later, Inger was through with work at the Dear Studios in downtown Rome. "But not quite," she told us.

"I have to have my hair washed and set every evening. But with the electric current so weak in this old *palazzo*, I'm afraid of fusing everything so I go to the local beauty parlor."

Inger explained that because of the two-hour afternoon siesta, the beauty shops stayed open late. "The shop is usually filled with *principessas* and their dogs," she laughed with that infectious laugh which was her trademark.

"I'm usually dressed in jeans and sandals and the *principessas* and their dogs look at me suspiciously. The dogs, usually tiny, growl ferociously as only small Italian dogs can!"

Two hours later, Inger would emerge from the shop and because of the huge curlers in her hair which she had to leave in until the studio hairdresser could comb them out the next morning, she could not go to a restaurant for a late dinner. Instead, she said, "I walk home, eat a cold dinner, usually chicken, and drink a glass of hot milk. I watch the news on television to improve my Italian and at 9:15 I get into bed, happy to be living in glamorous Rome." she laughed, halfheartedly this time.

"Before I conk out, I dial 114 and leave a wake-up call. You never know, one morning the church bells won't ring and the Romans will renounce their cars. I might even oversleep.

"Don't movie stars live exciting lives?"

We had to agree with her question in the negative as she meant it.

Why, as many people asked prior to Dr. Noguchi's ruling on the cause of her death, would Inger Stevens commit suicide? She had everything going for her.

- She had no financial worries;

- She had an active, busy and prosperous career;

- She was popular with members of both sexes;

- She was active as a contributing member of the Hollywood community.

Inger Stevens channeled her energy as a responsible member of the oligarchical society. She was appointed by Governor Edmond G. Brown to serve as a member of the Board of the Neuro-Psychiatric Institute at the UCLA Medical Center. She also served as Chairperson of the California

Council For Retarded Children and travelled throughout California on the Council's behalf, most of the time at her own expense. She spent hours with the children. She said they made her recall her own lonely childhood in the U.S. and in Sweden.

She had an extensive art collection in her Hollywood Hills home, read avidly, painted, swam every day in her pool which was heated for year-round use. She had a sauna installed in the house.

Why, then, would she take her own life and leave no word behind her?

Everyone who knew her felt there was a compelling and overwhelming need to do so, a reason no one knew of; not even her closest friend, Lola McNally.

Inger's death was ruled "death by barbiturate poisoning." But the Coroner did not at the time come right out and say her death was a suicide.

A compelling reason for her despondency occurred the night before her death and the previous weekend. Although Ike Jones and Inger had "officially" separated on March 17, Jones claimed he and Inger spent the weekend together at his home. He then drove her home on Sunday night. No one knows what they talked about; perhaps an equitable property settlement. Inger had already had her fill of paying off one husband.

The Monday night before her death, Inger dined at LaScala with Burt Reynolds and producer Aaron Spelling and his wife, Candy. They wanted to celebrate Inger's signing to star in Spelling's new "whodunit" series for ABC, **The Most Deadly Game**, which was to co-star Inger, Ralph Bellamy and George Maharis. The series involved a trio of highly trained criminologists and was scheduled to start shooting in Europe in June — two months following Inger's death. It was a location she was really looking forward to. It would get her away from Hollywood for a few months.

When Anthony Quinn, with whom she starred in **A Dream of Kings**, heard of her death, he told a reporter: "Inger didn't belong here. She should have stayed in Sweden, married a truck driver and had eight kids."

Quinn, who dated Inger for several months following her bust-up with Crosby, added: "She had idealism and purity, and maybe she came to a sort of desperation."

"The great competitiveness and phony sense of accomplishment in this damn town we have here can be very destructive!"

A close friend of Inger, with whom she worked on a regular basis ever since she came to Hollywood, said that Inger's life had never been

Bing Crosby and Inger Stevens in an intimate moment in Crosby's dressing room at MGM during the filming of Man on Fire. (Marvin Paige's Mot. Picture & TV Research Svc.)

happier — on the surface. She had finally attained some financial security after ridding herself of the contract with Anthony Soglio, whom she once referred to as a leach; a new series which would earn her a great deal of money; and a new love, Burt Reynolds.

Then what was it that caused Inger Stevens to take her life with a large dose of Tedral washed down with alcohol?

What verdict did Coroner Noguchi finally arrive at?

☆ ☆ ☆

On July 27, 1970, Jones again threw a monkey wrench into the final disposition of the star-crossed Inger's estate and her memory. He made a second attempt to gain control of her estate. Superior Court Commissioner A. Edward Nichols heard testimony concerning the purported marriage to Jones.

Ola Stensland flew to Los Angeles to testify that his sister wrote to him in Harwich Port, Massachusetts, where he ran a restaurant. He brought two letters in Inger's handwriting, which referred to the purported marriage between Jones and Inger. One letter was from Mexico City where Inger said she was "honeymooning" but to keep it a secret.

Deputy Sheriff Armando Acedo also testified. He said that at the request of the Los Angeles County Public Administrator, Baldo Kristovich, he went to Tijuana to search the records for proof of marriage. (*)

Acedo testified that he personally had checked all the marriage records in Tijuana without finding a trace of a marriage license or marriage of Ike Jones, Inger Stevens or Inger Stensland.

Kristovich opposed Jones' petition for the second time. The letters from Inger to her brother which, *for some strange reason were never produced at the first hearing*, swayed the Commissioner in favor of Jones despite the strenuous objections of Kristovich and the L.A. County lawyers.

Commisioner Nichols ruled that a marriage between Inger and Jones did take place on November 18, 1961. "The presumption of the marriage," intoned Nichols from the bench, "is fortified by eight years of holding themselves out to friends and family members as husband and wife."

Then why did Inger not "hold out" to Lola McNally that she and Jones were married?

(*) Another strange aspect of Inger Stevens' death is that she died *intestate*, without leaving a will. Under California Law, with the resultant bureaucratic *snafus* and unreasonable costs, the Public Administrator is charged wth locating lost heirs and administering such estates. During the last two decades, a Public Administrator has been charged with favoring relatives and others in the purchase of real estate and other property of people dying "*intestate*."

Under the *intestate* circumstances, ruled Nichols, all community property and half of any separate property would go to Jones. The other half would go to her father, Per Stensland, again living in New York, and her mother, Mrs. Lilibet Rubinstein, in Sweden.

Jones said afterward that his share of Inger's estate would go to a mental clinic in the name of Inger Stevens. No traces of any mental clinic bearing Inger's name, or that of Jones, could be located in 1988. Nor had one ever been heard of in Los Angeles, more particularly, South West Los Angeles.

☆ ☆ ☆

On August 4, 1970, the same day the Commissioner ruled in favor of Jones, Coroner Noguchi said that his "Psychological Profile," compiled with the help and cooperation of the Los Angeles County Suicide Prevention Center, concluded that Inger's death was "a suicide." Noguchi added that Inger's "emotional background," compounded by statements from her family and friends, and her previous suicide attempt in New York, should have been brought to the attention of Inger's doctors, insurance companies insuring her films, and others closely connected with the actress.

☆ ☆ ☆

But nothing in the Profile shed any light on *why* Inger Stevens, at the height of her career, a financially secure actress, would take her own life.

- Was it because she was overwhelmingly lonely?

- Was it because Jones told her that he would fight or contest any attempt to divorce him — *if, indeed, there ever was such a marriage* — and that it would ruin her career?

- Why did Jones file Income Tax returns as a "Single Man?"

- If there was a legal marriage to Ike Jones, why did Inger hope that she would marry Bing Crosby?

- Did she tell Burt Reynolds of any threats made to her by Jones about a divorce? And that because of this they "agreed to disagree" about their future plans?

- Why did Ike Jones not have Inger's brother and the letter or letters from Inger present at the first hearing in June when he first sought permission to administer the estate?

- Was Inger's suicide the result of the loneliness which she was always talking about? And what of the fact that Jones "was there" and befriended her eight years before: had she psychologically imagined they were married while they were only *living together*?

- Was it something that she could cling to; someone she could call her own and not be lonely anymore? Was it because of the "mixed" aspect of the relationship with Jones? Had she realized that, at least at this period of our history, they could not live openly for career reasons?

Inger Steven' career was moving forward and she could have eventually been a major star. That probability came crashing down on the kitchen floor of her home that April morning of 1970.

The untimely death of Inger Stevens, *nee* Inger Stensland of Stockholm, will always be considered one of Hollywood's Unsolved Mysteries which will never be definitively understood by anyone.

Was Loneliness a Contributing Cause ...?

INGER STEVENS' CHILDHOOD CAUSED HER PROBLEMS OF LONELINESS LATER IN HER LIFE DESPITE HER PROFESSIONAL SUCCESS

Inger Stevens told one interviewer ...

"A career, no matter how successful, can't put its arms around you.

"The thing I miss most is having someone to share things with. I always used to jump into friendships and give too much.

"You can't do that ...

"You end up being like Grand Central Station with people just coming and going.

"And there you are — left all alone ... "

1959's 'Fatal Attraction'

George Reeves as the original television "Superman."   (Marvin Paige's Mot. Picture & TV Research Svc.)

"I look upon every man as a suicide from the moment he takes the dice-box desperately in his hand; all that follows in his career from that fatal time is only sharpening the dagger before it strikes to his heart.

— *Richard Cumberland*
1631-1718
English Bishop

11 ... 1959's "Fatal Attraction" Murder Still Haunts

At 1:59 a.m. on June 16, 1959, a speeding bullet, faster than the speed of light, snuffed out the life of TV's indestructible Superman. By early the following morning, the newspaper headlines screamed "Superman Is Dead!"

Now, over thirty years later, the death of TV's first Super Star of the younger set, George Reeves, the first man to portray Superman outside the pages of a comic book or daily strip, still remains an unsolved mystery.

Officially, thanks to another "neat and tidy" solution requested by some powerful members of the oligarchy because of the prominence of the names involved, Reeves' death was listed officially as an "indicated suicide." Not definitely listed as a "suicide," but "indicated suicide." This was the compromise verdict reached by Beverly Hills officials to satisfy members of the oligarchy, especially by some powerful executives at the studio considered in those days to be The Second Coming: Metro-Goldwyn-Mayer.

The best friend and business manager of Reeves, Arthur Weissman, says that Superman did not commit suicide. What's more, the bizarre plot, as Weissman calls it, was brought about by the real life "fatal attraction" between George Reeves and the beautiful wife of Eddie Mannix, the vice president of Loew's Theaters, Inc., and the former Number Three man to Louis B. Mayer at MGM. Mayer was one of the most, if not the most, powerful executive in the oligarchy in the 1930's, and well into the 1950's. He was also common and uncouth and loathed by most people who knew him well.

Weissman, in an interview almost thirty years after his client and friend's death, broke his long silence about Reeves "murder," as he calls it. He thus has broken the code of the oligarchy. Weissman is retired.

Milo Speriglio the private detective, also states that George Reeves' death was a murder. "Nearly everyone in Hollywood has always been led to believe George Reeves' death was a suicide," said Speriglio. "Not everyone believed it then, nor do they believe it now. I am one of those who does not. I'm a professional investigator and criminologist and in my professional opinion, George Reeves was murdered."

Two voices from out of the long nights of silence of the oligarchy make the same claim.

So do we.

During the final two months of George Reeves' life, he received several death threats on his unlisted telephone — sometimes as many as twenty per day — mostly late at night. Most were hang-ups when the receiver was lifted. The final telephoned threat came just two hours before his death.

Taking the calls very seriously, Reeves filed a report with the Beverly Hills Police Department — "The Friend of the Stars" — then he filed a complaint with the District Attorney of Los Angeles County, which has jurisdiction over such matters.

Reeves suggested a suspect — Toni Mannix. As soon as that name reached the complaint desk, it would raise a red flag in both offices. It is almost certain that several members of the oligarchical society would have been notified of Reeves' action, probably including Toni's husband, Eddie Mannix.

Why Reeves thought Toni Mannix was behind the telephoned threats was never explained, but it was obvious to the oligarchy. Hollywood gossip and gossip columnists, including Parsons, Hopper and others, including ourselves, linked Toni and Reeves romantically — and very intimately. After an investigation, it was determined both Toni and George were receiving phoned threats. When that was disclosed, everyone then assumed it was Eddie Mannix who instigated them through employees or hired goons.

The last month of the actor's life was spent with his fiancee, Lenore Lemmon, whom he planned to marry within a very short time. Lemmon, an attractive brunette and former New York socialite, was known to be a jealous woman. She was once asked to leave, "bounced from" would be a better term, New York's Stork Club, for fighting with another woman over a man.

Sometime around 6:30 p.m., dinner was served at the Benedict Canyon split-level home of George Reeves. It had been prepared by Lenore for her soon-to-be husband and a house-guest, writer Robert Condon, who was there to do an article on Reeves and an upcoming exhibition Reeves had scheduled with boxing champ Archie Moore.

After dinner, the trio settled down in the living room to watch TV. On the large black and white set, they viewed **Tightrope** starring Mike Connors, **Garry Moore** and **Red Skelton**. All had consumed a great deal of wine and spirits. About midnight, they all retired.

Around 1 or 1:30 a.m., a friend of Lenore and Reeves, Carol Von Ronkel, came by with another friend, William Bliss. Even though the Benedict Canyon house was considered to be Grand Central Station West, Reeves did draw the line at visitors arriving after midnight. They banged on the door and Lenore got up and let them in. George got up, put on his bathrobe and started yelling at them for showing up so late at night.

Lenore finally calmed him down and soon afterward, after a night-cap, he went back up to his bedroom. At that point Lenore said something like, "Well, he's sulking; he'll probably go up to his room and shoot himself!"

Was she a clairvoyant? Or did she have some prior knowledge that a tragedy was about to unfold? Or did she know George Reeves' habits under such circumstances and his petulance?

The Beverly Hills Police Report would have you believe that while entertaining his fiancee and three others at his home, Reeves suddenly, and without explanation, impulsively decided to commit suicide. *It just doesn't happen that way, according to experts*. The report added that everyone in the house was very intoxicated, and it was very difficult to get a coherent account of the events of the night. Regardless, it is hard to believe, but the Beverly Hills Police Department report said, that Reeves went up to his bedroom, placed a pistol in his right ear and pulled the trigger.

But, Weissman does not dispute that description. He explains that Reeves was **not** trying to kill himself — he was just playing his favorite game, a practical joke he enjoyed with a gun that should have, and always had before, contained only a blank. That was the reason for Lemmon's outburst, according to Weissman.

The former business manager claims that, unknown to Superman, the blank was obviously replaced with a real bullet by either Eddie Mannix or someone hired by him to do it. Toni had a key to Reeves' house.

Toni Mannix was an aspiring actress and former model, and was gorgeous according to Hollywood standards. She was also 25 years younger than "Eddie the Ape," as he was referred to behind his back because of his looks. "Toni was madly in love with George Reeves," claims Weissman. Reeves' friends confirmed this.

"Their romance was an open Hollywood secret. It continued steadily for years, but appeared to come to an end when George announced his upcoming marriage to Lenore Lemmon."

According to other friends and business associates of Reeves, Toni became enraged over this sudden development. She bombarded George with hourly phone calls all night long. She threatened him with such threats as, "I'll get even with you if it's the last thing I do," and all the other familiar threats of a scorned woman.

Mannix, a powerful and proud man who was being openly humiliated by his wife's affair with Reeves, also would, by the very nature of the man, seek revenge. Both had the perfect opportunity.

George Reeves' friends knew that under the influence of liquor, he would sometimes fire a blank at his head in a mock suicide attempt, making certain his arm was far enough away so he wouldn't get powder burns on his face.

There were several mishaps that befell George Reeves in the months prior to his death.

George Reeves was not despondent. He had much to live for and nothing in his life to cause him to kill himself. His mother, Helen Bessolo, who had doted on her son as a youngster, was not satisfied, as a good Catholic, with the police "theory" of "indicated suicide." Bessolo retained Nick Harris Detectives of Los Angeles. At that time, Milo Speriglio was a novice investigator for the firm and played a small role in the investigation.

"Our preliminary findings" he said, "indicated a homicide. We ruled out suicide and no further investigation was required."

As the years passed, Speriglio became the director and owner of Nick Harris Detectives, named after a famous detective who founded the agency even before the FBI was in existence. Looking back, he says, Reeves' mother said she talked with George just hours before his death. "He was in great spirits. he was not depressed. She went to her grave in 1964 convinced that her son was murdered."

Things were going very well indeed for Reeves. Offers were pouring in to cash in on his **Superman** celebrity status. Just three days after his death, he was to have entered the boxing ring — he was a former Golden Gloves boxer — with the light heavyweight champion, Archie Moore. It would be an exhibition match and the nation would tune in on television, expecting **Superman** to defeat the champ.

"The Archie Moore fight will be the highlight of my life." he told a reporter. He then said that after the match, he and Lemmon would be married, and that they planned a honeymoon in Spain. Next, they would go to Australia for six weeks, where Reeves would pick up an easy $20,000 for personal appearances as his television character. The series had recently been sold to an Australian network.

Returning to Hollywood later in the year, he was set to star in a feature film which he would direct. He would then shoot some more **Superman** episodes for syndication and with a hefty salary increase.

Not the sort of future to cause a man to commit suicide —especially in Hollywood where you are only as good, or as popular in the oligarchy, as your last credit.

And George Reeves had a lot of credits yet to come.

In the months just before his death, Reeves suffered three mysterious auto mishaps that nearly killed him. The first time, Reeves' car was nearly crushed between two trucks on the freeway.

Another time, a speeding car nearly killed him, but he survived thanks to his quick athletic reflexes.

The third time, his brakes failed on a narrow, twisting road, because all the brake fluid was gone from the hydraulic system. A mechanic later found the system to be in perfect working order.

"When the mechanic suggested that someone had pumped out the fluid, George dismissed the notion," said Weissman. Weissman was then, and is now, convinced that those three automobile incidents were NOT accidents. Someone wanted George dead — and that someone could only have been Eddie Mannix.

George Reeves and his fiancee Lenore Lemmon at a Hollywood party. Reeves tried to end his relationship with Toni Mannix, the wife of a former executive of MGM, later theatre executive, when he became engaged to Lemmon.

In the film business, and in control of many theatres, Mannix had access to a lot of people not considered to be in the normal social whirl. They could maneuver two trucks on a freeway very easily — for a price. They also knew how to drain fluid from a car's braking system. Mannix also had access to "studio" drivers who knew how to eliminate someone walking down the street with a well-placed fender or bumper, and the right location to do it where it would not attract too much attention.

Furthermore, added Weissman, "It would have been no problem at all for either Mannix or his hired goons to enter the house with Toni's key, put a live bullet in the gun, replacing the blank George always kept there. Then it would just be a matter of time before he would decide to play his favorite game."

☆　　☆　　☆

Born George Bessolo in Iowa, the future "Man of Steel" was an accomplished athlete. Against his mother's wishes, he entered the Golden Gloves boxing competition in 1932. This was the year the Olympics came to Los Angeles. He hung up his gloves after having his nose broken nine times. But that did not discourage him from going into the acting field.

Reeves was not a tough guy, according to those who knew him. He was persuaded to take acting lessons at the Pasadena Playhouse, where he would meet his first and only wife, Eleanora Needles. They were married in 1940 and divorced nine years later. They had no children.

Like most struggling performers, Reeves was pleased to take any part offered him in a movie. What he did not know was that his first film would become an epic one, the most famous in history. Reeves played a minor role as **Brent Tarlton**, one of the red headed "twins" enamored of **Scarlett O'Hara** in **Gone With the Wind**. His other screen credits included **So Proudly We Hail, From Here to Eternity,** the 1941 version of **Blood and Sand**, and **Samson and Delilah**, the version with Hedy Lamarr and Victor Mature.

But Reeves' major claim to fame was that he was selected to play the mild-mannered reporter, Clark Kent — **Superman**. Later, Reeves' psyche led him to believe he really was the comic book character.

Sort of like Clayton Moore really believing he was **The Lone Ranger** long after the series had been cancelled.

Some people close to George Reeves claim he was self-destructive. He was a real-life Casanova and broke the hearts of many actresses he met during his days of film work. But, he was also known to have reached into the Danger Zone of the Oligarchical Society by having affairs with some prominent married women — wives of executives and actors; among them, one which turned into an ongoing, long-time relationship, with Toni Mannix.

Reviewing the Reeves case, the facts uncovered about Reeves' death proved that his mother's suspicions were well founded. Facts uncovered by the Nick Harris Agency in the original Bessolo investigation request, and facts which *should* have been uncovered by the police department — who ignored the Harris finding, included:

- The absence of powder burns on Reeves' face establishes that he did not hold the gun to his head, as stated in the police report for their "indicated suicide" theory;

- For the weapon not to leave facial powder burns, it must have been at least a foot and a half away from his head when the bullet was fired — totally impractical during a *real* suicide attempt;

- Immediately after his death, Reeves was discovered in bed, lying on his back. The single shell was found under his back. This is the bullet casing, the empty shell. Self-inflicted gunshot wounds are usually known to propel the victim forward away from the shell.

- Speriglio made a careful examination of the police report and noticed they listed the bullet wound as "irregular."

The agency reconstructed the bullet entry and exit. The slug exited Reeves' head and was found lodged high in the ceiling. His head, at the moment of death, would have been twisted, making a self-inflicted wound improbable. Said Speriglio, "I suspect an intruder, or perhaps a burglar, even, was waiting for Reeves, who noticed the assailant and grabbed for his gun. A struggle ensued, and **Superman** was overpowered, losing his weapon to the killer. The murderer fled Reeves' bedroom unnoticed."

This theory, however, is too far-fetched. There were too many people in the Benedict Canyon house for such a disturbance not to have been heard or discovered, even though they were all drunk, at least according to the police.

Another discrepancy: the official report said that George Reeves shot himself in the head, pulling the trigger with his right hand. Prior to his death, Reeves had been a victim of an auto accident. His Jaguar had hit an oil slick in the Hollywood Hills, crashing into a brick wall. As part of his story on the incident, a journalist at the time, reported, "Superman fainted after the crash!"

Reeves later filed a personal injury claim in Los Angeles Superior Court asking for half a million dollars in damages. *His right hand was disabled — the same hand the police say he used to fire the gun.* A German Luger has a mean kick when fired, according to the gun experts we talked to.

☆   ☆   ☆

Another aspect to the "investigation" of the Beverly Hills Police Department was that no fingerprints were ever taken in the Reeves bedroom. To them — probably with pressure — it was an open and shut case — the actor apparently took his own life.

But did he?

His death was never really investigated properly. The oligarchy had obviously moved again — very quickly behind the scenes.

Actor Gig Young was one of Reeves' closest friends. He said, "No! Absolutely not. George could never take his life....everything was going his way." The same could be said for Young nineteen years later. Alan Ladd, another friend, agreed: "I never saw him happier!"

☆   ☆   ☆

The background of George Reeves was clouded in mystery. The facts gradually started to come out following his death about his relationship with his mother, Helen Bessolo. Reeves' "biographer" in a book which never saw the light of day, said, "I would have to say that his mother's love for George was rather abnormal!"

Helen became pregnant in 1913 in her hometown of Galesburg, Illinois, eloped and was married in Iowa. She then quickly divorced her husband, took baby George and married a man in Pasadena, California. It wasn't until he joined the Army during World War II that Reeves discovered a number of chunks of his life that his mother had hidden from him — his true birthdate, the identity of his natural father, and the fact that his stepfather had committed suicide eight years after being divorced by George's mother.

This so disturbed Reeves that he wouldn't talk to his mother through most of the 1940's. The biographer, James Beaver, in an interview with Gary Deeb of the Chicago Sun Times, said George Reeves' mother was a very strange and possessive woman. "She used to have this picture of George on her piano with an eternal flame in front of it. George wasn't even dead yet; he was only in his thirties!"

Close relatives said that Helen Bessolo went to great lengths to discourage her son's youthful infatuation with boxing. She once actually saw to it that his opponent was an enormous bruiser who beat the hell out of George, thereby dampening his enthusiasm for the fight game. But in this case it backfired. George became interested in acting and the rest is history.

During his extensive research into his project, Beaver said the one thing he uncovered about George Reeves was that "apparently he was a totally decent person. I honestly never spoke to anyone who didn't like him a lot."

Beaver obviously didn't talk to Eddie Mannix.

☆　　☆　　☆

There it rests today — Toni and Eddie Mannix are dead and the unsolved mystery of George Reeves lives on. Weissman kept his charges to himself for the thirty years or so following his friend and client's death. He did not wish to incur the wrath of the oligarchy that would have happened had he made his charges public. Now 71, Weissman wanted to clear his conscience before he died.

Weissman did add a postscript about Toni Mannix.

"Twenty years after George's death, I visited Toni," he said. "By this time, her beauty had faded and she lived as a recluse in her Beverly Hills home. We spent most of the time watching — at her insistence — video tapes of George in his role as **Superman**.

"Through it all she sat transfixed, staring at the screen as if George were still alive. For the few remaining years of her life, she alone still had George Reeves and she never again had to worry that someone would take him away from her!"

The entire Reeves estate, valued at $71,000 went to Toni Mannix under the terms of his will. Had Reeves been contemplating suicide, it is almost certain he would have changed the terms in favor of Lenore Lemmon. But as to the extent of their previous friendship, it was strong enough for Toni to give George a luxury car — at the time — a Jaguar as a birthday present the year of his death.

From all the available facts, conjectures, statements, "guesses," analysis, and the background of George Reeves, and his zest for life, it is patently obvious to everyone that he did not commit suicide as reported by the police and coroner.

Every indication points to the fact that Eddie Mannix, with his connections into the deepest recesses of the underworld, had Reeves "eliminated" by having someone slip a real bullet into his pistol, knowing it would only be a matter of time. This when all else failed, such as the near fatal automobile "accident" on the freeway; the brake fluid being drained from his car; and the attempt to run him over in the street.

Mannix had the resources, both physically and financially to stage or order these events.

The death of George Reeves will always be another of Hollywood's Unsolved Mysteries.

(AP Photo.)

☆   ☆   ☆

'Superman' WAS Destructible!

THE DEATH OF GEORGE REEVES
SHOCKED THE WORLD

The death of George Reeves shocked the world, or at least that part of the universe which had television available at that time.

George Reeves — *Superman* — had a vast following — according to the Academy of Television Arts & Sciences, 34 million viewers watched the series religiously. It was also one of the first programs to have many segments filmed in color and was shown in the U.S. and in Britain in that form.

From 1951 to 1957, the Caped Crusader flew into homes in 30 countries. In all, 104 episodes were filmed, also according to the archives at the TV Academy.

The demographics at the time said that this was not a show for "kids only!" Nearly half the viewers were adults — but probably those were watching it with their children.

According to the records of the Academy, the late Emperor Hirohito of Japan sent Reeves a fan letter saying how much he enjoyed the series and that he watched it with his son, the present Emperor, Akihito, who ascended to the throne in 1989.

...Fade Out

Carole Landis, 1940's star of USO shows overseas and **Four Jills in a Jeep**. Did she commit suicide because of a lost love affair with British roué Rex Harrison or because of financial problems? (John Austin Collection.)

Thomas Harper Ince, a brilliant, early pioneer producer. Was he shot by Charlie Chaplin or by William Randolph Hearst on the latter's yacht in San Diego Bay? How did the oligarchy — and Hearst — cover up his death and manage to have it attributed to "food poisoning?" It was this yachting trip, it was said, which secured Louella Parsons' lifetime employment with the Hearst press. (John Austin Collection.)

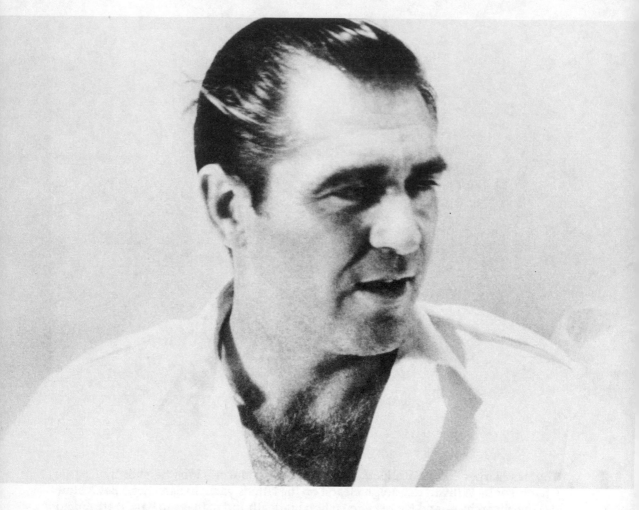

Movie "tough guy" Steve Cochran who died a still-unsolved death on board his yacht off the coast of Guatemala with an all-girl crew. When found, Cochran had been dead at least two weeks. (John Austin Collection.)

Epilogue ...

...And There Are a Lot More To Come!"

There you have them; some of the most famous of all of Hollywood's Unsolved Mysteries.

But there are more; many more, some dating back over five decades. They, too, still leave a lot of questions unanswered.

It will take another book to cover the rest; maybe two. What was the real story behind the death of Jean Harlow's husband, Paul Bern? Was he killed on the orders of Harlow's former lover, gangster Abner "Longie" Zwillman? Then there is the most famous of them all — Elizabeth Short — The Black Dahlia. Her body was found cut in half on a vacant lot in the Wilshire District in 1946.

Why had the venerable Los Angeles *Times* come out with the headline in its "Bulldog" (early) edition: **MOVIE PRODUCER SHOT ON HEARST YACHT** and then "pulled" it from all further editions? Was it Charlie Chaplin or Hearst himself who shot the film pioneer Thomas H. Ince? How did Hearst and the oligarchy manage to have his death attributed to "natural causes?" Was Hearst's mistress, Marion Davies, having an affair with Ince AND Charlie Chaplin?

The unsolved mystery of the death of **The Rebel**, Nick Adams, has never been explained. His death was put down as "Probable Suicide" from an overdose of paraldehyde, prescribed for "Johnny Yuma" for acute nervousness over his divorce and custody battle for his children. But when his body was found, there was no method of ingestion anywhere to be found. A telephone was less than a foot away from him.

The Wandering Walter Wanderwell and the all girl crew of his "International Police Force" is still a mystery which confounds the Long Beach, California police force. Wanderwell was found in his cabin on board his

Nick Adams as Johnny Yuma in **The Rebel** TV series. (John Austin Collection)

Lupe Velez, "The Mexican Spitfire." Star of the Mexican Spitfire films, she never met a man she didn't like. She is alleged to have committed suicide rather than give birth to an illegitimate child fathered by the 1930's cad, Harald Ramond, an actor. (John Austin Collection.)

Charlie Chaplin as Adolf Hitler in **The Great Dictator.** Did Chaplin shoot Thomas Ince to death on board William Randolph Hearst's yacht, or did Hearst himself? (John Austin Collection.)

yacht, the Carma — believed to be Wanderwell's cryptic version of *Karma* or retribution — shot to death.

Lupe Velez, "the Mexican Spitfire," never met a man she didn't like! She committed suicide, so they say, over a broken romance with the man who impregnated her. Being a devout Catholic, she refused to have an abortion. She feared that the scandal of being an unwed mother in the thirties would ruin her career. But, as a devout Catholic would she have committed suicide?

And did blonde beauty Carole Landis also commit suicide over the lost affections of the married British cad Rex Harrison, or was it because of financial problems?

Aspiring starlet Jean Spangler kissed her young daughter goodbye one afternoon on her way to an interview. She has never been heard from again over 40 years later. Kirk Douglas was one of those questioned about her disappearance.

The unsolved murder of Karyn Kupcinet, the daughter of Mr. Chicago, columnist Irv Kupcinet, still puzzles the oligarchy and the Sheriff's Department. Karyn was found dead in her West Hollywood apartment on Thanksgiving Day, 1963. She had been dead about three days when her body was discovered by actor Mark Goddard and his wife, Marcia, the daughter of well known publicist Henry Rogers.

Then six years and one month later, Marina Habe, daughter of actress Eloise Hardt and German novelist Hans Habe, disappeared from in front of the apartment she shared with her mother. It was within two blocks of Karyn Kupcinet's apartment. Marina had driven her small foreign sports car from the home of her date, Charles Hornburg, and disappeared. Her body was later found on the side of a hill and her murder was never solved.

Perhaps by the time another edition of **Hollywood's Unsolved Mysteries** is published, there will be others. One never knows in the highly charged atmosphere of Baghdad-on-the-Pacific.

☆　　☆　　☆

Over the years, Hollywood has been called many names and been publicized by many highly paid public relations experts as the center of the cinema art. Indeed, no other film producing country has ever been able to match the expertise and the popularity of films and filmmakers as those with the "Made in Hollywood, USA" logo on the credits.

At the same time, Hollywood has been word-painted by thousands of writers who have visited Tinseltown as Sodom-and-Gomorrah-on-the-Pacific. This is mainly because they did not take the time to learn the ins and outs of an industry which has millions of dollars riding on the talents, temperaments and expertise of a studio head, a major star or two, and a world-class director. If any one of three or four, even five, fail to do their job in any one aspect of a project — such as in **Heaven's Gate** and, more recently, **Ishtar**, then millions of dollars can be lost.

On the other hand, it is strange how many of the oligarchy's good deeds and world wide influence on people are forgotten in the heat of a scandal, a murder, or a sensational divorce case. It has always been that way.

Conversely, as we have mentioned many times in the preceding chapters, Hollywood is a "company town." You adhere to its policies, edicts and customs or you can say goodbye to a career in or around the oligarchy. If you are a journalist or reporter, you never write what you know, only what you are given — hand-outs, to be rewritten from the words of studio publicists and public relations firms.

During most interviews with top stars of the big or little screen, many publicists and PR firms insist on tape-recording the questions and answers. They then monitor every word of the interview when printed. If the interview answers are taken out of context, goodbye future interviews.

But, then, by its very nature, Hollywood lives and thrives on good publicity — the publicity it wants — nothing less. It is obvious that the world's press will never ignore Hollywood. The industry knows that most writers covering Tinseltown cannot earn a living without its cooperation. It is, in a sense, economic blackmail — but it has worked for many, many years and will continue to work.

The Hollywood neurosis is a unique one and it has bred its own peculiar brand of scandal. This might help to explain a lot of things, the reason for a lot of the cover-ups in some of these unsolved mysteries. Hollywood's excuse is that even in death the oligarchy must prevail, whether it be by suicide or murder.

We were in the business for many years as a second generation entertainment journalist covering the Hollywood scene. We traveled all over the world to write about and support the stars and the films of the Hollywood studios. The travel went with the territory and we are grateful for the experience and the "first class" travel we were always afforded.

We retired from the business several years ago and, with our companion, decided we could no longer live with the hypocrisy necessary to make a living in that fashion. Fortunately, we were able to do so and now indulge our whims in the countryside of California, and in Ireland several months a year. We no longer have the pressure to write what *they* want us to write; we can now write what we *want* to write.

However, *what* we write will *always* be objective — *never* subjective. Further, we will always be grateful for those many years we did spend in the industry; on the whole, many happy years. It was only when we sat down at our typewriter and realized that our scope was limited and our objectivity narrow, that we had second thoughts about where we had been for twenty five years, and where we were going.

We have no regrets.

As we said at the start of this epilogue, there are a great many more of Hollywood's Unsolved Mysteries yet to be recounted. There is the unsolved mystery of the high seas death of "tough guy" actor Steve Cochran. The 43-year-old actor was found dead in the wheelhouse of his yacht off Guatemala with an all-girl crew. The yacht had been drifting for several weeks before it was discovered and towed into port. The reason for Cochran's death has never been firmly established.

The deaths of three performers in what has become known as the "Jinx Film," **Promises, Promises**, has never been fully looked into. Jayne Mansfield was killed in a head-on collision in Louisiana not long after embracing a Satanic cult in San Francisco. Marie MacDonald, who also starred in the film, committed suicide, as did her husband, Don Taylor, who produced it; and comedian Tommy Noonan, whose idea the film was based on, is also dead.

And then there is the mystery of Diane Linkletter and her suicide leap from her sixth floor apartment. But, the strange part of Diane's death is the fact that a young man was with her and tried, he says, to save her, and more than two decades later, the same individual was with the **Tonight Show's** Matinee Lady, Carol Wayne, when she was found drowned off the coast of a Mexican resort. He fled the country before the *Federales* could question him about Wayne's unfortunate death.

There are other unsolved mysteries worth recounting as well — Charlie Chaplin, Jr., Dorothy Dandridge, Barbara (Mrs. Mickey) Rooney and her Yugoslav lover — a young man wanted by Yugoslavian authorities for draft dodging. There was also a mysterious connection between the Yugoslav and Cynthia Bouron.

Bouron had announced that Cary Grant was the father of her unborn child. When the child was born, it appeared to be the offspring of a black father. Bouron was once married to the Yugoslav in order to keep him in the USA because he faced deportation. Mickey Rooney then employed him as bodyguard to his wife, Barbara. Cynthia Bouron was later found bludgeoned to death.

Ah, but they are all chapters in yet another book to come. Very soon!

— Fini —-

Author John Austin with Mae West, a Hollywood legend, at a pre-filming cocktail party for Gore Vidal's **Myra Breckinridge** at 20th Century-Fox, circa 1970. West had a cameo role in the film which was not successful. (John Austin Collection)

End Papers

Bibliography

Crivello, Kirk. *Fallen Angels*. Citadel Press, 1988

Goodman, Ezra. *The Fifty Year Decline & Fall of Hollywood*. Simon & Schuster, 1961

Griffith, Dr. H. Winter, M.D. *Complete Guide To Prescription and Non-Prescription Drugs*. Body Press, 1988

Kirkpatrick, Sidney. *A Cast of Killers*. E.P. Dutton & Co., 1986

Milton, Joyce, and Bardash, Anne Louise. *Vicki*. St. Martin's, 1986

Noguchi, Dr. Thomas. *Coroner*. Pocket Books, 1983

Noguchi, Dr. Thomas. *Coroner at Large*. Pocket Books, 1985

Shevy, Sandra. *The Marilyn Scandal*. William Morrow, 1987

Speriglio, Milo. *The Marilyn Conspiracy*. Pocket Books, 1986

Wolf, Marvin, and Mader, Katherine. *Fallen Angels*. (*) Facts on File, 1986

(*) Strange, two books, same title, same subject(s) but two years apart.

"Hollywood is a fictitious, fabulous,
topsy-turvy, temperamental world that
is peculiar to its own way of life!"

> — *Federal Judge Ben Harrison*
> *King Vidor v Columbia Pictures*
> *Breach of Contract Suit*
> *Los Angeles, 1946*

"I wouldn't work in California for anything.
They don't have normal crime out there!"

> — *A N.Y.P.D. Detective,*
> *Third Homicide Division*